Labour and Management Co-operation

Labour and Management Co-operation

Workplace Partnership in UK Financial Services

STEWART JOHNSTONE
Loughborough University, UK

Routledge
Taylor & Francis Group

LONDON AND NEW YORK

First published in paperback 2024

First published 2010 by Gower Publishing

Published 2016 by Routledge
4 Park Square, Milton Park, Abingdon, Oxon OX14 4RN

and by Routledge
605 Third Avenue, New York, NY 10158

Routledge is an imprint of the Taylor & Francis Group, an informa business

Gower Applied Business Research
Our programme provides leaders, practitioners, scholars and researchers with thought provoking, cutting edge books that combine conceptual insights, interdisciplinary rigour and practical relevance in key areas of business and management.

British Library Cataloguing in Publication Data
Johnstone, Stewart.
    Labour and management co-operation : workplace partnership
    in UK financial services.
    1. Industrial relations--Great Britain. 2. Financial
    services industry--Management--Employee participation--
    Great Britain. 3. Financial services industry--Employees--
    Labor unions--Great Britain.
    I. Title
    331'.0413321-dc22

Library of Congress Cataloging-in-Publication Data

Library of Congress Control Number: 2010930647

ISBN: 978-0-566-08887-2 (hbk)
ISBN: 978-1-03-283820-5 (pbk)
ISBN: 978-1-315-59128-5 (ebk)

DOI: 10.4324/9781315591285

Contents

List of Figures

List of Tables

Abbreviations

Acas	Advisory, Conciliation and Arbitration Service
ACD	Automatic call distribution
ASLEF	Associated Society of Locomotive Engineers and Firemen
BA	British Airways
BACS	Bankers' Automated Clearing Services
BIFU	Banking, Insurance and Finance Union
BOG	Bank Officers Guild
CAM	Customer account manager
CARE	Career average revalued earnings
CBI	Confederation of British Industry
CIPD	Chartered Institute of Personnel and Development
CIT	Critical incident technique
COO	Chief operating officer
DTI	Department of Trade and Industry (now BERR)
EC	European Community (or) European Commission
EI	Employee involvement
EIRO	European Industrial Relations Observatory
ER	Employee relations
EU	European Union
FSA	Financial Service Authority
FTO	Full-time officer
FTC	Family Tax Credits
GDP	Gross domestic product
GMB	General Municipal Boilermakers and Allied Trade Union
HBOS	Halifax Bank of Scotland
HRM	Human resource management
HR	Human resources
ICO	Individual case officer
IDS	Income Data Services
IOD	Institute of Directors

IPA	Involvement and Participation Association
IR	Industrial relations
IRS	Industrial Relations Services
IVR	Interactive voice response
JCC	Joint Consultative Committee
JCNC	Joint Consultative and Negotiating Committee
KPI	Key performance indicator
MBA	Master of Business Administration
NEC	National Executive Committee
NHS	National Health Service
NUBE	National Union of Bank Employees
NWSA	NatWest Staff Association
PLC	Public limited company
PR	Public relations
PRP	Performance related pay
RBS	Royal Bank of Scotland
RMT	National Union of Rail, Maritime and Transport Workers
R&P	Recognition and procedural agreement
SERA	Security of employment and redundancy agreement
TGWU	Transport and General Workers' Union (also T&G)
TUC	Trade Union Congress
TUPE	Transfer of Undertakings and Protection of Employees Regulations
USDAW	Union of Shop, Distributive and Allied Workers
WERS	Workplace Employee Relations Survey

Preface and Acknowledgements

This book is concerned with workplace partnership agreements in the UK financial services sector. This is an area that has attracted significant academic and policy interest in the UK for the past decade, and similar debates have also been prominent internationally. Based on a research project conducted in the Business School at Loughborough University, the book presents in-depth case studies undertaken within three diverse banking organisations. The data was collected during the period December 2004 to December 2005. A particular aim of the book is to present the cases in sufficient detail to allow readers to obtain a feel for the reality of partnership working in the three organisations, and to provide comparative insights into the meaning, context, process and outcomes of partnership. Specifically, the study explores partnership across a variety of organisational contexts, particular attention is paid to what partnership actually means to organisational actors. It also focuses upon understanding some of the processes of partnership, in terms of decision-making processes and the nature of the relationships forged between the key actors. Outcomes for management, unions and employees are also assessed, with the efficiency, equity, voice framework developed by Professor John Budd (Budd, 2004), providing a useful analytical lens. The study also considers some of the main challenges to partnership in the UK. It is also worth mentioning that at the time of the research fieldwork the financial sector in the UK was reporting record profits, and the subsequent global economic downturn will undoubtedly provide a major test of the resilience of labour management co-operation agreements in these extremely challenging times.

I would like to express my gratitude to the people who made the project possible, in particular the managers, union officials, employee representatives and employees who gave up their time to share their views on labour management co-operation and workplace partnership agreements. I would also like to thank colleagues at Loughborough University Business School, especially Professor Adrian Wilkinson (who has since moved 'down under' to Griffith University) and Professor Peter Ackers. Their advice and encouragement was invaluable throughout the period of the research, and they also kindly provided detailed comments on the manuscript in its various incarnations. Martin West at Gower has also been helpful in progressing the manuscript, as well as answering my many questions along the way.

Finally, I need to thank my parents. Thanks also to my partner Jayshree who has shared the highlights (and lowlights) of the project. I hope everyone agrees it was worth it. Of course, any errors or omissions remain my own responsibility.

Stewart Johnstone
Loughborough

About the Author

Stewart Johnstone is a Lecturer in Human Resource Management at Loughborough University Business School, UK. His research interests include employee participation and representation, and he has published several articles on these themes in journals including *Employee Relations*, *Economic and Industrial Democracy*, *Human Resource Management Journal*, the *Industrial Relations Journal*, and *Journal of Industrial Relations*.

He is a Member of the Chartered Institute of Personnel and Development (Chartered MCIPD), the British Universities Industrial Relations Association, and the International Industrial Relations Association (IIRA).

1

Introduction and Overview

Background to the Study

Union decline in the UK since 1979 has been dramatic. Purcell (1993) questioned whether Britain was experiencing 'the end of institutional industrial relations' and Howell (1999: 26) also begins his analysis of British industrial relations by stating that 'trade unions are in crisis'. Metcalf has asked whether it is a case of 'resurgence or perdition' and his conclusions are decidedly pessimistic (Metcalf, 2004). Union membership has fallen from a peak of 13 million in 1979 to 5.5 million, and membership is heavily skewed towards public rather than private sector workplaces. Various explanations of this membership decline exist including the changing composition of the workforce and jobs, the business cycle, the role of the state, employer attitudes, employee reactions, and the strategies and structures of unions themselves (Metcalf, 2004). In addition, between 1980 and 2000, the coverage of collective agreements contracted from over three quarters to under a third of the employed workforce. This is compounded by evidence which suggests that even where unions continue to be recognised, their influence is still falling. Indeed, studies have revealed that the role of trade unions has faded over both wage and non-wage issues, with increasing emphasis on consultation and information rather than negotiation (Brown et al., 2000). Furthermore, WERS 2004 reveals that union officials spent most of their time supporting grievances on behalf of individual members, rather than negotiating terms and conditions (Kersely et al., 2006). As Terry has argued, 'local union representatives – shop stewards – are not the negotiators, the co-authors of "joint rules", that we have generally taken them for since the late 1960s' (2003a: 488). Even where collective bargaining continues, its impact appears to have diminished, and 1970s concepts such as 'joint control' and 'rule making' are generally considered to be outmoded. Few organisations outside the public sector still have specific 'Employee Relations Departments', and employee relations (ER) is now commonly seen to be only one component of the broader HR professional's remit. Indeed, for some, 'the language has echoes of a historical era that offers few insights into contemporary practice' (Emmott, 2005).

Overall, the emphasis has shifted from collective institutions, such as collective bargaining and trade unions, towards a management vogue dominated by more individualistic concepts of employee voice, commitment and engagement, and the management of the 'psychological contract' (Emmott, 2005).

Despite the general context of a decline in collective employment relations, labour management co-operation remains a perennial issue in British industrial relations research. Over the last decade interest has focused upon workplace 'partnership' agreements, which formed a key plank of the New Labour government's employment policy of 'modernisation' (Stuart and Martinez-Lucio, 2004a). In the British context the term partnership remains notoriously ambiguous (Guest and Peccei, 2001; Terry, 2003a), though most would agree that it concerns an attempt to shift the culture of employment relations away from zero-sum and adversarial relationships, towards co-operative employment relations, characterised by mutual trust and delivering mutual gains (Stuart and Martinez-Lucio, 2004a).

A rich literature on workplace partnership has emerged. Much has focused on whether partnership offers a valuable opportunity for the beleaguered trade union movement (Terry, 2003a and b), and the extent to which it delivers mutual gains (Guest and Peccei, 2001). Ideologically, the debate is polarised: pluralists tend to be more optimistic and view partnership as an opportunity (Ackers and Payne, 1998; Knell, 1999), while radicals remain decidedly suspicious and believe partnership presents a significant threat to unions and their members (Kelly, 2004; Taylor and Ramsey, 1998). Since unitarists believe that conflict is not an inherent or permanent feature of the employment relationship, they may take the view that partnership is unnecessary, as employer and employee interests can be aligned through (human resource) management policies.

Empirical evidence is mixed, though many recent empirical studies have been critical in tone (Stuart and Martinez-Lucio, 2004b), suggesting that – despite the mutual gains rhetoric – the 'balance of advantage' is often skewed in favour of management (Guest and Peccei, 2001). Some recent research, however, has been less deterministic, suggesting that a variety of employment relations outcomes are possible, and that partnership may not *necessarily* hold any single consequence (Heery et al., 2004; Kelly, 2004; Oxenbridge and Brown, 2004a, 2004b; Wills, 2004). However, there are several significant weaknesses of the current literature. Firstly, there is the issue of definitional ambiguity leading to the risk that researchers are actually comparing very different situations under the 'partnership' umbrella. For example, the literature identifies various different 'types' of partnership, such as union/non-union, formal/informal, public sector/private sector, but fails to engage explicitly with the potential implications of such a heterogeneity of arrangements. Studies also explore different sectors with very different product/labour market conditions and different industrial relations traditions. Researchers also overlook the importance of process, tending instead to favour fairly crude attempts at 'measuring' the outcomes, against very high measures of success often informed by a romantic historical view of industrial relations (IR) where trade unions and collective bargaining dominated the industrial relations landscape. Moreover, good process need not necessarily lead to good outcomes and vice versa, because of the influence of many other contextual variables such as economic conditions or corporate strategy. Of course outcomes are of interest, but it is argued that the impact of partnership on the broader regulation of employment relations is equally important (Stuart and Martinez-Lucio, 2004b).

Purpose of the Study: Context, Process and Outcomes

This study addresses some of these limitations, by presenting the findings of a three-year research study conducted in the British financial service sector. It is proposed that, in order to advance the debate, attention must be paid to the *context*, *process* and *outcomes* of partnership (Guest and Peccei, 2001; McBride and Stirling, 2002). Given the ambiguity of the term, context is important in order to ensure an instance of partnership can be reliably identified. Sensitivity to contextual variables is also important in order to establish why some arrangements appear to be more successful than others. Partnership is concerned with regulation and governance of employment relations (Stuart and Martinez-Lucio, 2004b), but relatively little is known about the process of decision-making and partnership. Rather, most research has focused upon the outcomes of partnership, but it is likely that outcomes cannot be fully understood and reliably interpreted without information regarding both context and process.

Thus this study addresses a number of research questions. Firstly, how does partnership play out in a variety of organisational contexts? There is a danger of assuming that partnership arrangements are homogenous, when clearly the typologies identified in the literature suggests that contextual issues are important. Important variables are likely to include union/non-union, formal/informal and greenfield/brownfield arrangements. Secondly, what does partnership actually mean to organisational actors, and what exactly is it expected to achieve? There is the risk that the expectations of IR academics may not be the same as those of practitioners and organisational actors. Thirdly, the research explores the process of partnership, and in particular the nature of decision-making processes and relationships in organisations espousing a partnership approach to employment relations. Does partnership change the way decisions are made and what does it mean in terms of the relationships between the key actors? Fourthly, what are the outcomes for management, unions and employees, as well as society more generally? Again, it is worth reiterating at this point that though outcomes are clearly of interest, they are notoriously difficult to measure given the plethora of non-HRM/IR factors that may also influence outcomes. Finally, the study considers some of the main challenges to partnership in the UK.

Research Methods

Accordingly, case studies were conducted in three diverse banking organisations, referred to by the pseudonyms NatBank, BuSoc and WebBank. Table 1.1 shows key characteristics of the three organisations.

This allowed insights into partnership in different contexts to be obtained.

Table 1.1   Key characteristics of the case study organisations

Organisation	NatBank	BuSoc	WebBank
Partnership	Formal	De facto	De facto
Union	Amicus (Unifi)	Staff union	No union recognised
Structure	Partnership framework	JCNC	Employee Forum
Status	PLC	Mutual	PLC
International operations	Yes	No	No, but owned by international finance group
Ownership	British	British	British
Site	Brownfield	Brownfield	Greenfield
IPA affiliation	Yes	No	Yes
Employee relations agreement	Partnership agreement	Recognition and procedures agreement	Commitment document
Unit of analysis	North East admin centre (1000 employees)	Midlands admin centre (2000 employees)	Midlands admin centre (2000 employees)

MAIN SIMILARITIES

The first similarity concerned the nature of the partnership arrangement. All organisations espoused commitments to the important aspects of the partnership ethos including information and consultation, legitimacy of representation, transparency and openness, and employment security/flexibility. They were also able to demonstrate a 'partnership infrastructure' as evidence of this. It was essential to confirm that the firms really qualified as displaying some evidence of a prima facie 'partnership'. The aim was not to find models or exemplars of partnership 'best practice', but rather to find companies illustrative of recent partnership developments in the UK, that were at varying stages of developing and refining their IR approaches. The second similarity was ownership. All organisations were British owned, reflecting the current structure of British retail banking where international operators are still rare. Thirdly, the unit of analysis was the same, as the project focused on call centres within large administration centres, as opposed to the wider branch network. Size is also a common factor as each centre studied was large, employing over 1000 people. The largest departments in these centres were related to customer sales and service and, again, these departments formed the principal focus of the study. Clearly, they are also drawn from the same sector and this was central to the design of the study, as sectoral differences such as product or labour markets could make comparisons very difficult (Kelly, 2004).

MAIN DIFFERENCES

However, there were several important differences as well. Firstly, there were differences in site history. NatBank and BuSoc both have a history of over 150 years. At each of the sites under study, the organisations had been major employers for over 30 years. WebBank, however, was established only seven years ago as an independent subsidiary of a major international financial services group, and the administration centre under study is only five years old. It is often assumed that human resource management (HRM) practices are more easily imparted in greenfield sites without baggage and history, and it was thought to be interesting to compare organisations which had very different histories (Hallier and Leopold, 2000). Secondly, union recognition was another important variable. NatBank and BuSoc have both recognised trade unions for many years. However, the BuSoc union is a former staff association, which has a history of co-operative employment relations and rivalry with other industry trade unions. WebBank, on the other hand, does not recognise a trade union. Thirdly, the different contexts allow comparisons to be made between formal partnership agreements and informal partnership agreements (Ackers et al., 2004; Oxenbridge and Brown, 2004a, 2004b). NatBank has a formal partnership agreement signed by senior bank executives and senior union officials. BuSoc has a traditional recognition and procedural agreement, although senior management and union officials agreed that in practice the agreement is almost irrelevant, and both parties confirmed that the actual relationship is much more co-operative and collaborative. At WebBank they have a Commitment Document, although this is not signed by the partners. The earlier partnership literature focused upon cases where formal partnership agreements had been signed, but there is now an appreciation of the possibility of informal agreements. Fourthly, corporate governance provided another variable. NatBank and WebBank are both public limited companies (PLCs) registered on the London Stock Exchange. BuSoc remains a mutual building society owned by members. It is often argued that one of the weaknesses of partnership in an Anglo-Saxon context is the pressure to deliver shareholder value (Heery, 2002; Deakin et al., 2004), and therefore BuSoc presents an interesting point of comparison to the two PLCs. Finally, another difference is the size and internationalisation of the organisations. NatBank is a large international banking group. BuSoc has focused very much on the domestic UK market and has no international operations. WebBank is owned by an international group but its operations are in the domestic UK market only. This provides an interesting comparison for various reasons. These include the fact that organisations like NatBank already had experience within European Works Councils before partnership, whereas BuSoc did not. Moreover, there is the likelihood that as an international bank, NatBank may have very different strategic priorities – and in turn employment relations practices – to smaller domestic organisations like BuSoc and WebBank.

The bulk of the data was collected by conducting over 50 one-to-one semi-structured interviews with a range of management, employees and representatives. Conducted during the period 2004/5, these allowed rich and detailed accounts of partnership in practice to be obtained. Interviews also have the advantage of allowing the interviewee to raise important issues not contained within the interview schedule. Accordingly, more structured interviews were *not* adopted, specifically because the aim was to obtain rich contextual data and to allow new patterns and themes to emerge. Equally, an open-ended ethnographic approach was not adopted as the aim was to obtain multiple perspectives and multiple levels, and therefore semi-structured interviews were deemed most appropriate, as they allowed sufficient commonality to allow a comparison of similar issues to be made internally between different organisational actors, and externally across cases. A danger with research into experiences of partnership is that the researcher may expect to find three basic attitudes (positive, negative, agnostic), and such attitudes may be clouded by recent events. For example, research may find positive attitudes to partnership after a recent pay rise, or negative attitudes to partnership where job losses have recently been announced. In other words, respondents' supposed attitudes to partnership may just reflect the extent to which there is a 'feel good factor' within the organisation at the time.

Inspired by 'critical incident technique' (CIT) (Flanagan, 1954) a particular aim of interviews was to 'capture the thought processes, the frame of reference and the feelings about an incident…which have meanings for the respondent' (Chell, 2004: 56), in an attempt to mitigate the risks of obtaining data which reflects vague underlying feelings regarding recent organisational events, as opposed to attitudes to partnership per se. CIT interviews, on the other hand, involve the discussion of significant occurrences (events, incidents, processes) identified by the respondent, the way they were managed and the perceived outcomes and effects. Another advantage is that interviewees often find such interviews enjoyable, as it affords the opportunity to take 'time out' to reflect on recent events (Chell, 2004). In practice, this method required interviewees to identify some of the main issues which have been prominent in the last five years (or since they joined the organisation if they had been an employee for less than five years). Typically, these would reflect a range of both positive and negative sentiments regarding the way issues were handled. For example, a respondent sometimes provided an account of some incidents which they thought were handled badly, and other examples where they believed the event had been managed more successfully. This method allowed a multi-dimensional picture of events to be obtained.

Accordingly, the study dissects decision-making processes in each case by mapping against the dimensions put forward in earlier research on employee involvement (EI) by Marchington et al. (1992). They propose four dimensions regarding the *degree, scope, form* and *level* of decision-making, and it is believed these dimensions remain relevant today. Degree refers to the amount of influence over decision-making. Form refers to the distinction between direct and indirect participation. Level refers to whether issues under discussion are high level or low level. Scope of decision-making concerns the range of issues under discussion, and as such is clearly linked to concerns regarding issues of agenda setting. The study also adds three additional dimensions derived from the partnership literature: *formality, representative level* and *timeliness*. Formality refers to the balance between formal mechanisms of decision-making such as committees and meetings, and informal mechanisms such as ad hoc telephone calls, lunch meetings and spontaneous chats between the actors. Representative level relates to the extent to which representation occurs at a high level, such as full-time officials, or at a local level, through lay employee representatives. Finally, timeliness concerns the point at which decisions are discussed, ranging from the early proposal stage through to the implementation stage where decisions may be presented as a fait accompli.

In terms of issues of scope and agenda setting, this was examined under the three broad headings: *pay and conditions*; *discipline and grievance*; and *organisational change*. These subject categories emerged from WERS data regarding the scope of decision-making in the UK, and the type of issues typically discussed at meetings between employee representatives and management (Kersely et al., 2006: 165). Respondents were also explicitly asked if there were any issues which were *not* on the agenda, or which had not been on the agenda. This typically elicited very candid responses, and interviewees discussed past incidents which were said to have been off the agenda and had emerged without consultation.

The research was also informed by an awareness of the critical literatures on partnership as well as labour process critiques of call centre working (for example, Kelly, 2004; Taylor and Bain, 1999) and these are discussed in detail in Chapters 2 and 3. The empirical data confirms that many of the topical issues raised in these literatures have indeed been captured through CIT, including controversies regarding redundancies, offshoring, performance/sales targets, as well as general pay and working conditions. Moreover, attempts were made to capture views on these issues across cases, even where they may have not been raised as a specific 'critical incident'. This was possible because of the heterogeneity of the case organisations selected. The study also triangulates responses regarding the scope of decision-making and agenda setting with other sources, for example, by comparing accounts between different actors groups (management, union officials, employee representatives, employees), as well as with other data sources obtained, such as internal and external documentation. Finally, notwithstanding the potential criticisms of CIT, it is crucial to reiterate the main strength of the CIT technique, in terms of eschewing glib, bland (and quite possibly meaningless) rhetorical responses from interviewees regarding whether partnership was 'good' or not, in favour of context-rich responses, drawing upon detailed organisational examples to illustrate the 'lived realities' of the partnership process. In addition, attitudes to recent 'organisational dramas' cannot be easily obtained from survey questions, and the CIT technique allows respondents' opinions to be placed in context, i.e. how they view the world. The interviews also allowed insights into organisational history, and views of the organisation from long-serving employees compared to new recruits, and views from the perspective of older workers as well as of young employees. The approach also enables comparisons to be made between the handling of a particular issue in one organisation compared with another, thus extending theoretical understanding (Chell, 2004). Table 1.2 summarises the interviews conducted in each of the case study organisations.

Table 1.2   Summary of interviewees

Company	Management	(Union) Representatives/ Officials	Employee Focus Groups
NatBank	(6) 1 Director of Sales and Service 1 Employee Relations Manager 1 Admin Centre Site Manager 1 Call Centre Manager 2 Team Leader Group interviews	(6) 3 Union Full-Time Officials 3 Union Representatives	(4) 4 employee focus groups from a range of functions
BuSoc	(10) 1 Head of Personnel 1 Personnel Consultant 1 Employee Relations Manager 1 Call Centre Manager 1 Senior Lending Manager 3 Lending Team Leaders 2 Call Centre Team Leaders	(7) 1 Union General Secretary 1 Union President 1 Individual Case Officer 1 Area Executive Officer 3 Constituency Representatives	(3) 3 employee focus groups from a range of functions
WebBank	(5) 1 HR Director 1 Team Leader	(5) 1 Employee Forum Chair 2 Full-time Employee Representatives 3 Part-time Forum Representatives	(6) 6 employee focus groups from a range of functions

This allowed rich contextual data to be obtained, and comparisons to be made across a number of variables including: route to partnership, IR history, union recognition, company history and corporate governance. Equally, focusing on one sector means some other variables are similar, for example, product market, competitive environment, labour market/process and technology. A particular focus of the study was to understand more about the process of partnership, in terms of the nature of relationships between key actors, and the system of decision-making. The study then explores the outcomes of partnership as perceived by the key actors, and employees in particular. In order to address the questions of decision-making and mutual gains, the study employs the framework proposed by Budd (2004) and asks to what extent does partnership balance the objectives of the employment relationship i.e. efficiency, equity and voice? This framework has not yet been employed in British industrial relations research. Thus the study makes two key contributions. Firstly, it offers a more holistic evaluation of partnership in terms of context, process and outcomes. Secondly, the study offers a test of the utility of the analytical framework proposed by Budd (2004). The bulk of the data is drawn from over 50 semi-structured interviews with managers, union officials, employee representatives and employees in the period 2004/5.

Structure of the Book

The book is divided into eight chapters. Chapter 2 sets the scene by reviewing some of the key contributions to the partnership literature. The chapter begins by examining the controversies surrounding the meaning of partnership. The chapter then reviews the polarised advocates/critics debate as well as more recent empirical evidence which appears to present typologies of partnership outcomes. It concludes by highlighting the limitations of the current research, including a strong ideological dimension to debates, lack of sensitivity to context and heterogeneity of partnership arrangements, as well as a tendency to focus on outcomes and to overlook the importance of process.

Chapter 3 provides essential context to the case studies which follow by providing an overview of developments in the UK financial sector. Some of the key changes in the last 25 years include changing markets, delivery mechanisms, technologies and marketing approaches. Such changes in business models have had significant HR implications in relation to pay, staffing, work organisation, skills and industrial relations. It also provides some context to contemporary issues concerning call centres and offshoring.

Chapters 4, 5 and 6 present the data obtained from the studies of NatBank, BuSoc and WebBank respectively. Each empirical chapter begins with a company profile and an outline of the unit of analysis. This is followed by a review of employment relations at the company and the background to partnership. The partnership architecture is then considered, including the definitions of partnership, structures and processes, and actors. The partnership process is then explored in detail, and focuses upon the nature of actor relationships, and the way issues are handled and decisions are made in each case. The final section of each chapter offers an overall evaluation of some of the outcomes, as well as the barriers and challenges. More specifically, Chapter 4 presents the data from the first case study undertaken at the NatBank credit card centre in North East England. Chapter 5 presents the case of BuSoc undertaken at the BuSoc administration centre in the Midlands. Chapter 6 explores the case of WebBank undertaken at the main operations centre and headquarters in the East Midlands.

Chapter 7 presents a discussion of the result from the three case study organisations, and offers detailed comparisons of differences and similarities. Following a broadly similar structure to the preceding three chapters, it begins by exploring the context and theory of the partnership process. The chapter then examines the realities of the partnership process in terms of issues and decision-making, and actor relationships. The final section offers an overall evaluation of partnership in practice, and asks whether partnership helps to balance efficiency, equity and voice. It then presents some of the main challenges to partnership, including a lack of a shared understanding, embedding a partnership culture, resistance to adversity, and representative efficacy.

Chapter 8 presents the conclusions of the study and suggests some implications for practice. It begins by suggesting the need to appreciate the heterogeneity of partnership arrangements in terms of route to partnership, corporate governance, union recognition as well as degree of formality. It then identifies three important points regarding the requirements for an enduring partnership. Firstly, the need for clear expectations and an understanding of the rules of engagement. Secondly, the importance of process, and the extent to which the partnership process can accommodate divergent interests. Finally, actor perspectives on partnership, and the extent to which outcomes can be considered mutually beneficial is discussed.

Overall, the evidence presented in the study suggests that the impact of partnership on employment relations in Britain is significantly more complex than the existing literature suggests. On balance, the study offers some support for the advocates, as well as some support for the concerns expressed by the critics. The research suggests that there is a need to pay much more attention to the *context* and *process* of partnership, as well as the difficult-to-measure outcomes which have dominated the existing literature. The study also demonstrates the utility of the framework of Budd (2004) as a useful tool in exploring the subtle processes of partnership, in terms of decision-making processes and actor relationships. Without this, only a partial understanding of partnership can be achieved. It is proposed that different trajectories of experience are possible, and indeed likely. The study also makes the point that the voice process is of intrinsic value, and must be considered separately from outcomes. Moreover, outcomes must not be compared only with the 'ideal' outcome but also with other possible alternatives. It also suggests that the context of contemporary British IR must be borne in mind when deciding whether the glass is 'half-full' or 'half-empty'. Importantly, the study found that in each case organisation there was little actor support for adversarial strategies, as well as evidence to suggest that partnership encourages management to think more strategically and long-term in relation to their HRM and employment relations policies. As with other forms of participation, 'initiatives are probably more limited than the enthusiasts claim, but more constructive than the critics admit' (Marchington and Wilkinson, 2005: 415).

2

Labour Management Partnership in the UK

The concept of partnership has become the defining feature of the 'new' industrial relations settlement for the Millennium (Stuart and Martinez-Lucio, 2004b: 410).

Introduction

In 1998 Ackers and Payne identified a new HRM trend, partnership, which promised to bring unions back into the heart of the employment relationship (Ackers and Payne, 1998). Partnership was also at the core of the 1998 'Fairness at Work' agenda set out by the Blair government (DTI, 1998), and the end of New Labour's 13-year term in office is an opportune time to take stock of the voluminous partnership literature which has emerged. The review begins by examining definitions of partnership. This is followed by a review of the conceptual advocates/critics debate, and some of the key empirical studies exploring trade union representative capacity/mutual gains outcomes. The review then highlights several limitations of the existing literature, and concludes by suggesting a need to understand more about the process of partnership, to clarify the meaning and expectations of partnership, and stresses the importance of evaluating partnership in context.

What is 'Partnership'?

The term partnership has become too diffuse to carry much meaning. (Oxenbridge and Brown, 2004b: 389).

Since the early 1990s partnership has attracted an enormous amount of attention from the New Labour government (DTI, 1998), the Trades Union

Congress (TUC, 1999), and most of the major trade unions, including Unison, TGWU, GMB, Amicus and USDAW. Partnership has also been endorsed by other bodies, including Acas and The Work Foundation (Acas, 2003). Though the partnership concept has attracted a rich research literature, definitions of partnership remain a matter for debate (Ackers et al., 2004; Ackers and Payne, 1998; Dietz, 2004; Guest and Peccei, 2001; Stuart and Martinez-Lucio, 2004a). As a result of the 'inherent ambiguity' (Bacon and Storey, 2000: 409), partnership has been described as 'an idea with which almost anyone can agree, without having any clear idea what they are agreeing about' (Guest and Peccei, 2001: 207). In reality, however, the concept has attracted significant controversy and support is far from universal. Indeed an element of ambivalence has been evident within the union movement (for example, RMT and ASLEF), employer bodies (for example, CBI and IoD) and employers (for example, anti-union campaigns) (Gall, 2004; Undy, 1999). In part this may reflect the lack of a common definition.

Academic definitions centre round the idea of 'co-operation for mutual gain' and 'reciprocity' (Martinez-Lucio and Stuart, 2002). For Gall (2004) the idea of 'mutualism' – where a successful employer is able to benefit all stakeholders involved – is a defining feature. Guest and Peccei (2001) also suggest that trust and mutuality are the key components of a genuine partnership agreement. Rhetorically at least, partnership appears to be hinged upon the proposition that, for employers, it can be both economically effective and ethically responsible to co-operate with unions and employees on issues of strategic organisational change (Stuart and Martinez-Lucio, 2004a). For Terry (2003a) commitment to business success, a quid pro quo between flexibility and employment security, and the representation of different interests are key. However, such definitions are inevitably vague and a useful definition 'should describe a set of organisational characteristics and practices that, firstly, do justice to the idea of managing employment relations in a 'partnership' manner and secondly, are readily observable in order to verify a genuine example in practice' (Dietz, 2004: 4; see also Guest and Peccei, 2001). To this end, more practical definitions are offered by the TUC and IPA and these are outlined in Table 2.1.

Table 2.1   TUC and IPA definitions of partnership

Partnership Element	IPA	TUC	Classification
A joint declaration of commitment to organisational success	Y	Y	Values (Marchington, 1998) Commitment (IPA, 1997)
Mutual recognition of the legitimate role and interests of management, employees and trade unions where present	Y	Y	Values (Marchington, 1998) Commitment (IPA, 1997)
Commitment and effort to develop and sustain trust between the organisation's constituencies	Y	Implicit	Values (Marchington, 1998) Commitment (IPA, 1997)
Means for sharing information (IPA)/Transparency (TUC)	Y	Y	Process
Consultation and employee involvement, with representative arrangements for an 'independent employee voice' (IPA)/Transparency (TUC)	Y	Y	Process
Policies to balance flexibility with employment security (IPA/TUC)	Y	Y	Outcome
Sharing organisational success (IPA)	Y	–	Outcome
Adding value (TUC)	Implicit	Y	Outcome
Improving the quality of working life (TUC)	Implicit	Y	Outcome

Source: Johnstone, S. Ackers, P and Wilkinson, A. (2009) The partnership phenomenon in the UK: a ten year review, *Human Resource Management Journal*

While the IPA definition is open enough to allow for the possibility of partnership in non-union contexts, the TUC believe trade union presence is essential to partnership, arguing that 'in companies without unions … consultation always risks being a sham' (TUC, 2002: 5). They argue that this voice is essential to act as a counterbalance to the power of management (TUC, 2002). The two models also agree on the need to balance flexibility with employment security, although care has to be taken with the definition here; a 'stable employment framework' is meant rather than a 'job-for-life' guarantee' (IPA, 1997: 2). They also agree on the desirability of positive employee outcomes, although these are defined slightly differently, with the IPA focusing on 'sharing success' with the financial connotations, whereas the TUC prefers the broader notion of 'improving the quality of working life' (TUC, 1999: 13). However, both include outcomes as part of their definition of partnership, and it is proposed here that it is important not to conflate partnership processes with employment relations outcomes. Employment relations outcomes (such as employment security or adding value) are better thought of as aspirations which need to be explored empirically, but do not constitute an integral component of the partnership process per se. Partnership may concern an attempt to achieve these outcomes, irrespective of whether or not they are achieved.

It is suggested that a more useful definition would offer some suggestions regarding the identifiable practices and processes associated with partnership. In terms of practices, employee voice is central to all definitions and this may involve a mix of direct participation, representative participation and financial involvement. However, most policy and organisational definitions suggest it is representative participation which is the bedrock of partnership, with or without trade unions, and this is also implicit in most academic research. At the centre of the process of partnership are issues of decision-making and actor relationships. Partnership decision-making is typically described as a 'joint problem-solving approach', characterised by a genuine process of early consultation and affording some influence over decision-making but not necessarily joint decision-making. Actor relationships are said to require trust and openness, mutual legitimacy and a commitment to business success, and as such the values and behaviour of organisational actors are crucial. Inevitably, there is likely to be some variety within this general framework, but it is proposed that these are the practices and processes which underpin a prima facie case of partnership and are likely to be mutually reinforcing.

Ideological Debates: Nirvana or Dead End?

Most commentators acknowledge a polarised conceptual debate in the early contributions between 'advocates and critics', regarding firstly the potential of partnership as a union revitalisation strategy, and secondly the extent to which the mutual gains are actually realisable (Guest et al., 2008; Martinez-Lucio and Stuart, 2004; Oxenbridge and Brown, 2004a, 2004b; Roche and Geary, 2004; Stuart and Martinez-Lucio, 2004b; Terry and Smith, 2003). Though excellent reviews of this debate are captured elsewhere (for example, Tailby and Winchester, 2005), a brief review is deemed necessary in order for the evolution of British partnership research over the last decade to be fully understood. For advocates partnership may offer an opportunity for unions to extend their representative capacity. Ackers and Payne (1998: 531) argue that partnership 'offers British unions a strategy that is not only capable of moving with the times and accommodating new political developments, but also allowing them a hand in shaping their own destiny' and 'provides an opportunity for British unions to return from political and economic exile'. It is certainly true that union elites appear to have been attracted by the potential of a new role in the regulation of work (Stuart and Martinez-Lucio, 2004b).

Advocates are also attracted by the idea of 'mutual gains' bargaining over employment security, flexibility, development and involvement (Kochan and Osterman, 1994). It is suggested that employers may benefit from a new cadre of representatives, improved relations with unions, and assistance with the facilitation of change. In turn unions may benefit from increased influence, greater access to information, job security and inter-union co-operation (Marchington, 1998). Employees are also said to benefit from greater job security, training, quality jobs, good communication and more effective voice (Guest and Peccei, 2001; Kochan and Osterman, 1994; Knell, 1999).

However, critics question the coherence of the partnership model, and point to the risks of adopting such an approach (Claydon, 1998; Danford et al., 2005a; Kelly, 1996; Taylor and Ramsey, 1998). Their primary concern is the extent to which partnership incorporates trade unions and may lead to compliant unions, thus limiting the ability of unions to attract members (Kelly, 1996; Marks et al., 1998; Taylor and Ramsey, 1998). It has been argued that some employers may view partnership as another union 'Trojan horse' and express a preference for free labour markets and individualisation of the employment relationship (Claydon, 1998). Indeed, WERS04 revealed that 77 per cent of managers agreed that they would rather deal with employees directly rather than through trade unions (Kersely et al., 2006). Managers may also be concerned that partnership may slow down decision-making, incur extra costs and challenge their managerial prerogative. Others simply doubt the putative benefits of such an approach. Critics argue that partnership may simply represent a pragmatic management decision rather than evidence of a long-term commitment to working with unions, as managers decide to 'involve' unions but only within strictly defined parameters, and very much upon their own terms (Ackers et al., 2004; Bacon, 2001). In other words, management will always be pragmatic in attempts to identify 'what works' (Edwards, 2003).

The most vocal case against partnership has been expressed by Kelly who defines the debate in terms of a choice between militancy and moderation (1996: 87). For Kelly, union militancy is a preferable option in light of what he perceives to be the growing hostility of employers to any form of unionism, the beneficial consequences of industrial action, the meagre consequences of moderation, and the continuing antagonism of interests between workers and employers. He concludes that 'it is difficult, if not impossible, to achieve a partnership with a party who would prefer that you didn't' exist, the growth of employer hostility is a major objection to the case for moderation' (Kelly, 1996: 88). Critics also express fundamental concerns regarding the British business environment and structure of corporate governance which focuses upon short-term performance, arguably meaning there is less incentive to engage in long-term partnerships (Ackers et al., 2004; Deakin et al., 2004; Heery, 2002; Suff and Williams, 2004) and the possibility the employer may renege on promises at any time, given the voluntarist framework of minimal juridification (see also Haynes and Allen, 2001). As Heery has stated, 'the dominant characteristics of British business ... do not furnish an environment in which union strategy of partnership can flourish' (Heery, 2002: 26). In short, the partnership debate is starkly polarised between the optimists and the pessimists, and these competing perspectives are summarised in Table 2.2.

Table 2.2   Polarised perspectives on partnership

Optimistic	Pessimistic
Union renewal, legitimacy, renaissance, organisation	Union incorporation, emasculation
Organisational success, competitiveness, productivity	Work intensification
Employee involvement, quality of working life	Surveillance
Win-win	Co-option
Greater job security	Employee disillusionment
Better working conditions	Zero-sum
Higher productivity	
Ackers and Payne (1998) IPA (2005), TUC (1999, 2002)	Kelly (1996, 2000); Claydon (1998); Gall (2003)

Source: Johnstone, S. Ackers, P and Wilkinson, A. (2009) The partnership phenomenon in the UK: a ten year review, *Human Resource Management Journal*

Empirical Evidence

The past decade has also seen a large quantity of empirical studies on partnership, most of which are qualitative case studies. Two main themes dominate the research: trade union representative capacity outcomes, and the delivery of mutual gains. A summary of the main studies is provided in the Appendix.

THEME 1: TRADE UNION REPRESENTATIVE CAPACITY OUTCOMES

Perhaps because of the bleak prognosis of early commentaries on the future of unions in the UK, many of the initial partnership studies focus upon trade union representative capacity outcomes (Howell, 1999; Metcalf, 2004; Ross and Martin, 1999), (see for example, Haynes and Allen, 2001; Heaton et al., 2000; Heery et al., 2004; Martinez-Lucio and Stuart, 2002; McBride and Stirling, 2002; Wills, 2004; Wray, 2004).

In one of the earlier studies, Haynes and Allen (2001) explore partnership at Tesco and Legal & General, and suggest that partnership not only led to the strengthening of workplace union organisation, but was actually founded upon strong unionisation. At Legal & General benefits were thought to include better training, jointly managed flexibility initiatives, a more open environment, and an increase in union members and activists. Tesco also experienced increased union membership, increased activism, and more effective consultative procedures in terms of issue resolution and quality of input (see also IRS,1999; Samuel, 2001).

Wills (2004) studied the Barclays-Unifi agreement, and found that partnership offered both benefits and risks for the union. On the one hand, the union had access to senior decision-makers in the organisation, greater employer support for the union, improved workplace representation, and more positive shop-floor management attitudes. On the other hand, tensions included difficulties in demonstrating union impact, and the risk of being perceived to be 'bought-in' to management decision-making, thus supporting both the positive (Ackers and Payne, 1998), and negative positions (Kelly, 1996; Taylor and Ramsey, 1998). Samuel (2005) investigated a partnership agreement between Legal & General and Amicus-MSF. He argues that partnership actually improved union organisation and increased influence in management decision-making, especially at the workplace level. In particular, he found a new cadre of proactive and competent union representatives were able to forge better relations with management. Though partnership was very much on management's terms, ultimately, union membership had increased, employee satisfaction with the union was good, and there was evidence of the union providing an important 'checks and balances' role.

Research in the public sector by Badigannavar and Kelly (2004) investigated the implications of partnership for trade unions in the UK civil service, and their conclusions are much more pessimistic. They conclude that partnership did seem to offer improvements in employee influence, information and training, but on the other hand, evidence on employment security and union influence was mixed, and they suggest that partnership appeared to be negatively related to grievances and union density. Their findings were said to 'lend little support to the idea that in the current UK context partnership arrangements ... are likely to contribute to union revival' (Badigannavar and Kelly, 2004: 22). Another public sector study in the NHS was also pessimistic (Tailby et al., 2004), where partnership was said to offer limited discretion and to be a process very remote from most ordinary employees. The study argues that there was a 'democratic deficit' primarily as a result of the performance regimes under which managers managed. Union decision-making was found to be centralised and distant from members, and the effectiveness was limited by the contradictory pressures of divergent targets, priorities and expectations (Tailby et al., 2004: 417).

Indeed, most of the early research partnership studies were critical. For some, partnership is doomed and a militant unionism is a more appropriate option. This is illustrated by the comments of Danford et al., who argue that 'partnership does not negate Kelly's militant unionism, it demands it ... high performance work systems and partnership do not resolve the structural antagonism between capital and labour' (Danford et al., 2004: 186). This view echoes Taylor and Ramsey (1998: 141) who argue that 'for unions ... an 'oppositional stance' to management remains justified and relevant'. Similarly, for Hyman the focus should be on partnership between trade unionists and not between management and unions. As he states, 'Trade unions should indeed embrace the principle of partnership. But its basis should be with other workers and trade unionists: nationally and internationally' (Hyman, 2004: 407). However, it is proposed that it is not necessarily the 'resolution' of antagonisms between capital and labour which is the main issue, but rather the moderation of a dynamic employment relationship characterised by periods of both conflict and co-operation.

Conversely, others argue that militancy is simply untenable in the current environment, with Ackers et al. concluding that 'partnership with employees is going ahead with or without trade unions (Ackers et al., 2004: 64), leaving unions with a choice of 'partnership or perish'. A similar conclusion is reached by Oxenbridge and Brown, who believe that there are simply limited alternatives to partnership and suggest that 'for unionised employment in Britain as a whole, the future will lie in greater co-operation. The economic and legal environment in prospect leaves little option' (Oxenbridge and Brown, 2004c: 157).

THEME 2: MUTUAL GAIN OUTCOMES

A second stream of literature focuses on the extent to which partnership can be argued to deliver 'mutual gains' to the various actors. Many studies have evaluated whether partnership delivers mutual or uneven benefits to employers, unions and employees (See Badigannavar and Kelly, 2005; Danford et al., 2004; 2005; Johnstone et al., 2004; Kelly, 2004; Kelly, 2004b; Oxenbridge and Brown, 2004b; Richardson et al., 2004; 2005; Suff and Williams, 2004). Much of the interest in this particular issue appears to relate to an influential article by Guest and Peccei (2001) on the 'balance of advantage'. Guest and Peccei, although in favour of partnership overall, concluded that there appeared to be unbalanced outcomes towards management. Importantly, they stress that this is not an argument against partnership per se, as they believe that a strong high trust partnership could *potentially* deliver superior outcomes for employers, unions and employees. The key point the authors make, however, is the need to take an integrated approach, and that in practice a lack of trust between parties was often a barrier to building effective partnership relationships. However, they argue that in principle a high trust partnership with extensive employee representation and direct participation should create benefits which flow to all stakeholders. They warn that a pick-and-mix approach is inherently risky and may simply become a disappointing 'hollow promise' (2001: 233) (see also Kochan and Osterman, 1994; Roche and Geary, 2002).

However, Kelly (2004a) suggests that partnership firms perform no better than their non-partnership counterparts. His research focused on the labour outcomes in partnership and non-partnership organisations, through the examination of issues including employment records and job losses, profits, wages, hours of work and holidays, and union density. He concludes that there was no impact on wage settlements, working time, holidays or union density. In terms of employment, in expanding industries partnership firms created more jobs than in non-partnership firms, but in declining industries partnership firms shed more jobs than non-partnership firms. However, it remains very difficult to quantitatively 'measure' the outcomes of partnership accurately.

In the public sector, Badigannavar and Kelly (2004) have also investigated the outcomes of arrangements for workers, unions and employers by comparing matched comparisons of partnership and non-partnership organisations in the NHS and civil service. They draw three main conclusions. Firstly, in only a few cases were employee outcome variables superior to their non-partnership counterparts. Secondly, there were significant differences in outcomes between the health service and the civil service, and in particular the finding that there was no difference in the employee outcomes between the two NHS trusts. In the civil service they actually identified superior outcomes in the non-partnership organisation. They argue that this could be because the NHS agreement was heavily 'employer dominant', whereas the union in the civil service partnership organisation had never been as well organised or achieved such high density as its non-partnership rival. Overall, they conclude that there is little evidence to support the mutual gains assertions in terms of union influence or better voice for workers. Another study in the non-union retail sector by the same authors also concludes that the partnership is 'precarious and well as ineffective' (Badigannavar and Kelly, 2005).

In aerospace and the public sector, Richardson et al. (2004) suggest that work intensification, stress and job insecurity may actually be the reality for employees in partnership environments, and conclude that 'the assumption that partnership leads unambiguously to mutual gains is highly questionable' (Richardson et al., 2004: 353). Similarly, Wray (2004, 209) concludes that 'in many instances, far from a situation of 'mutual gains', only marginal gains have been won for workers compared to significant gains for management'. He argues that this case organisation was characterised by a labour process based on exploitation and control rather than a collaborative relationship between capital and labour.

Less pessimistically, Suff and Williams (2004) found mixed results in their case study of Borg Warner, where management and union representatives generally argued that partnership had been a success. Employees also cited benefits, including better participation in organisational decision-making. On the other hand, employees did not really believe they had significant influence over decisions. Most employees also still felt insecure, and indeed thankful that they still had a job. However, with regard to rationale they found that 'the partnership concept is better viewed as a management device to secure enhanced organisational performance than an attempt to build genuine mutuality' (Suff and Williams, 2004: 4).

In sum, the partnership vogue has resulted in a fierce debate between critics and advocates. There are also those who support partnership in principle but – in response to empirical evidence – express doubts regarding the extent to which benefits have been achieved to date, and are conscious that barriers have to be overcome (Bacon and Storey, 2000; Guest and Peccei, 1998; Oxenbridge and Brown, 2004a, 2004b). It seems fair to conclude that the research in the first half of the last decade revealed little evidence of partnership leading to increased employee voice or mutual gains (Stuart and Martinez-Lucio, 2004b: 412).

Typologies of Partnership

Increasingly there is an acknowledgement in the literature that advocates/ critics debates were deterministic (Samuel, 2005), and that partnership may not hold any single consequence, and depends upon various conditions such as the underlying management and union strategies, the rationale for partnership, and the way in which it has been implemented (Heery, 2002; Heery et al., 2004; Roche and Geary 2002; Samuel, 2005; Wills, 2004). Given that partnership has been subject to various uses and interventions, and for different reasons, it is perhaps unsurprising that different outcomes appear to have emerged in the literature (Stuart and Martinez-Lucio, 2004b). After all, 'partnership is an imprecise term in employment relation, the meaning of which wanders from user to user and context to context' (Heery et al., 2004: 274). From the literature various distinctions can be drawn, including formal vs informal, union vs non-union, private vs public sector, as well as the variety of routes to partnership. This had led to typologies of partnerships emerging from studies in the second half of the last decade.

Wray (2004) draws a distinction between 'genuine' and 'counterfeit' agreements in his study of a light engineering company in the north of England. He argues that a genuine partnership depends upon how much voice partnership provides to employees, how far the relationship provides mutual gains, and how and for whose benefit the structures of partnership are operationalised. However, he suggests that the case in his study is best regarded as counterfeit. This was thought to be partly a result of the route to partnership which was characterised by the possibility of enforced recognition under the Employment Relations Act (1999), and a union signing the agreement primarily to increase membership. However, despite his critical stance, Wray (2004) does suggest the possibility that genuine partnerships may exist.

Kelly (2004a) makes a distinction between 'employer dominant agreements' and 'labour parity agreements'. He argues that given that most agreements have been signed within a context of restructuring or poor industrial relations, they are thus more likely to have taken the form of weak employer-dominant partnerships, for example agreements in utilities following privatisation, in banking following deregulation, and in motor manufacturing following intense Japanese competition. Labour parity agreements, he argues, are more likely where there are strong power resources such as with BA pilots and the Royal Mail. In reality, however, it is difficult to believe that such agreements are achievable in most private sector environments; indeed it is difficult to visualise what a true private sector 'labour parity' arrangement would look like.

Oxenbridge and Brown (2004a) examine the life expectancy of partnerships, and identify 'robust' and 'shallow' agreements. Robust relationships were identified as conferring a range of benefits to both parties, and were found in organisations where the employer supported trade union recruitment, wide scope of recognition, a history of trade unionism, high union density and extensive union input into decision-making. The primary benefits were from the informal consultative processes and the higher levels of trust. Shallow arrangements provided much fewer benefits for the union and were much less embedded. In these cases managers typically restricted union recruitment activity, and allowed unions limited involvement in workplace affairs. They conclude that while robust cases with employer support for the union and high membership appeared to be sustainable, the same could not be said for shallow cases characterised by a lack of employer support and employee apathy. Accordingly, they propose that partnership is more likely to be sustainable in large-scale manufacturing and the public sector, where a tradition of trade unionism is already deep rooted (Oxenbridge and Brown, 2004a).

Deakin et al. (2004: 115) suggest that partnerships can be either 'mature and enduring' or 'weak and disintegrating'. The former are characterised by union promotion of a high trust culture, and by management keeping their side of the bargain and investing in human capital. The latter scenario, however, involves a union role limited to that of dealing with the consequences of redundancy, with management offering a minimal commitment to employment security. Deakin et al. suggest that while a mature and enduring partnership is likely to survive an external shock, in weak partnerships actors are more interested in taking measures to minimise their exposure in the event of corporate failure, as opposed to genuinely engaging in a strategy aiming for mutual gains co-operation. Finally, Martinez-Lucio and Stuart (2005: 809) identify what they refer to as nurturing, transitional and coerced partnerships. Nurturing partnerships are predicated on an evolution of positive industrial relations. These are short-term, objective focused, and are often the result of an exogenous shock, in other words what they describe as a 'marriage of convenience'. They also identify coerced partnerships which they refer to as akin to shotgun weddings. These are elite level management-driven partnerships, devised by management to manage change and often exhibit union compliance. Both coerced and transitional partnerships appear to be incompatible with high trust enduring partnerships.

In sum, as Roche and Geary (2004) reflect, there appear to be *specific conditions* under which a robust partnership is likely to emerge. This reflects the arguments of Kochan and Osterman (1994) that partnership must be sufficiently institutionalised if it is to be enhancing or effective, and suggests that there is a need to understand the different types of partnership that are possible and to avoid asserting that partnership *necessarily* leads to a specific outcome (Haynes and Allen, 2001; Samuels, 2005; Wills, 2004). This suggests a need to understand more about what facilitates positive and negative consequences, and in particular the contexts and preconditions associated with each.

Limitations of the Existing Literature

It has been suggested that the early British partnership literature was characterised by a starkly polarised debate between advocates and critics. However, as Martinez-Lucio and Stuart state:

> *Accounts of partnership as a panacea for the future of employment relations are too simplistic, but so too are those that crudely conceptualise partnership as the latest management weapon for incorporating trade unions (Martinez-Lucio and Stuart, 2004: 421).*

The more recent literature, however, identifies a variety of possible outcomes, suggesting a much more complex picture than the ideological advocates/critics stalemate. Accordingly, it is proposed that there are ideological, contextual, methodological limitations to the current research. In addition, the early research failed to recognise the varieties of partnership relationship, and tended to focus on crude measures of outcomes. These are now discussed in turn.

IDEOLOGY

Firstly, there is a strong ideological dimension to partnership (McBride and Stirling, 2002). Views on partnership are inextricably linked to industrial relations frames of reference (Fox, 1974), and as such partnership is much more likely to be acceptable to those holding a unitarist or pluralist viewpoint. The fact that we have a 'highly polarised political debate' (Kelly, 2004b: 305), in the UK is therefore not surprising, as it is difficult to separate views on partnership from the ideological beliefs of researchers. For some, the institutional framework – without sectoral or industrial bargaining, and combined with short-termist corporate governance – *inevitably* leaves little scope for partnership

(Waddington, 2003). In addition, even although critics report *some* positive findings in their studies, these are sometimes overlooked in the conclusions of the overtly critical commentators. It also reflects the ideological constitution of British IR as an academic field, with many of the most pessimistic studies are written from within the critical IR tradition. On the other hand, the views of IR pluralists are more divided and uncertain.

CONTEXT

There is a lack also a lack of sensitivity to context. However, analysis of partnership should examine the context of the agreement as well as the relationships surrounding the negotiations (Jenkins; 2007; McBride and Stirling, 2002). As Marchington et al. (1994: 890) argue in their studies of EI, it is important to contextualise actor attitudes within the competitive and strategic environment in which businesses operate. They argue that there is a need to 'ground' studies of employee involvement in context, and the same is true for studies of partnership. For example, if only bad news is being delivered through the partnership infrastructure this could very possibly lead to negative attitudes towards partnership itself. Conversely, positive attitudes towards partnership could be symptomatic, perhaps, of a feel-good factor within the organisation because of recent good news such as a large pay rise. Workers' prior experiences of participation and in general, management's approach to employment relations, and the recent and future performance of the organisation are all likely to be important (Marchington et al., 1992, 1994). This leads to difficulties interpreting and comparing evaluations derived from both buoyant sectors and those in decline (Johnstone et al., 2004; 2009). Studies examine partnership in different sectors with very different product and labour market conditions, as well as different traditions of industrial relations. There is the possibility that partnership is likely to be successful in older industry sectors, with a history of unionisation, and buoyant sectors (Kelly, 2004a; Heery, 2002; Oxenbridge and Brown, 2004b). In particular, a clear distinction must be made between partnership in the public sector, where union density is often high, combined with strong state protection and insulation from market forces, and that in the private sector, where union density is often low, a tradition of unionism may be less entrenched, and market competition may be high.

METHODOLOGY

There are also several methodological issues. In particular, there is lack of data regarding worker responses to partnership. As Ackers et al. (2004) state, 'The attitudes and experiences of ordinary employees are central to deciding how successful a system of partnership or participation is,' given that managers and trade union criteria for 'effective' voice are likely to be quite different from those of 'ordinary workers' (Ackers et al., 2004: 56). Surprisingly, there has been a lack of emphasis on employee responses to partnership (notable exceptions include Richardson et al., 2004). As Suff and Williams note, 'direct evidence on the implications of partnership for workers in remarkably scarce' (Suff and Williams, 2004, 33). Rather, interviewees are typically trade union officials and managers, and few partnership studies have really engaged with debates on what workers want (see for example, Bryson and Freeman, 2006). In many ways this reflects the tendency of some industrial relations research to conflate the institutional interests of trade unions with the interests of employees, based on an assumption that what is good for the union must also be good for workers, and in turn failing to allow employee attitudes to be a shaping factor in the success or failure of partnership.

There is also a lack of comparative case study research. Kelly (2004a, 289) notes this lack of comparative case studies in the British literature, and suggests these may also be useful in the British context to complement the existing single case based research. Indeed, it is likely that comparative cases could assist with the process of 'theoretical generalisation' from the cases (Yin, 2003). Admittedly, the conduct of comparative case studies is not helped by the fact that it is difficult to identify a credible prima facie instance of partnership; given that partnership remains a nebulous concept it is perhaps unsurprising that the evidence presents mixed findings. This leads to the situation whereby Kelly (2004a) identifies Abbey National as a non-partnership organisation, whereas the IPA (2004: 1) describes the same organisation as having 'a formal partnership agreement which has been in place for a number of years and which was updated in July 2003'. Clearly, researchers need to question whether – and justify why – they believe the case investigated constitutes a prima facie instance of partnership, for example, in relation to the partnership criteria.

More generally, Kelly has commented how 'the level of methodological rigour in the empirical research is sometimes poor. There are numerous widely cited case studies of partnership firms that are often uncritical and journalistic in tone, excessively reliant on the views of a few partisan informants, and seriously under-theorised' (Kelly, 2004a: 270). While an important point, clearly the need for methodologically rigorous research applies equally to the conduct of quantitative partnership studies as well, for it is not only case study research that is problematic. The TUC (2002) for example, claim that evidence from WERS98 suggests that partnership organisations make fewer people redundant, have shorter average working hours and rarely declare compulsory redundancies. This is a somewhat dubious analysis given that WERS98 does not distinguish between partnership and non-partnership organisations, or indeed make any reference to partnership whatsoever. Moreover, much of the literature is limited to snapshot case studies at a particular point in time. Clearly, this is not ideal given that partnership is a dynamic process evolving over time, and like any relationship takes time to evolve.

VARIETIES OF PARTNERSHIP

A related issue concerns sensitivity to different types of partnership agreement. As the introductory section made clear, 'partnership is a loose word for many shades of the employment relationship' (Ackers et al., 2004: 17), and distinctions can be made in terms of several variables. For example, there has been a focus on formalised agreements (with the exception of Oxenbridge and Brown, 2004a), although some research has begun to make a distinction between 'de jure' and 'de facto' partnerships (Ackers et al., 2004). Oxenbridge and Brown (2004b) identify three broad categories of relationship in terms of formality: formal partnerships with explicit agreements; informal partnerships where the term is widely used, and co-operative relationships which may not actually be described by the parties as partnership. There is also the issue of the different routes to – and rationales for – partnership. In other words, was the desire to build a strong partnership to assist with the management of change, to sponsor weak unions, or to bypass unions? (see for example, Ackers et al., 2004; also Martinez-Lucio and Stuart, 2005).

There has also been a focus on partnerships between unions and management. However, as Ackers et al. (2004: 56) argue, 'it seems sociologically unproductive to rule out non-union consultative forms, whether voluntary or state regulated ... before examining the evidence'. The same bias is evident in wider discussions of voice which have also tended to be union centred. Non-union workplaces are crudely assumed to have no HRM and no IR, and often non-union voice is dismissed as inferior to union voice without reference to empirical evidence (Haynes, 2005). Again, where non-union voice structures do exist they are assumed to be merely cosmetic devices lacking the necessary power and authority to be effective (Terry, 1999), even though evidence on the efficacy of representation in non-union settings is mixed (Bryson, 2004; Dundon and Rollinson, 2004; Gollan 2001, 2005, 2007). In addition, while radicals may view voice as a means to an end, pluralists tend to perceive intrinsic value in the process of voice itself. This relates to the greatest limitation of the British partnership literature: the focus on outcomes.

FOCUS ON OUTCOMES

The tendency to focus on outcomes is odd given that partnership outcomes are notoriously difficult to quantify (Roper, 2000), and because partnership is about much more than just outcomes. As Stuart and Martinez-Lucio make clear:

> *Partnership is not just about outcomes, or its potential for trade unions ... partnership is a development that represents the emergence of a new approach to employment relations that attempts to reconfigure the form and content of management-union relations (Stuart and Martinez-Lucio, 2004: 11).*

In other words, partnership can be viewed more broadly as an attempt to reconfigure employment relations in light of the demise of old-style joint regulation (Terry, 2003). The narrow focus on outcomes is also criticised by Dietz, who suggests that it is not just the outcome which is important but also more subtle issues, such as the way issues have been handled. For example, in relation to job losses:

> *One need not express surprise when large scale redundancies take place under partnership. This issue is how they are agreed upon and handled. Training to enhance staff employability also plays a part (Dietz, 2004: 9).*

Partnership is also about subtle changes in attitudes and behaviours, which may not always be apparent if a narrow outcome focus is taken, requiring more attention to 'internal behaviour transformations and attitudinal improvements' (Dietz, 2004, 7; c.f. Walton and McKersie, 1965). Such factors would inevitably be missed by studies such as Kelly (2004a), where selected labour outcomes are used to 'measure' the success of partnership. A similar sentiment is expressed by Wray who explains how in his research 'it quickly became clear that a full assessment of the outcome would be impossible without a comprehensive understanding of the nuances shaping the process of negotiation' (Wray, 2004: 193).

It is not only the focus on outcomes which gives cause for concern, but also the way the outcomes of partnership have been evaluated and judged. In particular there is a lack of agreement regarding what partnership is actually expected to achieve, especially if the measurements for success are set unrealistically high. This has led to a situation whereby 'the expectations (both in terms of hopes and fears) generate by the term [partnership] means that it has become all too easy to set it up as a straw debate with aim of knocking it down' (Stuart and Martinez-Lucio, 2004b: 22). Consequently, outcomes are too easily offset against unrealistic announcements and agreements (for example, increasing transparency, enhancing training and development, creating a better quality of working life), or other equally ambitious aims such as the renaissance of the union movement, exceeding the expectations of even optimists like Ackers and Payne (1998). Much depends on how 'successful' partnership is defined and what it is expected to achieve, but it seems unrealistic that long-term partnerships will lead to harmonious, consensual and conflict-free IR (Terry and Smith, 2003). After all, the employment relationship consists of a blend of shared and contrary interests which inevitably lead to periods of both co-operation and conflict (Bacon, 2001). It also seems unrealistic to even suggest that partnership will lead to 'mutual gains' in the purest sense of the term, with gains flowing equally and harmoniously to all parties; indeed it is difficult to imagine what such a situation would look like.

Most commentators do seem to agree, however, that it essential to examine process in addition to outcomes if a more holistic understanding is to be achieved, as the following array of quotes illustrate:

> Good processes matter more than good institutions (Guest and Peccei, 1998: 9).

> Although there exists a wealth of published material governing the breadth and depth of participatory practices in UK workplaces, we have much less understanding of participation as a process (Danford et al., 2005a: 613).

> The study of partnership requires an approach that is sensitive to internal processes of decision-making, and the rationales that underpin the elaboration of strategies regarding work (Martinez-Lucio and Stuart, 2004: 421).

> Need to understand more about the substance of the relationships forged as a measure of robustness as opposed to the formality of the agreement (Oxenbridge and Brown, 2004c: 143).

Curiously, despite acknowledgement that process is important, and that without it only a partial view of partnership can be achieved, few British studies have explicitly focused on understanding the process as well as the outcomes, in order to achieve a more holistic understanding.

Implications

There are three main implications from this review. Firstly, it is important to examine partnership in context. Given that it is possible that an organisation could achieve positive ER and business outcomes without partnership and vice versa, a lack of contextual understanding could hinder a full understanding of partnership. Indeed, it is difficult to isolate ER/partnership outcomes from broader contextual issues such as corporate strategy and labour market conditions. In addition to a greater awareness of individual organisational contexts, there is also a need to locate partnership studies within the British IR context of union decline and less jointly regulated employment relations.

Secondly, despite the agreement that process is important, much of the British partnership debate has focused on hard-to-measure outcomes rather than on understanding process (Terry and Smith, 2003). It is proposed that two particular aspects of process are likely to be instructive. There is a need to be more sensitive to the mechanisms of voice, and to the ways in which partnership mechanisms influence behaviour and outcomes, for example in terms of decision-making processes. As Dietz states:

> *The litmus test for all partnerships – unionised or not – is the quality of the joint problem solving processes ... giving significant influence to employees over organisational decision-making early in the process, and in delivering regular, acceptable mutual gains for all parties (Dietz et al., 2005: 302).*

Sensitivity must also be paid to the presence or absence of partnership 'behaviours' in the employer-union relationship, such as the level of trust between actors and the way they interact, and this is really what is distinctive about partnership. Oxenbridge and Brown (2004b) suggest that a high trust relationship is likely to be characterised by a central and legitimised role for workplace representatives, trade union involvement at the earliest stage of management decision-making, explicit or implicit acknowledgement that each party benefits from the relationship, openness in dealings between the parties, and commitment to the relationship from managers at all levels of the organisation (Oxenbridge and Brown, 2004b: 156). It is important therefore to 'look beyond the superficial terminology to the relationships that underlie it ... the intentions that lie behind them' (Oxenbridge and Brown, 2004b: 157). In order to advance the debate, inspiration for future research in Britain may be taken from recent contributions from Ireland and the US examining the complex dynamics and processes of partnership. Such studies attempt to understand more about the preconditions for effective partnership, and the particular circumstances in which 'mutual gains' may be realised (see for example, Kochan et al., 2008)

Thirdly, there is a need to clarify the meaning and expectations of partnership before any attempt can be made to judge the outcomes. Definitions such as 'mutuality', 'reciprocity' are simply too vague. While they suggest a relationship between two parties, and the notion of an exchange where each party gains something, this reveals very little about the quality of the employment relationship; indeed even a Dickensian sweatshop could be described in such terms. 'Co-operative employment relations' is also ambiguous, as a co-operative relationship to one person could be perceived as co-option by another (Dietz, 2004). As a result, 'it has become all too easy to set [partnership] up as a straw debate with the aim of knocking it down' (Stuart and Martinez-Lucio, 2004: 422). A more useful definition would include identifiable practices (such as employee and especially representative participation) with specific processes, such as early consultation and a 'joint problem-solving approach' to decision-making. Relationships based on trust, mutual legitimacy and commitment to business success are also central. It is also important to draw an analytical distinction between partnership (defined as a combination of practices and processes), and employment relations outcomes which ought to be considered separately. For reformists, what really matters is the extent to which partnership delivers some benefits to employees, as well as wider benefits to the economy and society as a whole. There is a need to reconsider the benchmarks for success, and to pay more attention to the expectations and perceptions of the actors themselves, and not just those of academic theorists.

Research Framework: Transcending Polarised Partnership Debates

In light of the preceding discussion it is suggested that a fruitful approach for further research is to explore the meaning, context, process and outcomes of partnership (Guest and Peccei, 2001; McBride and Stirling, 2002). Firstly, in terms of context it is important firstly to justify how the organisation meets the criteria of a prima facie 'partnership organisation' else there is the risk of comparing pseudo-partnerships and therefore setting up the study to fail. It is also useful to explore how partnership is played out in different contexts, for example, between formal and informal partnerships, and union and non-union forms (Table 2.3). To minimise sectoral variables this study makes comparisons within the same sector, else there is the risk of contamination from the 'noise' of exogenous variables limiting the scope for useful comparisons to be drawn.

Secondly, this study benefits by paying closer attention to issues of process, which are often overlooked in the current literature. Key questions include the nature of actor relationships under partnership working, as well as the nature of decision-making and the way issues are handled in partnership organisations. Thirdly, regarding the final dimension of empirical partnership outcomes, it is argued that there is a need to re-evaluate the way the outcomes of partnership are judged. It is argued that the analytical framework proposed by Budd (2004) is a useful device for the analysis of the process and outcomes of partnership.

Table 2.3   Context, process and empirical outcomes of partnership

Context	Identifying partnership Routes to partnership Varieties of partnership (union/non-union, formal/informal, governance) Sector (for example, public vs private)
Process	Relationships Issues, decision-making and governance
Empirical Outcomes	Purpose and expectations of partnership Metrics of success Trade union outcomes Mutual gains outcomes (efficiency, equity and voice) Actor outcomes (employer, employees, unions)

Analytical Framework

Kelly (2004a) criticises the existing partnership literature on the grounds that there is insufficient reference to theory. At the centre of most discussions around partnership is the notion that it concerns a shift from adversarialism towards constructive co-operative relationships. Again, most discussions of partnership acknowledge that, in terms of process it suggests some degree of influence over some decision-making. In terms of outcomes the idea of mutual gains is central. In order to advance the debate, the analytical framework adopted has been devised by Budd (2004). He argues that the objectives of the employment relationship can be conceptualised as issues of efficiency, equity and voice. Given that partnership has been defined as 'an attempt to marry social and efficiency issues', and in the UK has pluralist notions of employee voice at its core (Martinez-Lucio and Stuart, 2002a: 254), this notion appears to chime with the idea of partnership.

Budd builds upon the traditional economic view of the employment relationship, in which capital wants to increase profits and workers want higher wages, and argues that equity and voice are equally important objectives (see Table 2.4). The narrow economic focus, he argues, must be balanced with employees' entitlement to fair treatment (equity) and the opportunity to have meaningful input into decisions (voice). He argues that extremes of either component are undesirable, and that a balance should the ultimate aim.

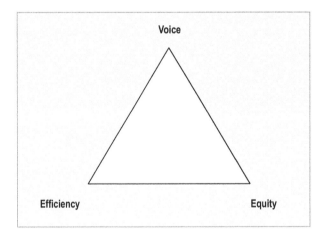

Figure 2.1   Balancing efficiency, equity and voice (Budd, 2004)

Table 2.4   Efficiency, equity and voice

Objective	Rationale
Efficiency	
• Market-based transactions and contracts	• Allocative efficiency
• Minimum labour standards (wages, hours, safety, family leave, advance notice, child labour)	• Externalities (social cost, purchasing power), asymmetric information
• Income maintenance (unemployment insurance, worker's compensation, pension standards)	• Asymmetric information, costly dispute resolution, liquidity constraints
• Industrial peace	• Externalities (social cost)
• Increased labour bargaining power	• Externalities (social cost, purchasing power) mobility costs
• Workplace public goods	• Externalities (free riders)
• Equality of opportunity	• Externalities (social cost)
• Employee representation/participation	• Co-ordination failure, asymmetric information
• Just cause dismissal	• Co-ordination failure, costly dispute resolution
Equity	
• Minimum labour standards (wages, hours, safety, family leave, advance notice, child labour)	• Human dignity (moral and religious)
• Balanced distribution of income	• Political equality/liberty
• Equality of opportunity	• Human dignity (moral and religious) political equality/liberty, due process rights
• Just cause dismissal	• Human dignity (moral and religious) political equality/liberty, due process rights
Voice	
• Industrial democracy	• Political equality/liberty/democracy
• Employee decision-making and autonomy	• Human dignity (moral and religious), psychological/social needs, property rights (stakeholder theory)
• Free speech	• Liberty/human dignity (moral)
• Political employee voice	• Political equality/liberty

Source: (Budd, 2004: 19)

Budd acknowledges that these ideas are not necessarily new, but build upon well-established debates. For example, as John R Commons stated in 1919:

> *Representative democracy is neither the imagined anarchistic equality of individuals nor the socialistic dictatorship of labour, but it is the equilibrium of capital and labour – the class partnership of organised capital and organised labour in the public interest (Commons, 1919: 43, cited in Budd, 2004).*

Again, a similar notion has been expressed by Kochan in 1980:

> *Industrial relations theories, research and policy prescriptions must be*
> *conscious of the relationships among the goals of workers, employers and*
> *the larger society and seek ways of achieving a workable and equitable*
> *balance among these interests (Kochan 1980: 21, cited in Budd, 2004).*

As Edwards comments, the employment relationship is inherently contested:

> *The employment relationship is a contest terrain embracing conflict*
> *and consent. From an employment relations point of view, there is an*
> *inherent management of uncertainty. For employees concerns include*
> *dignity and justice as well as economic interests (Edwards, 2003: 5).*

Similarly, as Hyman (1996: 67) acknowledges, 'uncompromising militancy is a recipe for defeat and exclusion; unqualified collaboration invites grassroots alienation and perhaps revolt. Any effective system of representation is a contradictory combination of conflict and accommodation'.

In other words, the comments reinforce the notion that some kind of accommodation is desirable. The idea is also reflected in the recent policy environment. As the UK government stated in 1997, in tune with their 'Third Way' objectives:

> *For those in work, the Government has two key objectives for the labour*
> *market: efficiency and fairness. We want to see efficiency because we*
> *want people to work well enough and hard enough to generate prosperity*
> *for the country as a whole. And we want to see fairness because people*
> *at work deserve to be treated decently – and they perform better when*
> *they are. Efficiency and fairness are wholly compatible. It is perfectly*
> *possible to have a modern, flexible and efficient labour market which*
> *is both a vital engine for economic growth and business output and a*
> *means for people to find well-paid and satisfying jobs (DTI, 1998: 4).*

Admittedly, in terms of rhetoric, a key DTI discussion document, 'High performance workplaces: the role of employee involvement in a modern economy', appears to be focusing on the business case, which may appear surprising given that the legislation emanates from European Social Policy. However, it is not really that remarkable given that all policies are couched rhetorically in terms of the intended audience, in this case the business community. Moreover, European social partnership also has a business case dimension as well. The Work Foundation also stress that information and consultation is not just about economic efficiency, but is equally concerned with issues of industrial citizenship. A similar point has also been made by Dundon et al. (2004), who argue that there is interest in voice for two reasons: high performance and high commitment, as well as issues of industrial citizenship, rights of workers to have their say, diversity, equality of opportunity and procedural justice. The links between employment and wider society are also underlined by Ackers (2002). Even Joseph Stiglitz – former Chief Economist at the World Bank – has acknowledged the importance of voice for broader economic, social and political reasons:

> We care about the kind of society we live in. We believe in democracy ... Democratic processes must entail open dialogue and broadly active civil engagement, and it requires that individuals have a voice in decisions that affect them, including economic decisions ... Economic democracy is an essential part of a democratic society (Stiglitz, 2000: 20).

The Budd model also allows a general comparison of various industrial relations trajectories to be made. The orthodox view is that the US model is characterised by free markets, voluntarism and, more recently, managerially driven HRM initiatives. This focus would put the US firmly in the bottom left of the triangle, reflecting the demise of the New Deal model. On the other hand, the European Social Model, with its emphasis on collective bargaining, employee representation, codetermination and neocorporatist social partnership would be placed towards the centre-right of the triangle, given the focus on voice and equity. It also illustrates how the European Social Model has been challenged in recent times and criticised on the grounds that it can be inflexible and inefficient.

Interestingly, recent arguments in the UK, US and continental Europe appear to demonstrate a degree of theoretical convergence. Mutual gains as promoted by Kochan and Osterman (1994) appear to be pushing towards the centre of the triangle, in attempts to increase the importance of voice and equity in US workplaces. A similar point could be made in relation to the 'new' European social model which has been traditionally strong on voice and equity, but has encountered criticism in relation to efficiency. In the UK context, it could be argued in the 1970s IR swayed too much towards voice and equity and was subsequently pushed towards a focus on efficiency at the expense of the other two objectives under the Thatcher government. British workplace partnership, US mutual gains models and the 'new' European Social Model could all be viewed as an attempt to redress the balance.

In the British context, as Martinez-Lucio states, 'it is generally accepted that in rhetorical terms, partnership is related to an approach to employment relations based on a belief – whether well founded or not – that there are employers that find it both ethically responsible and economically effective to co-operate with trade unions (and employees) on strategic matters of organisational change' (Martinez-Lucio and Stuart, 2004). This accords with Budd's proposition that 'debates over social partnerships can be interpreted as debates over balancing efficiency, equity and voice ... efficiency, equity and voice provide the dimensions for evaluating social partnerships' (Budd, 2004: 120). It therefore appears to be a useful analytical tool in terms of evaluating the processes and outcomes of workplace partnership working.

Two main propositions can therefore be made. Firstly, at the level of organisational decision-making, it could be speculated that a successful partnership would be characterised by attempts to accommodate the competing demands of stakeholders in some way. On occasion this may mean that the unions acknowledge certain demands would be uneconomical, while on others it would be expected that the employer would demonstrate due regard for employees in terms of the fairness of decisions. Secondly, in terms of outcomes of partnership overall, it could be speculated that outcomes in a successful partnership would be more balanced than they may otherwise have been. Again, it is important to note that though partnership is a process in which voice involves an attempt to balance equity and efficiency, this does not necessarily mean that this is actually an outcome, but rather that partnership is a process which involves such an attempt to balance equity and efficiency. This supports the argument that there is a need to draw an analytical distinction between process and outcomes.

Conclusion

This chapter began by highlighting the definitional ambiguity surrounding the notion of partnership, and reviewed the definitions offered by academic commentators, stakeholder bodies and organisations espousing partnership approaches. There was evidence from this review to suggest that there is a convergence around a common set of prescriptions and assumptions concerning ideas of employee voice, trust, a commitment to the success of the enterprise, as well as reciprocity and mutual gains. It has also been argued that it is important to explore partnership in the UK in context. Again, a desire to improve employment relations is certainly nothing new; rather IR reform and improvement was a perennial issue throughout the twentieth century. The bleak environment for unions and the decline of collective employment relations provide crucial context to the interest in partnership.

New Labour endorsed partnership as a central plank of their commitment to 'modernise' employment relations, underpinned by the Third Way notions of reconciling the interests of both the business community and workers. Partnership was also promoted by the long established Involvement and Participation Association, and the TUC took an interest, accepting that militancy was out, and co-operation was out. For unions, partnership arguably presented an opportunity for them to 'get their foot back in the door'. Perhaps unsurprisingly employer bodies have generally adopted pragmatic stances, often endorsing partnership but opposing regulation which compels firms to adopt systems which they argue may not meet specific organisational needs. Pragmatism also describes the attitudes of employers to partnership, and often partnership was agreed where there was a specific industrial relations problem. This chapter has also illustrated a starkly polarised debate between advocates and critics, with the debates focusing upon the likely impact on trade union renewal, and the reality of the mutual gains rhetoric. More recent studies, however, have begun to suggest that partnership need not necessarily have any predetermined consequences and that a variety of outcomes are possible.

Several limitations of the literature were also identified, including the ideological dimension, a lack of sensitivity to context, methodological issues, and a lack of sensitivity to different forms of partnership arrangement. The most important limitation is believed the crude focus on 'outcomes', despite the problem that such outcomes are notoriously difficult to quantify. Partnership is about much more than just outcomes. The impact on the regulation of employment relations simply cannot be deduced from 'measures' such as pay or holidays, as this may miss subtle but important nuances such as behavioural and attitudinal transformation which make partnership a distinctive social phenomenon. Indeed, it is simply too easy to set partnership up as a straw man with the aim of tearing it down (Stuart and Martinez-Lucio, 2004a).

This study aims to address some of these limitations by grounding studies in context and clarifying the meaning of partnership in each context. It also aims to reveal much more about the process of partnership, such as actor relationships and the way decisions are made, in addition to the outcomes. Of course outcomes cannot be ignored but there is also a need to reconsider how they are assessed. It is suggested that the analytical frameworks Budd (2004) provides are an excellent analytical device for this purpose.

3

Employment Relations in Financial Services

Introduction

An appreciation of the business and employment relations context is crucial, in order to fully understand the developments in the three case study organisations. The purpose of this chapter is to review some of the main developments and trends in the British financial service sector and then some of the more specific implications for industrial relations and human resource management.

Evolution of UK Banking

There have been significant changes in the nature of UK banking in the last 25 years, including changes in the structure of the markets, restructuring of delivery systems, and the development of a more sophisticated marketing orientation (Gardener et al., 1999). These three themes are now discussed in turn.

MARKET DEVELOPMENTS

Traditional retail banking in the UK was characterised by an oligopolistic market structure with limited price competition. High cost branch networks acted as an effective barrier to entry, and as a result there was steady growth and the major players remained moderately profitable. The financial services market was also traditionally demarcated. For example, until the 1980s, building societies operated in a market by themselves, enjoyed tax privileges, and interest rates were published by the Building Societies Association. Their main business was providing loans for house purchase; again there was little price competition, and the focus was upon the branch network and advertising.

Later, in the 1980s, banks entered the home loan market and eroded the building society monopoly. The 1986 Building Societies Act also allowed building societies to develop their diversification strategies into unsecured lending, property investment, estate agency, insurance brokering and personal pensions. Deregulation also exposed the clearing banks to competition, in what had previously been a clearly demarcated market. Banks and other financial institutions, and even non-banking organisations, began to compete for the same market. In particular, new entrants were cherry picking the most lucrative segments of the various markets, and were therefore able to operate on a much lower cost–income ratio. Intense competition led bank and building societies to focus heavily upon increasing profitability and efficiency, and retaining existing customers (Gardener et al., 1999).

Essentially, there has been a convergence, with various organisations now attempting to cross-sell entire ranges of financial service offerings rather than just focusing upon a select few. Consumers have also become increasingly sophisticated and able to compare the vast array of products available through the media, for example, newspapers and internet comparison sites. Banks, which hitherto benefited from a combination of customer loyalty and inertia, now have to deal with more savvy and fickle consumers. Retail banks have also become increasingly cost-conscious, as new competitors that have entered the market without an expensive branch network have selected only the most lucrative segments of the market. Key challenges in the 1990s included pressures on profitability, competition and new technology, putting pressure on the clearing banks to reduce costs. Since the 1990s, banks have also merged in order to reap scale economies. Initially, the focus was upon domestic mergers such as HSBC and Midland Bank (1992), Halifax and Bank of Scotland (2001), Lloyds Bank and TSB (1995), Royal Bank of Scotland and NatWest (2001). More recently, some of the largest UK banks have become part of international banking corporations, with Spanish Grupo Santander acquiring Abbey in 2004, and Alliance & Leicester and Bradford & Bingley in 2008.

RESTRUCTURING DELIVERY SYSTEMS

There has also been significant restructuring of delivery systems over the last 20 years. Traditionally the local branch network was essential in order to facilitate physical financial transactions, and this acted as an important barrier to entry. Technological developments have since meant significantly less reliance on physical transactions in favour of electronic transactions such as BACS and Direct Debit. In 2008, the Faster Payments system has also been introduced, which allows customers to make almost instant electronic payments. There has also been increased use of telephone banking, pioneered in the late 1980s by Direct Line, and online banking services have also expanded considerably in the past decade. These allow customers to carry out many transactions, such as checking transactions, transferring funds and paying bills, without any need to visit a physical branch. Increasingly, such activities can be carried out using automated systems without the need to speak to a customer adviser, or even by text message from a customer's mobile telephone. In the late 1990s, even 'bricks and mortar' banks created telephone and internet-based brands, including Cahoot (Abbey), Smile (Co-operative) and Intelligent Finance (HBOS). New competition from e-banks has led traditional banks to question the cost-effectiveness of their expensive branch infrastructure, however closing branches, especially in rural areas, often creates negative publicity. Leyshon et al. (2006) document a continuous decline in bank branches since the late 1980s, with banks closing 36 per cent of their branches, converted building societies 22 per cent and mutual building societies 17 per cent during the period 1989–2003. Between 1995 and 2003 banks closed 22 per cent of branches, converted building societies closed 19 per cent and building societies 5 per cent. They argue that investor pressure to cut costs may explain the different rates of closure, combined with intense competitive pressure, availability of new distribution channels, and changing consumer habits. However, their research did suggest corporate governance played a key role, with PLCs seemingly under particularly intense pressure to reduce costs and boost profits. Restructuring has occurred with a system of lead branches, shifting back office functions to large regional processing centres. Lead branches avoid the costs involved with replication of expensive management skills, while processing centres encourage economies of scale (Gardener et al., 1999). This has led traditional banks to reconsider how to best utilise the expensive high street floor space (Gardener et al., 1999). Many branches have been redesigned, becoming loss leading sales outlets, redecorated to offer a more open, friendly retail environment (Storey, 1995), in contrast to the traditional austere, high security environment.

DEVELOPMENT OF A SOPHISTICATED MARKETING ORIENTATION

Traditionally banks aimed to have presence in most financial markets and adopted a mass marketing approach. Emphasis has begun to shift to a target marketing approach, seeking favourable markets where the bank can earn the highest rates of return, and specialisation in particular markets where it is believed a competitive advantage can be achieved over competitors. Whereas previously the aim was to have representation across most product lines, banks have streamlined their product lines, and started to focus upon particular market segments. The growth of niche marketing is strongly related to developments in information technology which allow banks detailed insights into their customer profile and behaviour (Gardener et al., 1999). These changes are summarised in Table 3.1.

Table 3.1   Evolution of banking in the UK

	Traditional Banking	New Banking
1. Market characteristics	Oligopoly Stable growth Discrete and protected markets Unsophisticated market High barriers to entry Personal sector relatively neglected	Highly competitive Turbulent Sophisticated market Barriers to entry come down Erosion of traditional demarcation Consolidation Internationalisation Personal sector courted assiduously Deregulation and re-regulation
2. Delivery systems	Extensive branch network Branch network oriented	Reorganisation and reduction of branches Utilisation of IT 24-hour banking Online banking Call/contact centres Global delivery channels
3. Marketing orientation	Mass market Pricing based on cost Diversity of activityProduct oriented Collection of deposits Cheque and cash handling Loans Full suite of basic services at all main branches	Market segmentation Market position Pricing based on perceived benefit Focus on markets Customer oriented Proliferation of products but selectively targeted at segmented markets

Source: Adapted from Gardener et al. (1999: 90), Storey (1995), Stuart and Martinez-Lucio (2008)

Employment Relations Implications

Having mapped some of the key changes in the business environment over the last 20 years, the purpose of this section is to consider the implications for human resource management and employment relations. Six main factors will now be outlined in turn: culture change; pay; staffing; work organisation; skills and careers, and industrial relations (see Table 3.2).

Table 3.2 **Summary of HR/IR change in British banking before and after 1989**

Dimension	Traditional Banking Pre-1989	New Banking Post-1989
1. Culture	Conservative, risk averse, stable, paternalistic, cautious, hierarchical, command oriented	Dynamic, creative risk takers Marketing and sales orientation, commercial, flexible, performance oriented Commitment oriented, HRM, TQM, EI Cost efficiency
2. Pay	Stable, incremental pay system Uniform pay and conditions Cost of living increases Multi-employer bargaining outside the workplace Wages out of competition National collective bargaining	Introduction of PRP Individual performance management Inter-bank wage competition Localised pay Pay freezes/limited rises
3. Staffing	Secure, lifetime employment for career bankers Two-tier recruitment for clerical workers and trainee managers Steady recruitment and growth Paternalistic welfare policies	Less secure, segmented labour markets Rationalisation Jobs lost to technology Segmented recruitment policies Agency and part-time staff Offshoring/outsourcing
4. Work organisation	High street branches	Repetitive back office work Taylorised processing factories 'Satelliting'/regional hubs Flexibility High street 'Finance Shops'
5. Skills, training, career	Emphasis on lending skills and administration Job evaluation and multiplicity of job grades Steady promotion Internal labour markets 'All round bankers'	Increasingly specialised and fragmented Fewer job grades Diminution of promotion opportunities Reduced managerial responsibilities Recruitment of specialists Multiple tier entry
6. Industrial relations and governance	Diverse array of representative bodies Main role played by staff associations Rivalry between staff associations and BIFU Few disputes/industrial action Steady union density Moderate employer support for collectivism Stable/co-operative traditions	Containment of trade unions Maintenance of staff associations Consultation rather than negotiation 'Take-it-or-leave it'/hard-nosed employer policies Direct employee involvement Wave of industrial action/disputes Uncertainty about grassroots discontent Union unity/mergers/superunions

Source: Adapted from Cressey and Scott (1992), Storey (1995, 27) Stuart and Martinez-Lucio (2008)

CULTURE CHANGE

Firstly, it is important to outline the general shift in banking culture. In the post-war era the expansion of employment had enabled the development of stable paternalistic industrial relations, with a tradition of lifelong careers and (for men in particular) steady promotion through the ranks. Cressey and Scott (1992) describe the dominant culture as one of conservatism, deference, loyalty and risk aversion. Employment relations were characterised by low levels of conflict, high job security and oligopolistic competition. Employee representation occurred through both trade unions and in-house staff associations. Since the recession of the early 1990s, controlling costs has become an important strategic priority (Morris et al., 2001). This was believed to require a change in culture from the traditional conservative approach, towards a more dynamic culture of sales, performance and customer service (Cressey and Scott, 1992). While traditional banking was less cost-conscious or overtly profit orientated, with an emphasis on technical skills and lending competence, new banking was characterised by a shift towards a market orientated culture, stressing employees' sales ability and customer service orientation, as well as technical banking proficiency (Gardener et al., 1999).

In terms of pay, multi-employer bargaining collapsed in the sector in the late 1980s, followed by a shift to company level bargaining, and subsequently towards bargaining at the business unit level. Historically, pay was set by an incremental ladder with rises annually between ages 16 and 31, and normally a cost-of-living increase. Since the late 1980s, this has diminished since NatWest initially introduced performance related pay contingent upon profits and targets (Storey, 1995). Systems of collective bargaining and seniority-based pay have since been replaced by a more individualistic culture of targets, bonuses and key performance indicators. In addition, pay is now commonly linked to the evaluation of various employee competences, skills and behaviours (Stuart and Martinez-Lucio, 2008).

Traditionally, a job in a bank was considered to be a 'job-for-life', from leaving school or graduating from university until retirement. In the 1970s, banks introduced a three tier recruitment system for O-level holders, A-level holders and graduate entrants. Emphasis is now upon recruiting to specific functions rather than rounded 'general bankers' (Storey, 1995). As highlighted earlier, the sector has also been characterised by periodic job cuts over the last 20 years. For example, during the period 1990–1994 employment in financial services fell by 100,000, and between 2002 and 2007 a further 87,000 jobs were cut, the result of offshoring and other efficiency oriented measures (Stuart and Martinez-Lucio, 2008). Further waves of job cuts are expected to be particularly severe during the period 2009–2010 in light of the global financial crisis and economic downturn.

Changes in banking have also contributed to changes in skill requirements and career paths. There is no longer a uniform standard 'rounded' banking career, due to a preference in recruiting for specific functions (for example, technology, commercial, treasury and retail), and at different levels, such as graduate schemes, MBA schemes, and separate recruitment for specialist or administrative roles. There has also been a growth in the number of employment agency staff, females and part-time workers. In terms of skill demands there has been a shift away from administrative and clerical competence towards more proactive sales roles, and this has resulted in resistance from long-service staff (Storey et al., 1997). Employers are increasingly seeking an array of soft skills and competencies (Stuart and Martinez-Lucio, 2008), with the Barclays Graduate Scheme, for example, requiring leadership, determination, adaptability and team working among other specific behavioural traits.

CALL CENTRES

In terms of work organisation, since the early 1990s one of the main trends has been the creation of large centralised administrative centres, which have been introduced to provide customer service, processing and IT support. This is perhaps epitomised by the birth of the call (or contact) centre. A contact centre has been defined by the UK government as follows:

> *[A] contact centre will be said to exist where ten or more people work exclusively or for the majority of their time in a structured telephony environment (which may also involve electronic means of customer management), including either inbound and outbound operations. The operation will usually use an ACD (automatic call distributor) and this is a characteristic of a contact centre (DTI, 2004).*

At the end of 2003, 790,000 people in the UK were employed in call centres, typically in roles such as customer service, telesales, and management and support roles. It was estimated that there were 5320 call centre operations and 500,000 workers employed as call centre agents. The typical contact centre agent is female (70 per cent), and in their twenties, although at management level, gender is split more equally. Average tenure in a call centre is three years for a call agent and four years for a manager and the average age is 28. Typical worker profiles include school leavers, students, graduates and women returning to work after having children. The mean average salary is around £12,500 in the finance sector, with team leaders typically earning £19,000 and managers £27,250 (Datamonitor, 2004).

Issues of employment relations and work organisation in call centres have attracted huge academic interest. Managerial writers suggest that call centres are characterised by skilled, empowered employees providing high quality customer service (Durr, 1998; Hook, 1998). This positive image portrays call centre employees as empowered, semi-professional workers working closely with the customer and supported by advanced IT. To this end, working conditions are considered to be pleasant, offering interesting work, generous employment relations, teamwork and good physical working conditions. Most of the published academic research, written in a critical labour process tradition, has focused upon work organisation and management control, and has taken an overtly critical view. Studies have examined industrial relations developments in call centres (Bain and Taylor, 2002, Rose, 2002), human resource management (Hutchinson et al., 2000; Kinnie and Hutchinson, 2000) and union representation (Bain and Taylor, 2004), as well as labour process (Bain and Taylor, 2000), gender (Belt, 2002) and work organisation. Critics have described call centres as 'electronic sweatshops' (Garson, 1988), 'panoptical wired cage' (Menzies, 1996), 'twentieth century panopticons' (Fernie and Metcalfe, 1998), 'assembly lines in the head' (Taylor and Bain, 1999), and 'female ghettos' (Belt, 2002). Concerns have been raised in relation to the low status, poor pay, limited career prospects, high level of routine and limited discretion.

More positively, Frenkel et al. (1999) conclude that neither the deeply pessimistic, nor the optimistic views are a fair representation of call centre work organisation, arguing that complex hybrid forms of work organisation exist. They argue that elements of both coexist, as management grapple with two competing objectives: standardisation of processes and customisation of products. Frenkel et al. (1998: 91) conclude relatively optimistically that call centre workers do not 'fit the stereotype image of the technologically incarcerated, regimented front line employee' and 'the image of the service organisation as regimented is overdrawn and therefore invalid'. In fact their studies found evidence of environments where call centre jobs were interesting and challenging, and front line workers did appear to be valued. For example, 75 per cent of employee respondents reported *overall* satisfaction with their job (Korczynski, 2002). Deery and Kinnie (2002) suggest that there are limits to the 'engineering model' for three main reasons. Firstly, in some circumstances employees may need to exercise discretion or subjective interpretation in the interests of providing good service. Secondly, customers value the way service is provided, but this is limited in a tightly scripted and highly controlled interaction. Thirdly, given the fact the customer is part of the process, it is difficult to predict their demands and requests, therefore requiring scope for a degree of flexibility.

This apparent paradox between maximising efficiency on the one hand, and customer orientation on the other, has been addressed in work by Korzcynski (2002), and his theory of the 'customer oriented bureaucracy'. Clearly, then, there are evident tensions, and this leads to choices in employment relations strategies. In other words, do organisations adopt an 'efficiency model' with individualised pay, insecure jobs, and strict routine and discipline, or do they adopt an HR system based upon high training, supportive supervision and team-working? Organisations may make strategic decisions in relation to their business objectives, market segment and labour market (Kinnie and Hutchinson, 2000), and it is proposed that the employment relations implications may also be discussed in terms of the efficiency-equity-voice framework outlined in Chapter 2. A company which aims to maximise call volume and minimise costs is likely to pursue an approach with limited discretion, standardisation, surveillance and monitoring. In other words a high efficiency, low voice, low equity option. Conversely, an organisation aiming to provide high quality service may provide greater autonomy, wider skill utilisation, and technology focused on providing agents with the information they need to operate effectively. The aim of this approach would be to accommodate the interests of voice and equity as well as efficiency. These choices are similar to what Bowen and Lawler (1992) term the 'production line' approach and the 'empowerment' approach. Curiously, as manufacturing has shifted away from Taylorism and scientific management, research has suggested that this appears to be the dominant paradigm embraced by the service sector (Batt, 2002), and call centres in particular (Taylor and Bain, 1999). Recent evidence would seem to suggest however, that in reality, the constrained approach is actually inefficient (Deery and Kinnie, 2002).

OFFSHORING

However, financial service call centres have increasingly been viewed as high volume and low value added, and therefore most prone to offshoring (see Table 3.3). Labour typically accounts for over 70 per cent of a call centre costs, and therefore lower costs in terms of labour, IT and rent have contributed to an interest in offshoring to low cost economies, where it is estimated that costs can be reduced by 30–40 per cent. A summary of some recent offshoring activity is provided in Table 3.3.

Table 3.3   Offshoring activity of UK financial service organisations

Company	To	Activities
Lloyds TSB	India (2003)	Call centre operations
HSBC	India, Malaysia, China, Philippines (2000)	Back office processes
Abbey	India (2002)	Back office processes, call centre
Liverpool Victoria	Global	IT
Norwich Union/Aviva	India (2002)	Call centre operations
Zurich	India	Call centre operations
Royal and Sun Alliance	India/global	Software development
Allianz Cornhill	India	Business processes, IT
Scottish Widows	India	Back office processes
Scottish Provident	India	Data processing
BUPA	India	Invoice processing
Axa	India	Back office processes
Barclays	India (2003)	Back office processes, IT
JP Morgan Chase	India	Investment analysts
Capital One	India (2002)	Call centre operations
Prudential	India (2004)	Back office processes
Goldman Sachs	India (2003)	IT, back office processes

Source: Leyshon et al., 2006

However, some of the major banks, most notably RBS, HBOS, NatWest and Nationwide, have remained publicly negative regarding offshoring. The COO at Alliance & Leicester stated, 'I believe passionately that when a customer contacts us they should be dealing with one of our own staff, trained and managed by us and with a dedicated focus on our customers' needs and our products and services ... others might be happy to use call centres in overseas locations, but we don't intend to' (Company press release). An HBOS statement also claimed, 'The call centre operator is the voice of the company. It's a big enough challenge to ensure that all of our people in the UK are aware of changes in everyday issues, without having to worry about an operation that is 3000 miles away' (Company press release).

WORKER REPRESENTATION AND ENTERPRISE GOVERNANCE

The recognition of trade and staff unions in financial services can be traced back to the 1960s, and membership has been relatively robust (Gall, 1993). This has been attributed to factors including moderate employer support for representation, increasing employment concentration in large centres (excluding the branch network) and considerable employment growth from the post-war period until the end of the 1980s. Employee representation in the finance sector has been characterised by one main union and numerous staff associations. The main industrial union was the Banking Insurance and Finance Union (BIFU), known as the National Union of Bank Employees (NUBE) prior to 1979, with origins prior to this in the Bank Officers Guild (BOG). UNIFI was formed by a merger of three unions in 1999: Banking Insurance and Finance Union (BIFU), National Westminster Staff Association (NWSA) which organised NatWest staff, and UNiFI from Barclays (the former Barclays Group Staff Union). The Lloyds TSB union remains independent and is not affiliated to the TUC, and UNIFI merged with Amicus in 2005. UNITE, created in 2007 by a merger of Amicus and Transport and General Workers Union, currently has over 180,000 members in the financial service sector (Stuart and Martinez-Lucio, 2008). There are also many building society staff associations, and indeed there has been a historical contrast between the traditionally moderate, cautious approach of building society staff associations as opposed to banks, although even BIFU was considered to be a fairly moderate union (Gall, 2001). Employment relations in the sector have been generally stable; however, during the 1990s the sector was 'far from strike free and docile' (Gall, 2001). Union density peaked at 54 per cent in 1994, in stark contrast to the general industrial relations trends of the time. This was in response to major business changes including attempts to extend branch opening hours and the introduction of performance related pay, and the resulting 'restructuring and erosion of the psychological contract in the finance sector' (Gall, 2001: 361).

Most of the largest financial service organisations in the UK still recognise trade unions and/or staff associations. Indeed, in 2004, 72 per cent of financial services workplaces recognised trade unions, and aggregate union density was 32 per cent (Kersley et al., 2006: 119). Comparable figures in manufacturing were 23 per cent and 31 per cent respectively. In addition, 56 per cent of financial services workplaces have a union density greater than 50 per cent, compared to only 11 per cent in manufacturing. However, it must be noted that the categorisation of financial services combines insurance and banking, though density is typically much higher in banking than in insurance. Nevertheless, besides privatised public utilities, the financial service sector is interesting as it is the only private sector industry where union recognition is still the norm. (Kersley et al., 2006: 120). In 2004, 85 per cent of financial services workplaces had arrangements for employee representation, in turn making representation available to 80 per cent employees in the sector. Non-union banks are certainly in the minority, and include organisations such as internet banks Capital One and Egg, and Bristol & West building society. Nevertheless, most non-union financial service organisations also have formal representative structures, such as the Partners Council at Bristol & West, and the 'LINK' representative council at Standard Life.

Following a hostile period of industrial relations in the sector in the mid 1990s, several organisations signed partnership agreements with the trade unions, in an apparent acknowledgement of the untenable nature of a poor employment relations climate. In particular, service organisations are especially vulnerable to the bad media publicity that strikes attract. In addition, the need to get unions on board may have reflected the limited success of effecting organisational change and restructuring without their support (Stuart and Martinez-Lucio, 2008). Poor IR and a general context of industrial action and job cuts appeared to be the impetus at Barclays, Co-operative Bank, NatWest and Lloyds TSB. In some other cases, including Legal & General and Scottish Widows, the rationale seemed to be an attempt to cement existing relationships (Gall, 2001). Interestingly, many of these partnership agreements appear to have been enduring (Bacon and Samuel, 2009), and several have been subject to academic scrutiny (see for example, Haynes and Allen, 2001; Samuel, 2005, 2007; Wills, 2004).

Conclusion

Following 'firm-in-sector' theory (Smith et al., 1990), it is suggested that there is a need to place organisational developments within the wider context in which they operate. Again, a clear advantage of studying organisations drawn from a single sector is the degree of homogeneity it affords which could not be achieved, for example, by comparing a retailer with the NHS. Indeed, it is proposed that there are many similarities between financial service organisations, which may represent a degree institutional isomorphism. Undoubtedly, the financial service sector is a major component of the UK economy. It is also one which has experienced massive change from stable oligopolistic 'traditional banking', to turbulent and intensively competitive 'new banking'. This has contributed to perceived need to change organisational culture, pay structures, staffing, work organisation, careers and industrial relations in the 1990s, and resulted in a significant rise in disputes and calls for industrial action. The rise of adversarialism in a traditionally stable employment sector, may partly explain why workplace partnership has been embraced by many organisations in this sector (Bacon and Samuel, 2009), as unions and management had to address the end of post-war stability, and deal with the issue of falling profits, intense competition and industrial relations unrest. This context provides an excellent leading edge test of partnership i.e. to what extent can partnership working help regulate the competing efficiency, equity and voice forces, in an industry where such forces had generally been balanced in the post-war era? The study focuses upon the experience of call centre workers. Again, this forms an important contemporary component of UK working, and the financial service sector is the biggest employer of such workers. Moreover, call centres may be considered to be more representative of 'modern' employment relations, and have many interesting characteristics including the profile of employees and HRM/IR practices adopted, in a sense suggesting that if partnership is the future, this provides an excellent context in which to evaluate it.

4

Partnership with a Trade Union at NatBank

Introduction

This chapter presents the first case study undertaken at the NatBank credit card administration centre in the North East of England. It begins by providing an outline to the case organisation and the site under study. This is followed by a discussion of the background to employment relations within the organisation, and at the centre. The partnership structures and understanding of the concept within the organisation are then examined. The chapter goes on to examine the process of partnership by focusing on the nature of the various relationships forged between managers, union officials, and representatives and employees. This is followed by a review of some of the key issues within the organisation in recent years, and in particular the way decisions have been made. The final sections evaluate the outcomes of the NatBank partnership, before concluding with some of the key barriers and challenges to partnership at NatBank.

Company Profile

NatBank is part of a major UK-based financial service group, established in London 300 years ago, and currently one of the largest in the world. The bank is currently developing a growing international presence, and has over 100,000 employees across 60 countries. In the 1960s, the bank created a separate credit card division, and the credit card business is one of the leading credit card organisations in Europe, with significant international operations in Africa and North America. The credit card business holds significant autonomy from the rest of the bank. It has over 12 million credit card holders in the UK and over 5 million internationally. The credit card business is also a significant player in the corporate credit card market, with over 550,000 corporate cardholders, as well as in the transaction processing market where it has relationships with one third of British retailers.

The Case Site: North East Credit Card Centre

The credit card business has four main administration centres throughout the UK. The bulk of the research was conducted at a large credit card administration centre in the North East of England. The local area is synonymous with the industrial revolution, and is an important port for coal, iron and steel due to its abundant natural resources. It is also famous as the birthplace of the railway industry and a centre for bridge building, constructing major bridges throughout the world. In the post-war era, the area experienced economic decline and over the last 30 years employment loss in traditional industries exacerbated already high unemployment. The region has since embarked upon a significant regeneration strategy to re-invent itself as a centre for inward investment and for service industries in particular. The riverbank that was once dominated by engineering and shipbuilding is now a modern business park, part of a major redevelopment project. The business park has attracted investment from several financial service organisations as well as a local university, management consultants, legal services, architectural and engineering consultancies, and now employs around 5000 people.

The case site itself employs around 1000 people. Most are employed as customer account managers (known as CAMs), resolving inbound telephone queries from customers, and promoting credit card products and services. Callers are connected to the interactive voice response (IVR) system to determine the nature of their query and route them to a suitable adviser. These are automatically routed through the automated call distribution system (ADS), which is also used to generate various statistics regarding the efficiency of the call centre. The employee profile ranges from school leavers and graduates who have recently joined, to long-serving former clerical staff with over 20 years experience.

Partnership Structures at NatBank

The partnership agreement at NatBank was born out of a very poor climate of industrial relations in the late 1990s, culminating in industrial action over the proposed introduction of performance related pay in 1997. Union representatives admitted that there was a need to end the hostile 'everybody out mentality' that prevailed within the bank whenever an issue arose. The Employee Relations Manager for the credit card division is based at corporate headquarters, and is responsible for employment relations issues across the four sites. He explained how, when he joined the organisation in the 1990s, the industrial relations climate was poor:

> When I first joined the organisation the relationship was absolutely shocking. Within the three months of me joining the organisation there was industrial action. Not because of anything I'd done! There was industrial action in the branch network. As I began to find out that was the culmination of a lot of things going badly in terms of the overall relationship. During the 1990s the relationship between the union and the company had been quite fractious, every odd year there would be industrial action and every even year they'd be long days and evenings at ACAS trying to solve problems (Employee Relations Manager).

Similarly, the Union National Secretary, who had been heavily involved during the 1990s disputes, suggested the union was kept at arm's length:

> In 1995 the bank tolerated the union and both the unions were kept very much at arm's length, weren't allowed into the banks head office, had no relationship with the business-end of the bank, had no relationship with the senior HR or other managers in the bank … the only relationship they had was with the Employee Relations Director. And in autumn 1997 we had the most horrendous strike in NatBank, we were out for three days, it doesn't sound much but in finance industry terms that's pretty big. I didn't speak to the bank for about 6 months (Union National Secretary).

Management and union respondents agreed that the 1990s situation was untenable. A formal partnership agreement was signed at a national level between NatBank and the recognised union in 2000 and, following a formal review and ballot, was subsequently renewed for another five-year period in 2005. The partnership agreement was based upon an adaptation of six principles of partnership espoused by the TUC (TUC, 1999). The six main principles are summarised overleaf (see Appendix for the full document).

THE PRINCIPLES OF PARTNERSHIP:

1. to secure and promote the long-term success of NatBank

2. to promote the interests of employees, customers and shareholders

3. to ensure that NatBank meets customer expectations by having people with the right skills in the right place at the right cost

4. to facilitate the management of change

5. to ensure employees are managed fairly and professionally

6. to promote equality of treatment and opportunity for all, valuing diversity.

There are currently three accredited union representatives on site, while for a period before there were none. Typical duties include providing advice to members, delivering joint union–management communications, recruitment, liaising between management and members on issues, and representing members during discipline and grievance procedures. All are long-standing employees of the bank and have been in the role as representatives for around two years. They decided to get involved following several related incidents within the organisation concerning a poorly received pay deal which apparently resulted in a pay freeze for many long-serving staff, attempts to harmonise contracts, and plans to offshore certain administrative functions to India. Before this shift in emphasis, the centre delivered a wide range of back office banking functions and up until the 1990s around 90 per cent of staff employed at in the credit card business were in administrative roles such as data processing/input or cardholder servicing. This shift resulted in many previously non-customer-facing staff being transferred to new telephone-based customer service and sales roles, as well as a review of the pay and conditions associated with the new roles.

A key motivation for the current union representatives to stand for election was in response to the suggestion that flexible call centre oriented contracts were to be introduced. As one representative explained:

> *I thought, I'm going to need to get more involved here, it cannot come in!*
> *It cannot come in to the centre. Because what they were looking for was*

to get everyone off the original NatBank contracts which were fantastic contracts, and get them all on these flexi contracts which are pish! Very little pay, and also staggered start and finish times, you don't know when you are in from one week to the next really. They've streamlined a lot of it since then, but that's why I got involved. I thought, it's not happening. I'm not letting it happen. And I haven't let it happen! (Union Representative).

Another representative offered a similar explanation:

We didn't have a rep here and there was loads going on. I just thought bugger it, I'm going to go for it and see if I can make a difference. And I went for the interview and I got the role (Union Representative).

Representatives receive two days per month for union duties, although there is scope for scheduling of extra time if union duties require it, and the representatives suggested that this is normally granted by their line managers. The representatives also have weekly meetings together to discuss issues, fortnightly meetings with the call centre managers, and monthly meetings with the Head of Site. They also hold quarterly meetings for members. The representatives also have frequent contact with the central union, receiving various weekly mailings through the post, and can also email and telephone for important enquiries. They appeared to be fairly active, suggesting that they deal with at least one union issue each day. They described the role of the NatBank full-time union official as one of 'mentor' offering advice and support when they feel they need to escalate an issue, although many decisions are devolved locally. The credit card division full-time official suggested that it was an explicit aim to build a solid cadre of local representatives, not just because this was desirable for practical reasons, but also because partnership working required competent and knowledgeable local representatives. The FTO suggested that the role of representatives is twofold. Firstly, to deal with day-to-day discipline and grievance issues with members, and secondly, to provide local expertise at negotiating meetings. This was believed to be extremely useful as they can bring valuable first-hand insights into how issues are experienced at the front line. However, they are not allowed to agree changes to contracts or terms and conditions without the involvement of full-time officials.

Though partnership was described as primarily in terms of mechanisms of representative participation between the employer and the trade union, the business also utilised an array of direct employee involvement mechanisms.

These included newspapers and magazines, 'buzz' team briefing sessions, memo 'desk-drops' and the company intranet. Though much of the emphasis was on downward communication there were also some upward mechanisms, for example, the Head of Site also holds occasional informal feedback sessions with employees over coffee. She believed this offered her a quick snapshot of the concerns of 'ordinary' employees. At a business level there were also employee attitude surveys and suggestion schemes. There was no evidence to suggest that these practices competed with representative participation; rather they appeared to operate in parallel.

Definition of Partnership within NatBank

According to the Employee Relations Manager partnership concerned a modern, sensible approach to the management of industrial relations centred around a joint commitment to business success:

> I think [partnership] is about sensible modern industrial relations. From a trade union perspective what they are interested in is long-term business success because without the business being successful, well trade unions rely on businesses being successful in order for themselves to be successful. There is a mutual self-interest here. We want to make lots of money for our shareholders, and the union would like us to make lots of money so we can continue to employ lots of staff who can in turn contribute to the union's funds. That means that the central core of partnership is about long-term business success, but that the perspectives the employer and trade union are coming at it [from] are completely different (Employee Relations Manager).

Management suggested that in practice this meant more dialogue and interaction with the trade union, and considering decisions from an *employee* as well as business/financial point of view. Without a partnership approach, the Director of Customer Service suggested that the union wants what is best for the union, and the business simply wants what is best for the business:

> When you don't have partnership, the trade union wants to get a result which is good for the trade union. And the company wants to get a result which is good for the company ... [with partnership] when you take an issue to the table, everybody wants to get it solved (Director of Customer Service).

Local managers also suggested that partnership concerned a more proactive problem-solving approach, and understanding the rationale behind decisions and business pressures. As the Site Manager explained:

> *Working together to get the best outcome ... it's thinking about what we're doing in advance and that we need to talk to the reps ... it's not an afterthought anymore (Site Manager).*

For the Call Centre Manager, clarifying the rationale for decisions was central to the approach:

> *The idea of partnership for me is that we work on things together ... they [the representatives] have the absolute and full logic behind decisions (Call Centre Manager).*

The Site Manager offered a fairly unitarist definition:

> *I think the value of employers today and the values of the union are more closely aligned. Unions want sustainable jobs and the employer wants to be profitable. And profitable businesses are more likely to deliver sustainable jobs. I think there has been a meeting of minds in a way (Site Manager).*

For the Union National Secretary, 'partnership' also concerns problem-solving and closer interaction between the union and the management team, but warned that perhaps the term 'partnership' itself is a misnomer:

> *Respect, transparency, a move from 'institutionalised' conflict to problem-solving. The whole ethos around partnership is problem-solving. But partnership is not the right word. It can never be a partnership. NatBank are running a business which makes £4 billion per year profit! What it does mean is that we are now in the tent rather than out the tent. In terms of interfacing with the main leaders of the bank, in terms of business decisions and the impact on staff. Dealing with staff in a totally different way. Dealing with staff as a real resource that the bank want to train and keep (Union National Secretary).*

In other words, he believed it was possible to get involved in a debate as to whether partnership offered an 'equal' relationship, overlooking the benefits such a framework offers, including access to key business decision-makers, better information, and a greater respect for each party's point of view. Full-time officials also suggested that one of the key components of partnership concerned both management and the union understanding each side's point of view. The National Secretary suggested that senior management now had a clearer idea of the operation of trade unions, and equally full-time officials now had a greater appreciation of business issues. In other words, in terms of approach, partnership was quite distinctive from traditional zero-sum arm's-length adversarialism.

As for the representatives, they described partnership as a less conflictual approach, and suggested that they now had to consider decisions from a staff and business point of view, whereas previously they may have only looked at the staff point of view. They also suggested that partnership concerned early consultation regarding issues as opposed to discussion at the implementation stage which they believe characterised non-partnership relationships. Representatives offered the following definitions:

> A 50:50 way of sorting things out ... meeting in the middle without strikes and ballots. There's nothing daft. Sat round a table sorting things out before it gets any further (Union Representative).

> Partnership is working together to try and solve issues. Not in conflict. It's both working for the best possible interests for the members, well it's not just the members that benefit but the staff. That's my understanding. That's my idea of partnership (Union Representative).

> As a rep it's a fine balance. You are there for the staff, but you are also there for the business. Basically in that in-between bit. Obviously we are more there for the staff than the business, but the business does pull on us as well (Union Representative).

It was made clear by the management team, however, that the union representatives do not need to *agree* or 'rubberstamp' decisions. Rather, the focus is on early consultation regarding developments and the opportunity for representatives to provide feedback and input while decisions are still at the 'design stage'.

When no agreement can be reached locally, representatives have the option of escalating issues to national consultation meetings. These meetings take place monthly at the different sites, and involve the divisional Employee

Relations Manager, full-time union officials, and other relevant management and representative guest members. The Employee Relations Manager made clear that under partnership the business retains the right to make the final decisions:

> *The union is not always going to agree with us. We are not always going to agree with them. Big deal. In a large organisations it's about being adult and grown up about that, it's OK to have rows. It's OK to have diversity of opinion. It just means one side has to convince the other that their arguments are stronger. But ultimately the business will make the decision. Because it's the business that has to answer to shareholders. It wouldn't necessarily stop us from doing something. Sometimes it might stop us from doing something, but ultimately we would proffer the view that we are dealing with the shareholders not the trade union (Employee Relations Manager).*

Indeed it was suggested by the Call Centre Manager that if employees perceive that the trade union actually agrees with all decisions this can lead to misunderstandings between representatives and union members:

> *I think the reps get themselves into a bit of a corner sometimes, because I think they like people to think that they agree everything and that nothing can happen until they've said yes, so when something does happen they don't agree with, staff are up in arms with them. So I think it's in everyone's interests to be very clear, the union reps do not need to sign everything off, but they will understand why we've done what we've done, and I think that they learn that more and more as we go forward. The more experienced union reps absolutely know that. Your life is a nightmare if the staff think that they agree everything. Because they get attacked. So it's far better, that everybody understands that relationship. (Call Centre Manager).*

Union representatives, however, suggested that sometimes the way decisions were communicated through joint statements contributed to the employee perception that unpopular decisions have been 'agreed in conjunction with the union'. As one representative explained:

> *Sometimes staff might think the union agree to anything but they don't know what the starting point was, and they can't be told. They can only be told what the outcome is. It's part of the restriction the bank place on*

it. Quite a lot of things. If it's bad news it says NatBank and the union have agreed this, that makes them look in a better light. And we can't say what the starting agreement was, and that what we ended up with was a hell of a lot better! (Union Representative).

However, as the Employee Relations Manager put it, *'Ultimately we are responsible to shareholders, and even if fundamentally the trade union is opposed and we wanted to do something, we'd go and do it.'*

Relationships

The purpose of this section is to explore the realities of the relationships between the key partnership actors. These are now discussed in turn.

SENIOR MANAGEMENT–UNION RELATIONSHIPS

Senior managers and union officials unanimously agreed that at a senior level management–union relationships were healthy. The Employee Relations Manager suggested the key issue was creating a dialogue which attempted to balance employee interests with commercial realities and shareholder expectations. However, he commented that the nature of the relationships forged under partnership were *'oceans apart'* compared to pre-partnership, *'arm's-length legislative compliance, rather than real enthusiasm'*. He proposed that at a senior level the relationship can work well, with union officials acknowledging business rationale, and senior management acknowledging the value of union dialogue, as an insight into employee opinion and likely reactions. This positive management assessment of the union–management relationship was echoed by the Customer Service Director, Site Manager, and Call Centre Manager. The union National Officer suggested a need to evaluate the relationship in relative terms, and on this basis he proposed the relationship was actually better than most others in the industry. Likewise, the Employee Relations Manager concluded that the NatBank relationship was very good in comparison to many others in the UK. In other words, how you measure success appeared to be important.

REPRESENTATIVE–MANAGER RELATIONSHIPS

Senior managers and union officials agreed that typically relationships were less strong at a middle management level. A full-time official suggested this was because middle managers are not rewarded on the basis of 'partnership behaviours' but rather on the basis of delivering quantitative business targets, and sometimes this would mean issues concerning involvement and consultation would *'fall by the wayside'* in order to achieve the business demands placed upon them. The Employee Relations Manager also suggested that a range of line manager attitudes to trade unions existed, and was to be expected:

> *Further down the organisational food chain you've got a mixed bag really of people who are very pro the trade union, and the role they can play as the representatives of staff, to people who are agnostic about the role the union can play, to people who are damn right hostile. Well that's no different to society. It would be a very odd organisation if we didn't reflect that (Employee Relations Manager).*

However, the representatives agreed that local relationships had improved immensely within the North East centre since the partnership agreement. In particular, it was believed that the fact that the union representatives and most of the management team were long-serving employees had helped to promote a strong relationship. For example, the current Site Manager is a former union representative, and actually recruited one of current representatives to the union many years ago. Many of the site management team are also members of the union. As a representative commented: *'We can go and talk to anybody. We don't always get what we want, but we know we are heard ... I'll even go for a ciggie with the managers, it's really no problem!'*

Local management were also positive, describing relationships as *'quite open and honest'*, and were good at bringing views *'from the floor'*:

> *I would say we have a good relationship ... it's not without its problems ... we don't always agree but it's not about agreeing, and it's not about rubber stamping, it's about talking to each other, and trying to get the best possible outcome for everybody concerned (Site Manager).*

> *We've got a good relationship, quite friendly really ... I've worked with these people for a long time (Call Centre Manager).*

Management and local union representatives openly admitted that there has been conflict and some very heated debates, but suggested that this was a normal part of a healthy partnership agreement, and was therefore to be expected:

The relationship should be strong enough to withstand heated debates.
Some people would probably be offended by it. But because you know
the people as individuals you can do that (Call Centre Manager).

Both sides emphasised the need to build relationships, and to understand the highly political nature of the partnership process and negotiations, and that each side is just playing their role. This was described as hard work but rewarding.

Team managers were also positive about the union role, although it is worth noting that knowledge of the role and involvement of the local representatives was patchy. Nevertheless, all knew who the local representatives were, and had a general knowledge of their role. Line managers primarily viewed representatives as the advocates of employees on day-to-day individual issues such as discipline and grievance procedures:

I think the union are there to ensure things are run fairly and effectively,
not to catch management out. From my own experience of that situation,
that's how I find it (Team Manager).

It's another voice really, you need it for clarification on a lot things. I
suppose it's a secondary mechanism there if you want to resolve issues
(Team Manager).

EMPLOYEES AND UNION REPRESENTATIVES

It also appeared that the union representatives had a good relationship with employees, and most employees knew who their representatives were. Employee understanding of the exact nature of the union representative's involvement and relationship with management was patchy, but most employees perceived the management–union relationship to be reasonably good, and were aware that such a relationship existed. Overall, most employee respondents admitted they did not really know much about representative involvement in collective issues but took the view that *'no news is good news'* and *'I wouldn't pay £10 a month if I didn't think they were doing something'*. Most employees agreed that the union representatives were well known and that there was trust in them doing a good job, as illustrated by the following quotes:

Everybody knows the union reps, they are all characters, you definitely
know them!

We don't get to see what they do for us. We don't know all the ins and outs. But you'd rather pay your funds because you think, if I didn't what would happen?!

I guess there must be trust in there somewhere otherwise you'd withdraw from the union.

They are very active and do seem to play a part. And I think they are really approachable. I wouldn't hesitate if I had a problem.

I think they are a lot more approachable now. A few years ago you wouldn't have had a clue who they were (Employee Focus Groups).

A union representative also believed that they had managed to establish some credibility with members over the last few years, suggesting they had received various compliments in relation to their achievements. This is an interesting finding, given than many employees had previously withdrawn from the union in the late 1990s because they believed they were being *'sold down the river'* by the trade union, and appears to suggest an increase in confidence and trust. Representatives stressed that one of their main tasks when they became accredited representatives, was to try and recruit many of the disaffected former members who had previously cancelled their subscriptions.

Issues and Decision-Making

The North East centre had experienced significant organisational change over the five years preceding the fieldwork. A key objective was to explore the way some of the key issues had been handled, and how various decisions have been made. This section begins with a discussion of traditional union issues such as pay and working conditions and then explores some other issues specific to the company.

PAY AND WORKING CONDITIONS

As discussed earlier, pay had been one of the main sources of industrial relations conflict, culminating in the 1997 industrial action, when the bank introduced PRP as a replacement for traditional seniority-based pay. For management, the negotiation of pay and conditions has improved under partnership, and a three-year pay deal has since been agreed with the union on three occasions. For the Employee Relations Manager the nature of pay negotiations had improved significantly under partnership, suggesting it is one of the main benefits of partnership working:

> *By working with the trade union we have been able to have at least three pay deals that have been agreed on and voted on by members of the union. And to my mind that's a strong endorsement that staff buy-in to how we are going to pay them, their reward. From an employer perspective it gives us a level of clarity in terms of being able to plan for the future, so we are not constantly in pay negotiation mode. I've taken quite an open book approach in terms of what we can and can't afford, and them having the opportunity to influence that at the start of our thinking on pay. They have been able to gain more influence through partnership than they might have otherwise done. And likewise we've been able to get a lot more planning done that we might have, if we hadn't had partnership. (Employee Relations Manager)*

Full-time officials agreed that they *'get very involved in the whole pay and reward'*. As the National Secretary explained:

> *We discuss all terms and conditions. Pay. Equality and diversity. Holidays. You name it. We don't negotiate bonuses but we have an influence and a debate. Well factually we don't negotiate bonuses (Union National Secretary).*

This was contrasted with pay negotiations pre-partnership:

> *The bank would tell us about changes an hour before. It was all done and dusted … This is what we are offering and we ain't moving. You can do what you like. Now we sit down and negotiate. Now we have a pay formula. PRP. Inflation plus a formula (Union National Secretary).*

Indeed, members voted 9:1 to accept a recent pay ballot, and this was cited by both the National Secretary and Employee Relations Manager as a positive endorsement of the success of pay negotiations under partnership.

Representatives were also positive regarding the pay agreements under partnership, whereas pay had been a major issue of controversy prior to partnership, with many employees leaving the union in the belief it was letting them down. As a representative commented:

Employees that have been here donkey's years like us came out of the union because they didn't get a pay rise for a few years because of the union. The union did sell us down the river and there is no hiding it, they did. About five years ago. Even I came out of the union, I cancelled as well. I thought I will get an extra £120 a year because I'll cancel my subs. And I did (Union Representative).

The representatives explained how this had made them absolutely determined to try and get a pay rise for all employees, and despite intense negotiations, this appears to have been successful:

Because I'm long serving and didn't get a pay rise last time, I went and sat on the board to make sure we got a rise this time. This year we all got a pay rise. And it's only through the union. People said well done (Union Representative).

Everybody who was in the top bracket or the high bracket, or moderate gets a pay rise regardless of what salary they earn. The pot was divided. That took about four days of arguing with management. Loads of arguing. They weren't going to give in. The top management were at that meeting (Union Representative).

Overall then, representatives clearly believed that under partnership pay negotiations have improved. However, they also suggested that it was still sometimes difficult to 'sell' the success of the pay negotiations when union members do not know the detail of the actual negotiations, but only the final outcome. For example, the final deal may be much greater than the bank was initially prepared to offer, but employees would be unaware of this, and may pass judgment based upon the level of the increase alone. This was quite different to more transparent traditional bargaining processes where collective bargaining worked as a useful rhetorical device in terms of demonstrating value to members.

This is clearly significant, as for most members the key role of the union was the negotiation of pay. Indeed, when asked about the role of the union, even those with a minimal interest in union activity remarked, '*I know that any pay deal goes through the union, and has to be sanctioned by the union, apart from that not much*'. Fortunately for the union, there was a feeling that pay negotiations had improved under partnership, as the following quotes illustrate:

I actually got a rise last year, it was my first rise in four years. And I think that was something, that had been pushed through the union that we'd get a minimum rise, and I thought last year, oh that's a one off. About £25 a month, at least I got a rise. Well it'll pay the water rates, at least you are getting a rise. I think that's the union pushing that through (Union Representative).

In short, pay negotiations – previously one of the main employment relations flashpoints throughout the late 1990s and early 2000s – were said by management, full-time officials and the union representatives to be better under the partnership process. Between the union and the management there seemed to be a mutual understanding that, on the one hand, employee pay was already competitive and the company could not afford massive rises, and on the other hand, that no pay rise for several years is unfair and demoralising. Employees were generally pleased too, because they were receiving pay rises whereas prior to partnership many employees were not, leading to disillusionment with the union.

DISCIPLINE AND GRIEVANCE

The management of discipline and grievance was another key area of union involvement at NatBank. The Employee Relations Manager suggested that under partnership, they now have established jointly agreed procedures for managing discipline and grievance. It was proposed that this has created clarity for the organisation in terms of their expectations of employee conduct, but also provides clarity for the union in terms of raising claims against the organisation when they have reason to believe the process has been unfair.

The union representatives suggested that among young employees in particular disciplinary cases were common regarding issues such as sickness, absence, time-keeping and underperformance. It was proposed that for many of these employees the union was viewed as a source of help should they end up in a discipline and grievance situation. Indeed, after successfully defending an employee in a disciplinary hearing the representatives would commonly provide the member with a bundle of membership forms and ask them to find new members to demonstrate their appreciation of the union service! The representatives believed that their success at dealing with disciplinary hearings was a good form of word-of-mouth marketing, especially among the younger employees who may not otherwise have been interested in joining the union. It was argued that overall due process was being followed more often under partnership, and representatives believed that cases of arbitrary treatment had been declining, as line managers increasingly paid attention to formally agreed procedures. As a representative explained:

> *I think it's better, I think managers think about the process more before they put people through disciplinaries. We don't seem to be getting so many stupid ones now. We won every one for six months because they just didn't follow process. They were silly. If you weren't a union member you could have got the sack through that. Now it's starting to hurt when you're losing them, but you realise that there is a process, and people do things wrong (Union Representative).*

Nevertheless, assisting those in trouble had proved to be a double-edged sword. On the one hand, it had increased membership amongst a cohort of younger employees they have had difficulty persuading to join the union. On other hand, some managers believed this was a cynical and untenable approach. For example, the Director of Customer Service argued that the union should not be focusing their efforts on defending people with poor attendance, and that that, *'they should be protecting the people who come in every day and carry the people who are consistently sick'*. Equally, it is possible that some employees would also resent this situation if they shared the view that the union effectively 'carried' the weakest members of staff.

For line managers, direct interaction with representatives occurred primarily during the discipline and grievance process, and many viewed them positively as a useful party acting as a *'checking mechanism to make sure people are dealt with fairly and consistently'* and that due process was followed. As one young team manager explained:

> *I pretty much see them as people who come to disciplinaries to see you dot your i's and cross your t's … I don't think we as team managers are made fully aware of the background. It would be something we would have to proactively find out as opposed to having to know about it as part of your role (Team Manager).*

Other team managers would proactively seek out the representatives before a hearing to try and establish different sides to the story. Indeed, on the day of one interview, a representative had found a cake on her desk, apparently from a line manager keen to get some advice on dealing with a problematic employee. Overall, the general view was that processes had improved since partnership.

In addition, it was suggested that very few formal grievances are now raised by employees at the centre.

MANAGING CHANGE

The third main issue concerns the management of change, and in particular the implications of transforming a back office administration centre into a call centre. Several related issues are of particular interest: outsourcing to India; re-grading and flexible contracts; targets, and the sales/service split. These are now examined in turn.

Outsourcing to India

The main issue to affect the centre in recent years was agreed to be the offshoring of several back office administrative functions to India. This involved the relocation of some of the more routine jobs to India, in areas such as correspondence and 'charge-backs', i.e. when the buyer requests that their card company claims back a payment from a merchant. The Head of Site suggested that this meant *'India was on everyone's radar'*, and had inevitably resulted in concerns regarding job security. In practice, the change meant that many employees previously engaged in other non-customer-facing clerical roles were offered roles as telephone-based customer agents. Managers suggested how *'It's quite a change in culture to put a headset on and answer the phone call after call ... a lot of the old school took very hard to that change'*. Again it was believed that the union lost many members at the centre because of the offshoring issue, as *'people thought the union were pretty crap'*. The representatives (who were not representatives at the time) believed the announcement was *'out-of-blue'*, with minimal information provided to employees from management or the union.

Employees suggested that the news of offshoring was published on the internet before NatBank had even made a formal announcement, and that *'it was just a major hoo-ha, we were all very worried'*. Since the fallout of the offshoring, the union and the bank have signed a 'globalisation agreement', outlining various commitments regarding offshoring practices. At the centre of the agreement is a framework to avoid compulsory redundancies in the event of offshoring. The key provisions of the agreement are:

- voluntary redundancy register across geographic regions

- enhanced use of voluntary job matching

- redeployment into alternative employment where a role is undertaken by a contractor or agency staff trial periods and no loss of redundancy option

- £2000 gross training support for external career retraining

- in-placement and outplacement support by consultants

- three months advanced notice plus three months displacement

- TUPE transfers and globalisation such as redundancy terms and pension provision

- International Labour Standards – freedom of association in international operations

- rolling management information on job transfer possibilities.

There is also the possibility of an industrial action ballot if compulsory redundancies arise. The Union National Secretary suggested that this meant the bank now has *'hoops and barriers they need to jump across'* to mitigate the worst excesses. As he commented, *'It doesn't' stop the off-shoring happening but it does protect the existing staff.'* Without such an agreement, he speculated that the union would not be consulted as early as they have been, and that the bank might only make minimal, cursory efforts at redeployment. To date nobody has lost their job as a result of the offshoring programme; indeed according to the representatives, many older members have been interested in pursuing the attractive voluntary redundancy packages.

Management suggested that the main difference under the new framework is that there is the agreed process for managing business change, even if the union inevitably opposes such decisions. The Employee Relations Manager suggested that having an agreed process means that now such change is upfront, with early union involvement, as well as union appreciation of competitive pressures and business rationale. In a similar vein, the Director of Customer Service suggested a need to confront tough realities and that in the current climate there is no such thing as a 'job for life', and the priority should be treating people correctly if they are made redundant. Full-time officials agreed that the union role is to mitigate the effects of such decisions through redeployment, training and earlier consultation, and believe with a non-partnership situation the bank may make less effort in managing redundancies, or offer a less generous severance scheme. Representatives agreed, however, that a reality of the current climate is that the union cannot stop offshoring. Instead, they suggest a need to focus on ensuring employees affected get the very best possible deal, either in terms of redundancy package or finding alternative employment, and that they are treated fairly and with respect.

Re-grading and flexible contracts

As the administration centre became a call centre as a result of offshoring, most employees were to take customer-facing telephony roles as customer account managers. Moreover, management believed that as technology had developed, decisions were now more systems-based and the job roles were to be re-evaluated to explore this. The re-evaluation of job roles meant that call centre agents could potentially have ended up on a lower grade (known as grade B2 rather than the current B3).

The job evaluation concluded that the new CAM role was more suited to grade B2. The management and union explored the various options and a decision was made to leave existing employees unaffected, to avoid conflict. The Call Centre Manager suggested that without the partnership process it may have been a fait accompli, with minimal consultation, seeking union input at a late stage if at all. As the Employee Relations Manager explained, without the extensive dialogue through the partnership process, a 'logical' business decision might *'have been imposed from on high without much consideration'*. Under partnership protocol, the decision followed a long period of consultation and discussion about the potentially disastrous impact on morale. The final decision was therefore to leave existing staff on their B3 grade, but to recruit new hires on the new B2 grade which the management team believed better represented the market rate and reflected the demands of the new roles. This was described by the union representatives as an example of a *'good win'*, as it reflected compromise and a degree of success. Representatives argued that the final decision did not benefit the business as much as management may perhaps have liked and neither did it satisfy the union fully, but ultimately they suggested it was the best outcome for both sides given the constraints. The Call Centre Manager also commented how *'it wasn't a great shock, it was the most palatable option. They got their win really'*.

As she explained:

I talked to them [the representatives] from day one so they knew everything I was doing and it wasn't a great shock to them, and I think it was the best approach to take. And they're not stupid. They knew it was absolutely the right thing to do (Call Centre Manager).

She contrasted this with the general approach before partnership:

Previously we would have done that 100 per cent behind closed doors. It would have just been delivered. A fait accompli just dropped on them. I have been involved in things before where it was absolutely cloak-and-dagger behind closed doors (Call Centre Manager).

For the union representatives, the compromise was the best approach for both sides:

Although it's not ideal, it's not benefiting the business as much as they would like to have from a money perspective. It made everybody happy. They knew the score (Union Representative).

This demonstrates a clear difference in terms of process between pre-partnership and post-partnership decision-making in terms of the level of engagement, and the fact that representatives were involved from an early stage.

A second issue concerned the introduction of a new flexible contract to replace the traditional 9–5 contract existing staff had. From a business perspective, it was believed to be important to be able to deal with customer enquiries in the evening rather than just during office hours, as is the case with many customer service operations. For many long-serving employees, however, the new contract was seen to represent a significant diminution in their terms and conditions. For example, the new contracts pay a lower premium for weekend working and have variable shift patterns. Of course, both the business environment and role of the centre have changed considerably since the 9–5 contracts were first issued. Again, it was eventually decided to keep existing staff on these contracts to avoid the potentially negative impact on morale. New bank employees, are of course, recruited on the basis of the new flexible contract.

Management suggested that without discussions with the union providing an insight into how potentially damaging this could prove in terms of employee morale and attrition, the decision might simply have been imposed. As the Employee Relations Manager explained:

> If we hadn't had that ongoing dialogue with the union, there is no doubt we would have imposed something from on high, would have pissed a load of people off, would have moved our attrition rates up, and would have cost us more in the long term. Because people would have left, and we would have had to recruit people, and trained them, and invested in them, and so on. We had people stay on those contracts, keep them happy and working. And did not make radical changes when we didn't need to (Employee Relations Manager).

Representatives also managed to negotiate a 25 per cent premium for weekend working:

> We got them 25 per cent. And that was a big win. Because management came in and said there was no way they were going to budge. But we got 25 per cent. Even though it was still crap it's better than nothing. Nothing like what we get, but times have changed, and they need to change. That was a good one (Union Representative).

Clearly, then the approach appeared to have enabled management to take a more holistic view of the situation, and to look at the impact of decisions on a longer timeframe.

Targets

Another topical issue concerned targets. The representatives argued that the targets were too stretching and a controversial issue was the proposed reduction of 'not ready' time between calls from 20 seconds to 15 seconds. As a representative stated 'these are people we are dealing with, they are not battery chickens'. It was argued that this was leading to low morale as a result of the constant flow of calls, and little time for social interaction. At the time of the research the issue appeared to have reached stalemate and was due to be escalated to a formal business consultation meeting with the senior management and full-time union officials. The Site Manager suggested that throughout the change programme there had been regular meetings with the local representatives and full-time union officials. The Call Centre Manager argued that the *way* targets were to be set had been agreed in consultation with the union, but that the *actual* quantitative targets remain at the discretion of management depending upon business change and employee performance. She contended that the targets were achievable for most employees – and that many advisers were already achieving them – and that the representatives would need to build a more convincing case to oppose the issue.

The Employee Relations Manager suggested that most of the issues regarding targets could be attributed to a lack of communication as to why the targets were being raised and why the management team believed they were achievable. This view was echoed by the Customer Service Director, who argued that most employees *were* already meeting the proposed targets, and the business was not catering for a minority of low underperforming employees. Again, this raises the concern of unions which are perceived to be defending the lowest performing members of the organisation. His view was that employees need to be stretched if the company is to achieve its goals:

> The bank needs to raise targets to become a top five world bank. It's not achievable via mediocrity. People don't come to work to bugger about and have a chat and go home. Sorry we don't have jobs like that (Customer Service Director).

The credit card division FTO was less impressed, arguing that *'they don't give a damn provided they produce profits … they are taking the piss'*. At the time of the research this issue was still unresolved.

Sales and service split

In light of intense competition in the credit card market, NatBank has been keen to make the organisation much more sales oriented, encouraging employees to cross-sell a range of products and services on even the most routine calls and queries. The IT systems are designed to advise employees if a caller is a good prospect for additional services, and prompts them with product offerings such as insurance. The Call Centre Manager explained that there was a need to change the call centre culture to become more of an income centre generating new leads, as opposed to a service centre merely reactively servicing customers' problems. However, the response to this change towards a more intense sales culture was not positive, with many customer advisers feeling uncomfortable working with the new pressure to sell on even the most routine calls, and many staff have actually left the organisation as a result. Eventually, it was decided after long consultation with the union that customer advisers would not be forced to sell, but that those adopting a 'sales and service role' would be receive greater rewards. As one manager commented:

> For a long time, because we hadn't thought of it quite frankly, we resisted the unions call for splitting the sales and service. And then – lo and behold – there's nothing so zealous as a recent convert, we suddenly 'came up' with the idea. Oh, wouldn't it be good to split sales and service. And the union said we told you so. It's another good example of where we have worked together (Employee Relations Manager).

For the union representatives this was another example of successful consultation exercise. They argued that there is a need to be a certain type of person to be good at sales and many long-serving employees had no experience in sales, and the found sales roles too stressful. The Employee Relations Manager echoed this view:

> It's a bit of a double win really. The people who like to sell get the best people to sell to ... and the people who don't want to sell don't. So it worked out really well because everybody got their first choice (Call Centre Manager).

He argued that the consultation process meant there was a greater understanding of the day-to-day dynamics of call centre work, and the views of grassroots employees rather than just a pure technical model.

Line managers were pragmatic, proposing that the key issue is ensuring employees understand the business rationale for the sales culture, in order to maintain market share and remain competitive. Again, for the trade union it raises the problem of protecting – or being perceived to be protecting – the lowest performing employees in the organisation. Nevertheless, it highlights how partnership facilitated discussions around the business rationale, and identified potential flaws and pitfalls based upon the particular culture and historical context of the credit card centre.

Outcomes

In terms of outcomes, there was clear evidence of several benefits compared to the pre-partnership days at the North East administration centre. These include the influence and regulation of decision-making, improved employment relations locally, and increased union legitimacy.

INFLUENCE AND REGULATION OF DECISION-MAKING

One of the key benefits concerns the influence and regulation of decision-making. Management suggested that when the representatives challenge proposals it can be constructive, as it means pre-emptive changes may be made, leading to the greater legitimacy and acceptance of decisions. As one manager explained:

> *I might have an idea, and I might think it's appropriate but the union may say 'hmm, this has been an issue elsewhere', and I can then use their intelligence and they can also use mine. So you get both sides of the story early on, and can actually come up with something better ... I guess it's common sense really (Site Manager).*

This was echoed by a union representative who explained how *'Management can come to us and get our feedback on anything they've got. And we can say "that won't work", or "brilliant, get that it in"'*. The Employee Relations Manager argued that the union do have an influence, and that with partnership management now carefully weigh up the potential cost and benefits of business decisions, and the implications from an employment relations perspective.

Similarly, the Employee Relations Manager suggested the partnership framework resulted in more thorough decisions which had been considered in detail, and evaluated from a colleague (employee) as well as business perspective, thus encouraging a longer term perspective than may have otherwise been the case. As he explained:

> *Imposing changes often causes disgruntlement, it can slow things down significantly, it can mean morale goes through the floor, because something has been imposed rather than introduced with people. Having the union in at early doors, having them work with us, keeps the ER climate quiet and it means we can facilitate change quicker than we could without partnership (Employee Relations Manager).*

The Site Manager argued that the union adds value if both parties engage upfront, allowing management to benefit from the intelligence of representatives and union officials and their feedback. She argued that by engaging in discussion early there is additional brainpower, sharing of different experiences and perceptions, and more ownership and buy-in to the final decision:

> We go to the union and say that we are looking at doing X, they might say 'well fine, but have you thought about this, because if you go forward with X this might be an issue.' We can come up with a better compromise. By working together I hope that 9 times out of 10 that it'll actually be better received because we've considered all options, and we haven't just considered it from the business point of view, we've very much considered it from the colleague aspect as well (Site Manager).

Similar sentiments were expressed by the Call Centre Manager, who admitted that the partnership process can often be hard work, but that better outcomes do result:

> If you didn't have the union to jump in and say 'hang on' sometimes, you would just jump in and make dictatorial decisions with no idea of the impact. Create so much disruption and it's too late to do anything about it because you've already done it! I really value the relationship. It can be a pain sometimes, don't get me wrong. But they put the other side and that's what they are there for. It's a useful process to go through (Call Centre Manager).

The local union representatives were also positive, suggesting that they had an important role in trying to ensure decisions are as fair as possible:

> I think it's very effective. It'd worry me if we lost it. I think we need somebody to keep it going and to keep management thinking 'we can't do that' because of them. I think our roles are a bit like the police. To make sure they treat people fairly. We are here for that (Union Representative).

> If we weren't here they'd have walked all over us by now (Union Representative).

Encouraging news for the union is that their influence was acknowledged by employees, as the following quotes illustrate:

> The bank don't seem to go as far as they could sometimes. They seem to show some respect for their employees.

*Every employee's dream is to have some say in what the company does,
and we believe we do get asked our opinion. It might not always suit
everyone, but at least we have been asked (Employee Focus Groups).*

One employee cited the introduction of flexible contracts as a good
example:

*[The bank] could have chosen to scrap everything and start again. Those
contracts don't exist anymore. You need to sign new ones. But it doesn't
choose to do that. It chooses to leave those people on those contracts, and
let things change slowly through time. They won't issue those contracts
now. The demands of the business and customer have changed. But they
don't choose to do that (Employee Focus Group).*

IMPROVED EMPLOYMENT RELATIONS LOCALLY

It was clear at NatBank that partnership appeared to be operating at multiple
levels, and management and union representatives agreed that another benefit
of partnership was more local decision-making. Representatives explained how
'We iron a lot out locally so management have a quieter life because of partnership',
and it was suggested that the formal escalation process is used infrequently by
the North East centre. Moreover, there was evidence to suggest that the union
representatives were well informed and aware of business issues. Full-time
officials stressed that creating a capable and well-trained cadre of local union
representative was a key priority.

It was also suggested that before partnership employees were less likely
to speak out because they did not want to be perceived to *'being negative'* or
a *'trouble-causer'*. There is now less hierarchy, following a restructuring of the
management team, and the use of first-name terms was thought to be symbolic
of a more approachable management team. This was contrasted with the
traditional staid banking culture. There was also evidence of significant respect
for the charismatic Head of Site, as she was a long-serving employee who
began her career in clerical work at the centre, but had steadily risen through
the ranks into management. It was suggested that employees now know who
the management team are, whereas previously this was not the case. Managers
share the open plan office space as opposed to traditional private offices. Line
managers agreed that generally NatBank is *'just a better place to work than it
was before'*, and the change in management style was also acknowledged by
employees:

When I first started, the management was the man at the end of the corridor. You saw him once every three months because you had an appraisal, and you put your best clothes on. But he didn't have a clue who you were. Now you see the managers walking around the building and they give you the impression that they are more approachable (Employee Focus Group).

UNION LEGITIMACY

The third main outcome is increased union legitimacy. It was suggested that before partnership the representatives had very few facilities or resources, and that much of their work was expected to be undertaken at home. This had led to difficulties finding volunteers to fill the representative vacancies, meaning for periods of time the centre was completely without union representation. Prior to partnership the role of a representative was described by a full-time union official as a passive *'letterbox rather than an activist'*, and as one representative remarked, *'Nobody wanted to be a rep before partnership ...it was a hassle and a lot of work.'* Since partnership, credible and active representative roles have been created, and at the time of the research all union committee positions were filled, and there was evidence of improved workplace organisation. The representatives are now allowed to hold a recruitment day in the staff canteen every three months, and have a stand with an abundance of leaflets, photos, promotional materials and information on how to contact them for advice. They are also given 15 minutes during induction sessions to promote the union to new recruits, as well as the ability to post information on the staff intranet. Representatives were also satisfied with other arrangements such as access to private meeting rooms, internet use, and ad hoc time off for union business above the allocated slots.

The union representatives also recently won a union award as a result of the success of their recruitment campaigns. One of the representatives was so enthusiastic about her new role that she had successfully applied for a two-year secondment to work full-time for the union at a regional level, representing members, dealing with enquiries and casework and supporting the union representatives. The centre also has one union learning representative responsible for helping members find learning and development opportunities both inside and outside the workplace. The National Officer cited the competent union representatives as evidence of success.

Another theme which frequently arose was the provision of information at an early stage, as opposed to after a decision had already been made, as the following quotes illustrate:

> *We engage early on ... they [the reps] have an input at the design stage (Call Centre Manager).*

> *We know a lot about issues ... displacements, job losses, knocking down walls ... we know a lot longer, months before it happens (Union Representative).*

> *They virtually run everything past us and ask for our feedback (Union Representative).*

Indeed, one representative suggested that by the time the Site Manager formally announced a decision, she had often heard months before from other sources. When asked if there were times when union representatives would not be involved the Call Centre Manager remarked: *'Even if it's things they won't have influence over we still tell them in advance and get their feedback. Nothing is absolutely set in stone and rigid.'* The representatives also agreed that on balance they know well in advance of upcoming issues, typically a long time before things actually happen.

Challenges

Despite the advantages of partnership some challenges remained. The main challenges included: understanding of the meaning of partnership, embedding a partnership culture, communication, representative efficacy and resistance to adversity. These are now discussed in turn.

SHARED UNDERSTANDING OF THE MEANING OF PARTNERSHIP

This concerns actor understandings of the meaning of partnership, and in particular in terms of working relationships and decision-making. There was a feeling that sometimes the partnership becomes 'woolly', and that this could result in confusion and unnecessary tensions. As the Call Centre Manager explained:

> *It gets a bit muddy really ... they [the reps] think its their role to agree ... it's not their role to agree ... it's their role for me to show them how we arrived at it [decisions], and so they know the rationale, but they don't have to agree with everything (Contact Centre Manager).*

It was made clear by senior management and union figures that partnership did not mean joint decision-making, or that the union had to 'sign off' all proposals. Rather, the key components of partnership were consultation at the design change, an explanation of rationale, and an opportunity for the union to comment, question and propose alternatives. Another central component was that both sides agreed to consider both the business and employee point of view when making business decisions, but ultimately the final decision lay with management. It was suggested that some representatives within the wider business remained dissatisfied with this approach, preferring traditional bargaining over consultation which they believed to be 'second best'. Despite these criticisms, the comments from management and union representatives at the North East centre were generally sanguine, although representatives believed that partnership did benefit the bank more, commenting how, *'It's good, it does work, but I still think it works for the bank more.'* However, they took a pragmatic point of view that, overall, things were now significantly better than they had been prior to partnership. The Call Centre Manager echoed this positive assessment, saying, *'I would hate to go back to a position where we locked horns with the unions all the time ... I'd far rather work with them and I hope they'd say the same.'*

EMBEDDING A PARTNERSHIP CULTURE

Embedding a partnership culture throughout the entire organisation was another challenge, especially at the middle management level. In this particular case, relationships appeared to be strongest between senior management and union officials, as well as locally between the local management team and representatives. However, the main manifestation of tension was at the line manager level. One FTO suggested that often local issues escalate because *'management start to play hard and fast with the rules'* and take short cuts, despite the formal procedures and processes in place. He argued that line managers are under pressure to deliver profits, and when things are tough *'the first thing to go out of the window is proper negotiation or consultation'*.

The union National Officer agreed that managers either forget or are sometimes not aware of agreed process, and implement local decisions without due consideration of the consultation procedures. It was also suggested that some more old-fashioned managers still resent having to consult with union representatives about decisions. He proposed that many older managers who joined the bank when the union was kept very much at arm's length may find it difficult to change their traditional mindset. Line managers also appeared to occupy a space outwith the partnership system, and patchy relationships with middle managers were also highlighted by union representatives:

> Some team managers are fine. Take on board what you say and sort things out. Other team managers couldn't give a shit, want to make a name for themselves, want to go up the ladder and are pure bastards (Union Representative).

In addition to getting the buy-in of middle managers, another challenge was engaging employees. There was a feeling that some employees still have little interest in the union. Of course a diversity of views is not surprising, and as a team manager stated, non-members often think they will not need the union until it is too late:

> I still think there is some apathy amongst people towards the union. What can they do for me? They won't do anything? It's like a life preserver on a boat. You don't' need them until the boat starts to sink. And then they think, oh, where is my life preserver! (Team Manager).

Yet employee attitudes towards trade unions generally were positive, and the quote below was fairly typical:

> I think what they do is ensure there is a degree of fairness. If a company makes a change in policy whether it be to type of contract, hours you work, health and safety – just ensuring fairness. They will certainly fight your corner in that respect and do it well (Employee Focus Group).

Although, as mentioned earlier, many employees did have trust in the union to work effectively behind the scenes, others were less convinced, and demonstrating their effectiveness presented another challenge to the union:

I personally don't think they are a lot of help to us.

I think the unions are in a difficult position. Not just here but at other companies as well. This is what it's going to be, end of story. No more discussions and that's it. In lots of companies the unions have their hands tied. They have nowhere to go.

The only thing I hear from the union is vote for this and vote for that in the mail (Employee Focus Groups).

COMMUNICATION

Another component of partnership was the idea that there should be 'no surprises'. It was agreed that one of the main barriers to the partnership process was the communication with staff which one union representative described as *'simply atrocious'*, an issue that also recurs in the annual staff attitude surveys. Documentation reveals, however, that issues of improving communication have been an explicit strategy throughout the NatBank Group in recent years. This was especially true in the call centre environment, where the work environment was described as an impediment to good communication. As workers are on the telephone for most of their day, they simply do not have time to read or digest the frequent information bulletins provided. Attempts had been made to address the issue through team brief sessions between customer advisers and team managers, but these were often irregular or cancelled due to fluctuations in call volumes. Representatives also joked that often they still find things out 'from the floor' or 'in the smoking shelter'.

Managers acknowledged that communication was a major problem, and that although downward cascades of information were plentiful, there were significant issues getting feedback from the floor. Much of the communication relied upon the use of paper 'desk-drops' and notices on the electronic bulletin boards. This was attributed to the 24-hour environment, diverse shift patterns and the fact that customer service agents are on calls for most of the day, making face-to-face interaction very difficult. Employees also raised the issue, suggesting that to a great extent the work environment inhibited communication, and that time set aside for communication sessions was often cancelled. Many expressed frustration regarding the fact that even when communications were available they had no time to read memos and emails, or to browse the intranet. This suggests that good communication is more difficult, yet even more necessary, in the call centre environment.

REPRESENTATIVE EFFICACY

There was also the concern by union representatives that they were sometimes perceived to be 'in the bank's pocket', as staff were sometimes unaware of union achievements, and representatives were bound by strict embargoes on information. This was compounded by the fact that bank and the union release joint statements state that *'The Bank and the Union have agreed...'* leaving members unaware of the starting point, how successful or heated negotiations were, or whether a compromise was reached. The representatives stressed that there was a need for a great deal of trust from members that they *were* actively involved on their behalf and not management poodles. Yet representatives sometimes felt unable to advertise their successes. One representative suggested how she would ideally like to create a document listing their achievements but suggested that it would not be possible as it would be seen to be against 'the spirit of partnership'. As she explained, *'You don't want to advertise everything because you don't want to step on their toes really.'* There was a perception that advertising successes under traditional bargaining would be a lot easier. However, they suggested that small individual successes (for example, discipline and grievance cases) were often spread through word-of-mouth, but that employees generally have a more limited knowledge of collective issues. As one representative remarked, *'Members need to trust us to fight for them even if they don't know exactly what's going on'.*

Nevertheless, the Site Manager proposed that the representatives are very credible, and commented, *'They're good at promoting what they do and I think their people know when they've intervened, and when we've had discussions and maybe changed something.'* The Call Centre Manager, however, acknowledged that sometimes it may be difficult for the representatives, because if members perceived that the role of the representative is to agree everything, they will inevitably be *'attacked'* if the final decision is unpopular. The Employee Relations Manager proposed that unions *'need to re-assess their very member proposition'*, suggesting that whereas militancy afforded unions a high degree of visibility to members, partnership relationships are significantly more low key, making it more difficult to explicitly demonstrate influence to members. While some members took the view that no news was good news, on the other hand, no news also meant no credit for the union.

RESISTANCE TO ADVERSITY

Another concern was the sustainability of partnership over time. The National Officer proposed a key challenge could be if economic times are much harder and the bank has to make very tough decisions arguing that *'a major announcement for example, closure of a centre or takeover could tear it to pieces very quickly'*. He argued that, though mitigation of the worst effects had occurred during initial small-scale offshoring, he questioned how sustainable this will be if the bank decides to offshore on a much larger scale. Other management and union respondents also queried how sustainable the partnership is if 'champions' were to leave the organisation or if there was a shift in government policy. Despite the challenges outlined above, most management and union respondents remained sanguine. Finally, employee views were also positive, with the majority expressing support for more co-operative employment relations, and few expressing a desire for a more traditional adversarial relationship between the company and the union.

Conclusion

This chapter has presented the findings of the first case study conducted at NatBank. Contextually, it is proposed that the partnership is interesting for several reasons. Firstly, NatBank has a long history of working with trade unions. Though employment relations were thought to have been historically stable, intense market pressure and attempts to reconfigure the business resulted in a long period of industrial relations conflict in the 1990s. Inspired by the partnership model being promoted by the government as well as organisation such as the TUC, IPA and Acas, a formal partnership agreement was signed in 2000. The founding principles included joint commitments to the success of the bank, employees, customers and shareholders. Employees were to be treated fairly but equally, the union committed to the principles of business flexibility and the need for organisational change. The approach was summed up as one of joint problem-solving.

In contrast to the frosty times of the 1990s, relationships between senior management and union officials, as well as between local management and local representatives, appeared to be very good. The main challenge was changing the attitudes of some line managers who were loathe to work with the union, as well as restoring employee interest and support for the union. Indeed, in the late 1990s many employees cancelled their memberships. Local representatives, who were previously described as 'letterboxes' rather than activists, were now involved in a range of issues, including pay and conditions, discipline and grievance, and organisational change. Before partnership, representative roles at the North East centre were often vacant; now they have a highly enthusiastic team. They acknowledged that their role now concerned persuading, challenging and questioning rather than simply opposing. For representatives, the key issue was devising a strong case to convince management on the basis of both employee impact and business rationale. The examples of re-grading, flexible contracts and the sales/service split all illustrate that they did appear to have an impact.

Through the process of partnership, benefits included the regulation of decision-making, increased union legitimacy and better employment relations. Management benefited from the union input regarding negative consequences of decisions, and the union benefited from the opportunity to comment and question. The union has also benefited in terms of legitimacy and revived weak trade union organisation. Most management and union figures agreed that the hostile relationship which characterised the 1990s was ineffectual from both a union and management point of view. Lastly, from an employee point of view there also appear to have been improvements. Employee comments were generally positive, an important finding given the significant changes which have occurred within the bank in recent years.

Naturally, challenges remain. There is still some disagreement about what partnership actually means. The partnership culture is not embedded across all levels and especially in relation to line managers and work teams. Representatives have a tough job demonstrating their effectiveness to members as a result of a more low key approach. Communication is also problematic and is exacerbated by the nature of the work environment. Finally, it is difficult to assess how the partnership framework will cope with future business challenges, or the impact key champions leaving the organisation could have. Nevertheless, it seems reasonable to conclude that within the context of the NatBank North East centre, a partnership approach appears to be fairly well rooted, and has demonstrated a reasonable degree of success, delivering a variety of benefits to actors.

5

Partnership with a Staff Union at BuSoc

Introduction

This chapter presents the second case study, undertaken at the BuSoc administration centre in the Midlands of England. The chapter begins with an introduction to the case organisation and to the site under study. A brief background to the evolution of employment relations and the partnership structures at BuSoc is then provided. This is followed by a discussion of the meaning of partnership in this context. The chapter then explores the process of partnership in detail by firstly examining the nature of the relationships forged between the key actors. Secondly, recent and issues and decisions within the organisation, including pay and conditions and discipline and grievance processes, are examined. The chapter concludes with an evaluation of the BuSoc partnership, and discusses some of the main benefits and gains, as well as the challenges to partnership at BuSoc.

Company Profile

BuSoc is a major British building society providing mortgages, loans, savings accounts and insurance products. The current organisation is the result of a series of mergers between many regional and national building societies, and historically, the roots of the society can be traced to the 1850s. The most significant merger was in the late 1980s when the society merged with a major competitor, but the society struggled to bring the two organisations together. These problems were exacerbated by arrears problems as a result of early 1990s recession, a downturn in the housing market and a significant rise in bad debt. A combination of low output, high unemployment and high inflation also posed a significant challenge to the society, and public relations at this time were very poor. Since these crisis years, BuSoc appears to have had some success in reinvigorating the business. In 2006, BuSoc's assets reached a record £120 billion with pre-tax profits exceeding £500 million. This gives BuSoc a position within the largest UK financial service organisations, and within the top three in terms of mortgage lending. It currently has over 10 million customers (known as members). Though the society entered into the provision of personal banking services following the deregulation of the market in the 1980s, the primary business remains residential mortgage lending to individuals. The organisation has received various awards as an 'Employer of Choice', 'Top 100 Company to Work For' and 'Investor in People Champion', and has developed a reputation as a good employer. It also retains a commitment to its mutual status and has used the fact that it continues to be owned by members to give it a distinctive marketing edge compared to the 'profit-driven' high street banks and converted building societies. The society claims that mutuality allows both a more customer-focused and employee-focused approach, due to the absence of stock market pressure.

The Case Site: Midlands Administration Centre

The organisation has 16,000 employees in the UK across 700 branches and two large administration centres. As a result of a merger in the late 1980s, BuSoc has two main administration centres, as the two companies decided to retain their respective headquarter buildings. The bulk of the research was conducted at an administration centre in a large Midlands town. Traditional employers in the area include brewing and engineering, although current growth industries include financial/customer services, communication, transport and logistics, and creative industries. The administration centre site employs just over 2000 people across a wide range of roles including customer sales and service, information technology, finance and law. The offices are located on a major business park on the outskirts of the town. As the former headquarters of one of the merged building societies the building represents a very traditional office environment. The primary functions at the administration centre are mortgage administration and customer services.

To maintain consistency with the other case studies, the focus was on customer service and sales departments, including lending control and the contact centre, and such typical roles as 'lending advisor' and 'customer advisor'. Lending advisors deal with customer arrears issues where customers have fallen behind with payments on their mortgages, personal loans or credit cards. This often involves calling customers who have payment difficulties, and arranging payment plans. It can also involve arranging the sale of repossessed houses and liaising with other parties such as surveyors. Customer service advisors are involved with inbound customer account management issues in the call centre which answers 300 customer calls a day. The most obvious difference between the lending and call centre environment is that in the former, employees have greater autonomy in managing their workload, whereas in the call centre environment, the automated system distributes a constant flow of calls. Lending agents also have more time 'offline' completing paperwork, whereas in the call centre environment almost all time is spent answering calls. Before the opening of the call centre, many of the long-serving staff had been working in administrative roles, including filing and reprographics, and so there was a feeling that call centre roles were a lot more pressurised than traditional administrative work. In the call centre environment, agent activity is monitored and compared to targets. The call centre is typically very busy and advisers normally deal with a steady flow of calls for the duration of their shift.

Partnership Structures at BuSoc

Representative participation at BuSoc centres around the recognised staff union. The union has been recognised by the Certification Office as independent from the employer since the late 1980s (it was formerly a staff association), and has been representing BuSoc employees for over 30 years. Until the late 1980s, the association did not have full-time officials; rather a Chairman was appointed on a seconded basis. He was supported by external consultants who would provide specialist advice. However, in 1990 the staff associations of the two merging organisations also merged to form one new association. The union was run by a General Manager, and this was said to be symbolic of the kind of association it was: a business union rather than a campaigning union. The staff association represents all staff below general and senior management. Membership of the staff union is currently around 75 per cent and it is affiliated to the TUC but has no formal political affiliation. In 2006, union membership at the administration centre was 54 per cent. This compares to membership of 64 per cent at the Southern operations centre and an average of 75 per cent in the branch network. The union has 14 staff members, and membership is officially encouraged by the society.

Currently, the main formal mechanism for information, consultation and negotiation is the Joint Consultation and Negotiation Committee (JCNC), chaired by the Divisional Director of Personnel. The Union President, General Secretary, Assistant General Secretary, and some representatives from the NEC also attend these meetings. The General Secretary is the Chief Executive of the Union, and Chief Negotiator. The President – who is seconded from BuSoc for two years – acts as Chair of the NEC and National Conference, and is the Chief 'Lay' Officer. Most of the society members are from personnel functions, although one senior manager from the branch network also sits on the JCNC. Formally, the JCNC convenes for the Annual Pay Review, with the majority of other issues advanced through informal 'corridor conversations'. There is a list of negotiable items in the recognition agreement, and the business has resisted abandoning this list despite union pressure. Formally at least, negotiation still remains limited to the issues summarised below:

- pay ranges

- the amount of money available for distribution in general salary reviews

- number of hours in the basic working week

- annual holiday allowance

- overtime pay rates

- shift payments

- Saturday morning payments

- compensation for employees using their own car on BuSoc business

- payments for working on Public Holidays

- on-call and call-out agreements

- additional responsibility payments

- unsociable hours payments

- London allowance

- lunch time payments

- maternity leave and benefits, adoption leave and paternity leave

- employment break

- subsistence allowances.

This does not mean that items not on the list are not discussed, but that the union would be unable to take the society to formal arbitration. If they fail to agree at JCNC, another meeting has to be scheduled within 14 days and this would be attended by a senior executive. If there is still a failure to agree, the union can raise the issue with Acas for pendulum arbitration. Pendulum arbitration would involve the arbitrator choosing between the position of the trade union or the employer, without any option of 'splitting the difference' and suggesting a third solution or compromise, as this is meant to encourage each party to make sensible demands. However, the union acknowledges that this is a high risk, worst case scenario strategy, as each side risks losing everything through the arbitrator's decision. Nevertheless, this is an extremely powerful tool for the union. It is important to note that at the time of the fieldwork the infrastructure fell short of the demands of the Information and Consultation Regulations because the focus of the current structures is very much on personnel as opposed to general business issues, and a new employee involvement structure was intended to be in place later in the year.

Constituency Representatives are allocated four days per year plus additional time at the discretion of their line manager throughout the year. Area Executive Members receive six days per year, Health and Safety Representatives are also granted six days per year, and those with both roles receive both allocations. NEC members receive 12 days per year. In terms of ability to get time off for union duties the evidence was mixed. As the Area Officer explained, *'It all comes down to the line manager/business needs. If the team's workload is so high the union role has to take a bit of a backseat. It's balancing the business needs.'* Much appeared to hinge upon the attitudes of individual line managers. For example, there has been poor attendance at Area Council meetings even though the meetings are planned months in advance. As the Area Officer argued, if representatives do not attend meetings, they cannot properly represent their members. However, despite these difficulties, there appeared to be an acceptance that union work is very much secondary to their full-time job. As the Area Officer explained, *'We are not employed by the Union. We are employed by the Society. At the end of the day they are paying us to do a job. The union work is voluntary'*. The Union President highlighted that the role of the local representatives is to collect views, provide feedback and relay information *'but they are not there as negotiators'* and that they are *'not like traditional shop stewards who negotiate terms and conditions'*.

Although most actors believed partnership primarily concerned representative participation, like most UK organisations the business also employs various direct employee involvement mechanisms. These include, for example, team briefing sessions, company videos, intranet, suggestion schemes and attitude surveys. In the call centre, monthly focus groups had also recently been introduced to provide a forum for call agents to air some of the day-to-day concerns regarding working practices or other issues of concern.

Definition of Partnership at BuSoc

Although there is no *formal* partnership agreement between management and the union, it was argued by senior management and union actors that the relationship between the business and the union could be described as a partnership relationship. This was thought to be a result of contextual factors such as the history of mutuality and the resultant management style. Indeed, the management style was typically described as 'benevolent' and 'paternalistic' by both union and management respondents. Management were keen to stress their commitment to being recognised as a responsible/ethical organisation and employer, and believed that it was complimentary to the partnership ethos.

The partnership notion of 'working in partnership with the union' is also mentioned on the company website: The Personnel Director suggested that BuSoc has always had good personnel policies:

> *BuSoc has always had good employment policies. I felt that when I came in. I was very impressed with the caring attitude. I worked in the City before and you would be out of the door much more quickly. I think over the last 15 years we have made a concerted effort to say we want to be a leading edge employer, and we have deliberately gone out to see what is best practice and where we can go beyond best practice (Director of Personnel).*

She argued that historically building societies were *'caring organisations'* and suggested that internal research had confirmed a sound business rationale for investing in employees. Similarly, the Employee Relations Manager suggested that there was a feeling that good employee relations were complimentary to good customer service and in turn business success. As he explained:

> *We used to say we knew BuSoc was successful when customers said it would be their first choice, where business experts would recommend BuSoc as their first choice, and employees would say BuSoc is where I want to work (Employee Relations Manager).*

Senior personnel managers suggested that this may partly be related to mutuality, which means the organisation does not have the pressure to impress shareholders:

> *A traditional city organisation would be looking at maximising shareholder value. We don't have shareholders so our focus is how do we maximise values for members. But I think culturally the difference is greater, and I'm convinced it's related to our mutual structure. It sounds clichéd but there is something different (Personnel Director).*

> *I think we have it right because we are a mutual organisation, and our competitors are PLCs. They have shareholders to satisfy, and maybe they have to be a little more astute with some of their policies. Whereas we deal with fairness which sits comfortably with me, and the way they treat employees, mutuality is a very big positive. At the end of the day it's about working for the members: people with mortgages, savings and investments. And to make sure at the same time the workforce are equally rewarded and treated as well (Personnel Consultant).*

Of course, a more rigorous approach is needed to establish whether the relationship at BuSoc can be considered to have the typical characteristics associated with partnership organisations, as there is no automatic link between employer paternalism and partnership. For this reason, it is useful to review the commonly cited TUC principles of partnership:

- a commitment to the success of the organisation

- a focus on the quality of working life

- a recognition of and respect for the legitimate roles of the employer and the trade union

- a commitment to employment security

- openness and transparency

- adding value to all concerned.

Firstly, it is argued that there is sufficient evidence to suggest that the union and management shared a commitment to the success of the organisation. Most of the union officials are employees or ex-employees of the society and all stressed the importance of BuSoc delivering to members as well employees. Policy documents also state how *'BuSoc and the union have a common objective in ensuring the efficiency of BuSoc and its employees'*. This resonates with the TUC principle of a shared understanding of and commitment to business success. The second TUC commitment concerns quality of working life. Again, there is evidence to suggest that BuSoc has demonstrated a commitment to working life by implementing many pioneering HR initiatives and exceeding statutory requirements on most aspects of UK employment law. With regard to the legitimacy of the union, the fact that the society funds the seconded President post, and that union case officers have offices in the two administration centres suggests a level of support for the union. The employee manual for new staff also encourages membership of the union. The fourth TUC principle concerns employment security, and a flexibility/employment security agreement is at the core of many partnerships. On this issue the union and the company have a security of employment and redundancy agreement (SERA), which outlines the consultation process to be followed, and *'BuSoc's need to be flexible with employees needs for stability in employment, affording maximum protection for employees and their earning potential'*. SERA exceeds statutory requirements in that BuSoc agrees to consult with the union regarding redundancies, regardless of union membership, number of redundancies or length of service. Another TUC partnership principle concerns openness and transparency. In accordance with this, the recognition and procedure agreement expresses a management commitment to *'hold regular meetings with the union, and maintain effective communication and exchange information on business issues ... effective consultation and negotiation are instrumental'*. The final TUC principle concerns adding value to all concerned, and this is reflected in a policy document which states how *'BuSoc and the Union have a common objective in ensuring the efficiency and prosperity of BuSoc and its employees ... good employee relations ... will in turn promote the well-being of BuSoc and its employees'*.

In short, the evidence suggests that the arrangement does appear to have many of the ingredients of a prima facie partnership. Interestingly, despite the positive comments regarding 'partnership relationships', union officials were reluctant to engage with the formal language of partnership, pointing out that they had discussed the notion of establishing a formal partnership agreement, but had subsequently rejected the idea. As the President explained:

> *A number of years ago we did look into putting in place a partnership agreement … I think it's fair to say that around the National Executive table there was quite a concern that the Union, was possibly too bought into – and certainly perceived to be – too bought into Society strategy and decision-making (Union President).*

In other words, the union was keen to maintain a degree of distance from the company, and perhaps also reluctant to give up the power the pendulum arbitration clause affords. As the President explained, *'we will and probably do have a very partnership style approach to the way we operate … I doubt we'd be in a hurry to call it a partnership though … the word just wouldn't sit well with it … but it'd be that in all but name perhaps.'* The General Secretary also highlighted the need to be seen to be independent of the Society:

> *Those who are aware of what is going on, are aware that we are very independent. But I guess if you asked somebody working in a branch in Oban or something, they'd probably think we are just another department of BuSoc. It's really strange (Union General Secretary).*

These concerns notwithstanding, there was a feeling that the actual name is not important. The Union President cited examples of partnership agreements in the finance sector which he believes have meant very little in practice, with little differences from traditional recognition and procedure agreements. In short, the partnership 'badge' was not thought to be so important. Yet despite the union reluctance to use the formal language, it was agreed that the operation/relationship is generally reflective of a de facto partnership. As the Union President stated:

> *Our role is to look after the people who work for BuSoc. I have always maintained that we can look after people who work for BuSoc a lot better if we have a relationship which is constructive … because if you don't, it's dead easy for the employer to just keep saying no (Union President).*

He argued that even in the context of a good employer, issues still occur and the union role is to challenge and ensure employees are treated responsibly. Equally, union involvement was said to make issues easier to manage, leading to better outcomes for the business as well. As the General Secretary summed up, *'I want a balance between we'll work with you, so you'll work with us, it's very much a two-way thing.'*

For the Employee Relations Manager, one of the key differences between partnership and non-partnership working was the stage at which the union is engaged with decision-making. He suggested that with a traditional decision-making process in an organisation, consultation would often begin after a great deal of time had elapsed, and much of the management chain would be consulted before union involvement began. He proposed that the partnership concerns early consultation to allow ideas to be considered and refined, providing more of an opportunity to fine tune and discuss the plan.

He also suggested partnership concerns a co-operative approach:

> *More constructive because you are going forward with a joint plan, you know what the union reaction is going to be, you know the communication the union is likely to give out to employees, and you can go forward almost with one voice, and everybody is very supportive and they feel that they've influenced and got something out of the process, and the business has also. And you can deliver much more quickly, and there's not so much conflict. That's the ideal model (Employee Relations Manager).*

He suggested that the main benefit was that the business had insight into likely reactions, union commitment enhances the legitimacy of the decision, and that ultimately both parties gain some value through the process.

It was also clear that, as a small union, the operation centred around a few key figures at the elite level, and in particular the long-serving General Secretary. The Employee Relations Manager explained that having a close relationship between a few key players can be very beneficial, but on the other hand creates significant problems in relation to succession. As he explained:

The General Secretary is very well known around the business, he takes the whole shooting match on his shoulders really, and he is the union. He is known to be the union. He has a huge network and gets to know lots of things ... and that makes the union very effective, he's got his finger on the pulse, but frankly if he was run over by a bus tomorrow the union would struggle (Employee Relations Manager).

This was also implied by the Union President who remarked, '*It would be really easy to say that the key relationship exists between me, the people in personnel and the Chief Executive, and there is an element where that's true.*' For example, the Chief Executive and Deputy Chief Executive go out for dinner three or four times a year with the General Secretary, and often deals are struck during lunch meetings and 'corridor conversations' rather than at formal union JCNC meetings.

In terms of union influence, the Union President described an important distinction between *negotiation* on certain items such as pay and conditions – and *discussion* and *consultation* on most other issues. The General Secretary acknowledged union influence may not always be obvious to employees as much is behind the scenes:

Because we have a partnership/collaborative approach, a lot of things BuSoc were going to do get stopped before anybody even knows they were thinking about it. So, from that point of view, employees' perception of BuSoc is that it's actually a pretty nice place to work. You think if we didn't do our job for a month, they would still think that? But that's just the way of the world isn't it? (Union General Secretary).

However, management admitted that – at least formally – the union has traditionally had limited access to high level business information beyond private discussions between senior management and the General Secretary. In short, partnership appeared to be much more about relationships in this particular case.

The Employee Relations Manager suggested that the union was an influential force, and that it did act as a useful regulator on business decision-making:

I've always seen the union as a bit of a regulator on us. Making sure we do the right thing. It doesn't mean that they should stop the business making the right decisions for the business, because both parties have got the same vested interests: making BuSoc a viable business proposition, for the prosperity of customers and employees (Employee Relations Manager).

He added that sometimes union input can be valuable in preventing the business making short-sighted decisions which actually overlooked major problems with business proposals:

I think there have been examples where the business wants to do something and the union have come back and said well have you thought about this, have you thought about that. And whilst it might have sounded like a good idea for a particular business department, in the context of fairness, employment law, regulation and the business as a whole you sit back and think yeah, actually brainstorming is very well but that wasn't a good idea (Employee Relations Manager).

The Personnel Consultant agreed the union do have influence, again through the strong senior relationships:

As a collective group, I think yes, the union do have influence and that's down to the relationship the General Secretary has with the Directors and Executive Directors. And also with the membership numbers behind them it gives them quite a bit of weight there, to make sure their voice is heard (Personnel Consultant).

Union interviewees also believed the union did have influence. As a case officer explained:

I think quite a lot of influence. They do listen to us and they do value our opinion. I think the society take the view that if the union is coming to them, it's not because they are wanting to be difficult. It's because their members have genuine issues. ... I think a lot of the issues are cost driven ... I think they take the attitude that if the union is saying it's a problem, then at least we need to listen. I don't think it's oh, no, they don't have enough to do so they're banging this drum again (Case Officer).

Local union representatives were less clear on the extent of influence because so much occurred at a high level, but they speculated that the union is influential. As one representative noted, they do not actually know what happens at negotiations:

> *I would hope there is influence. I think there is. But again I've got no evidence of that. Our messages come through saying it's a joint statement from the General Secretary and whoever, but I don't know about the negotiations or how they have gone, you just take on board what they've said. But it appears to me there must be some pretty good working relationships to get what we get (Union Representative).*

A similar view was taken by another representative who believed that the dialogue promoted the interests of the union, employees and the company:

> *I think it should be fairly amicable but at the same time it's got to be positive enough for both of them to put their case forward and talk positively and openly about issues. And come to an agreement that will suit everybody: the staff, the company and the union. I feel that's what they do but it's only my opinion. I've never sat in one of their meetings so I don't know for sure (Union Representative).*

One criticism raised by the representatives was that the union is more concerned with company-wide issues and policies, and local representatives do not always feel they receive sufficient assistance to deal with local concerns, for example, stress and morale in the call centre. It was suggested that this had upset some members who believed it *was* a union issue, but were advised to take up issues directly with managers, but *'people don't want to put their neck on the line directly'*. Again, it was suggested by team managers that sometimes departmental issues are introduced with minimal consultation and *'they'll probably implement it and then sort out the fallout, rather than have the union involved there and then'*. It appeared that departmental issues are generally channelled through a monthly meeting between managers and lay 'reps' from each team, but there was a feeling that this was not effective, as often employees did not want to be seen to be 'complaining'. In other words, although there were other employee involvement mechanisms available for day-to-day issues, sometimes the result was that employees felt their issue was perhaps too small or specific to be a 'union issue', but lacked the confidence to raise it through direct mechanisms.

Relationships

The purpose of this section is to explore the relationships between the key partnership actors. These are now discussed in turn.

SENIOR MANAGEMENT–UNION RELATIONSHIPS

The first issue concerns the relationship between the trade union and senior management. The President explained that there was *'generally a very good relationship, the dialogue is constructive but I'd hesitate to call it friendly. It's carried out in a reasonably conducive environment to get a good result'*. However, he expressed a slight concerned that the relationship had not really been tested recently:

> *You do worry that there have been no really significant disagreements between us [the union and management] for a couple of years. So how much of that is genuine and how much would evaporate if we said actually, no, you can't do that on something that they thought was significant. Or if we just dug our heels in about something and they thought we were being obdurate ... How much is it dependent that things are running pretty smoothly between us, and how much is actually a genuine commitment on everybody's part to make things work even when we do disagree? (Union President).*

In other words, it is difficult to test the strength of a relationship when things are going well. The central relationship, however, involved the General Secretary and senior management. The General Secretary is heavily involved in a myriad of meetings and committees and has an extremely busy schedule.

Senior HR managers also described a good working relationship with the union, again suggesting that the union adds value. As the Employee Relations Manager explained:

> *The union have helped no end ... We would say we have a good relationship with them, we try to involve them in new employee type issues, at an early stage in terms of policy and procedure design. The business, and certainly Personnel, values the relationship with the union (Employee Relations Manager).*

Managers particularly valued the fact that most union officials are former employees, suggesting that this enables them to take a more balanced view on issues. A similar view was expressed by a Personnel Consultant:

> *I think it's a good relationship. It used to be the staff association. And that to me suggests a very close link between the union and BuSoc. A lot of union officials are former employees and have a good understanding of what BuSoc is trying to do. And therefore, when they become reps and we enter into discussions, they have a good idea of where we are coming from and it can be quite harmonious. But at the same time they are ready to challenge if they think something is not right. Which is good. It makes us think are we doing the right thing (Personnel Consultant).*

However, the extent to which good relationships extended beyond the personnel department was less clear. As the Call Centre Manager remarked, 'Presumably they [the union] are having a positive effect from their perspective but who knows. I don't get involved in negotiations.' A senior collections manager in the mortgage division also admitted she did not have a great deal of knowledge of the union, but speculated that the relationship was probably healthy:

> *I would say it's very healthy. It's not them and us, we work closely together. In terms of policies and people we are very likewise thinking I feel. Whatever dealings I've had with the union, it's always been amicable, professional I feel. We are looking to achieve the same thing for the business and individuals really. We want the same. We work well as far as I'm concerned (Senior Collections Manager).*

Nevertheless, a Personnel Consultant suggested that periods of disagreement are a normal part of healthy relationship:

> *I imagine there is some healthy debate there sometimes, when there is disagreement. What is the right thing to do? I'd say it's healthy. There have been some firm, strong challenges, but people move on from that (Personnel Consultant).*

The Personnel Director also suggested that the union can add value to the process because they have a good level of business knowledge, and can bring a different perspective to decision-making. As she explained:

> *I'm always very impressed with the level of knowledge the union people have, around what goes on in BuSoc ... it makes it more transparent because you can't pull the wool over each other's eyes. You both understand what you are dealing with (Director of Personnel).*

There were also examples where individual managers had approached the union for advice, for example, how to deal with a specific employee who is underperforming, or on the procedures for dealing with an employee who is on long-term sick leave. However, in terms of union dialogue most appeared to occur at a senior level between senior HR figures and union officials. As the Senior Collections Manager explained, *'I think the most involvement is above my level really. We don't have a lot of contact with the union ourselves really ... in terms of liaising/looking at policies with them, I don't really have any involvement with that.'*

Union representatives also described a good relationship, suggesting that it was *'generally civilised and not militant'* which they believed could actually prove counterproductive as the following comments illustrate:

> *We work in liaison ... not confrontational ... we are not that kind of union.*

> *I think we work a lot closer ... a dovetailing of interests ... we know the business has to be successful as well.*

> *It's pretty civilised. I don't get involved there, obviously but I feel it's civilised, yes, a good relationship.*

> *You don't see what goes on behind the scenes when they have meetings about pay and all that. I'd like to think it's a nice positive relationship, and a productive one, but obviously you have got BuSoc on the one side wanting to do this, and the union saying no we want to do this, so I'd like to see what it's really like in the heat of the battle (Union Representatives).*

Union representatives were dismissive of adversarial relationships, and most used terms such as 'civilised' but 'challenging' to describe the relationship.

REPRESENTATIVE–MANAGER RELATIONSHIPS

It was suggested by both management and union respondents that despite a fairly robust senior management–union relationship, the failing point is 'old-school' middle management, who still view union involvement as unnecessary or inconvenient. As a case officer explained:

> *In general terms I think management-representative relationships are a lot better ... and that there has been a lot more understanding of what the union is trying to do. But I feel there are still certain people in here, that have a quite hostile attitude to unions. We are here to cause trouble (Individual Case Officer).*

As the Employee Relations Manager explained, middle management may sometimes perceive agreed policies to be impediments to 'good' business decision-making. He suggested that this was actually short-sighted, however, and that managers should be pleased to be working with a generally co-operative internal union, rather than a national union. The disinterest of middle managers was also a topic of discussion at a recent union Area Council Meeting. The Call Centre Manager expressed a feeling that legislation means that the discipline and grievance process is now *'very long winded, it seems like there all sorts of barriers put in the way of line managers to actually manage the business effectively. There is obviously a good reason but it's not always apparent'.* One of his main objections was that discipline and grievance procedures make it very difficult to end the contracts of underperforming staff:

> *If you want to get rid of someone who is not good, even if they have just joined you need to get into a process with many steps, eventually a hearing between you, the people and the union ... It can be very frustrating, someone is constantly sick on a Monday, and results are not good. They don't give a damn about working here but you can't do much about it ... it's just a very long winded process ... you just want to say goodbye to this person (Call Centre Manager).*

Given the mixed managerial attitudes to the union, it is unsurprising that the relationships between line managers and union representatives were also mixed. As one representative working in the call centre explained:

> *I can say what I feel, I can ask them if they have a spare five minutes. I*
> *don't think there is a problem. I know I can say to either of them I need*
> *some time, can we discuss something. And they'll say yes. I don't find*
> *it a problem (Union Representative).*

Another call centre representative was less sure, suggesting that she *'would like to think we have a good relationship but I don't know'*. There was evidence of representatives experiencing difficulties with managers who were not supportive of the union, particularly in the call centre. As a representative explained:

> *I think the manager/rep relationship is good except for the really*
> *negative senior manager and he's just really hard. He's not interested*
> *in the union at all so I won't go and see him; if I need something I'll*
> *go and see the other one. What their personal feelings are and how they*
> *handle it affects how they deal with you (Union Representative).*

She also explained that following the centre refurbishment the manager had declined her request to put the union notice board back up, ostensibly for 'aesthetic reasons':

> *They don't like you putting up anything about the union around the*
> *call centre now. Posters and leaflets. So we have to sneak them up when*
> *no-one is looking. Our department has been refurbished. It's all purple*
> *and 'new and wonderful'. They don't want a crappy notice board on*
> *their new purple walls apparently (Union Representative).*

EMPLOYEE AND UNION REPRESENTATIVES

The relationship between employees and representatives appeared to be very limited. Most of the employees interviewed were uncertain of who their representative was. Conversely, attendance at an Area Council meeting confirmed that many representatives were also unsure of whom their constituents were, and most had not been active in the six months prior to the meeting. Nevertheless, employees perceived the union–management relationship to be generally co-operative, although most admitted they could not say for certain, due to a lack of knowledge:

*I think it's amicable. I'm not sure but I'd say so. You get more done on
a friendly basis.*

*I think they work closely, I think the relationship is quite amicable
between the union and the society. They are not a militant union
(Employee Focus Groups).*

Again, the nature of union communications may also partly explain the
employees' lack of knowledge. Union newsletters and magazines appeared to
only offer very limited factual information such as the number of discipline
and grievance cases, employment trends, prize draw winners and adverts to
fill the many representative vacancies available.

Issues and Decision-Making

In comparison to the other case organisations, the pace of change at BuSoc in
the five years preceding the research appeared to have been more incremental.
A key objective of the research was to explore the way some key issues have
been handled in each organisation in order to enrich understanding of the
reality of the partnership process. The next section begins with a discussion
of traditional union issues such as pay and working conditions, and discipline
and grievance, and then reviews some other issues specific to the company.

PAY AND WORKING CONDITIONS

Unsurprisingly, the negotiation of pay and conditions was considered to be one
of the main issues for the union by management, union officials and employees
alike. In 2005 staff received increases worth 3.93 per cent of the pay bill, and
a corporate bonus of 12.8 per cent. This was described as an *'excellent overall
settlement'* by the General Secretary. However, he also expressed great concern
that BuSoc have been *'holding down'* basic pay and placing increased emphasis
on the use of bonus pay. As he explained, *'Ultimately people will recognise that
actually their pay in the market place is dropping behind, because they are getting
bonus pay rather than pay which goes on their salary, and pay going into their pension.
It really pisses me off!'* The issue centres around the fact that basic pay is formally
negotiated with the union, but the bonus is not on the list of formal negotiable
items. The union remains resolutely opposed to the increased use of bonus pay,
viewing it as sacrificing basic pay, a stealth diminution in terms and conditions,
and increased vulnerability for employees. Although the bonus scheme is not

a formally negotiable item, union officials suggested this has not prevented the union from raising issues and concerns regarding the operation of the various bonus schemes.

A senior collections manager argued that bonus dependent pay was creating a recruitment problem in her department. She speculated that when people are searching for a job they make 'bottom line salary comparisons' and therefore consider BuSoc to offer low pay because they do not factor in the benefits and bonus scheme.

For many employees, the role of the union is predominantly negotiating pay rises. As some employees remarked:

> I am part of the union, but I do always tend to think the union – probably wrongly – is there for more important issues like your pay rise.

> We just got a rise the other week, and they've been fighting to get our standard pay up and stuff. They do a lot on our behalf behind the scenes. I'm aware of what they do (Employee Focus Groups).

Team managers suggested that generally employee opinion on BuSoc as a place to work is sharply divided depending on whether employees are achieving their bonuses or not, suggesting a notion of 'winners' and 'losers'. Among employees, bonuses remained a controversial topic. Employees cited examples of departments where employees often achieve 300 per cent, and others where employees seldom meet their targets. Most employees believed that, overall, they have a good package of terms and conditions, but that their basic pay appears to be low compared to other similar local employers.

The union has also been involved in improving the holiday purchase scheme. The ability to buy extra holidays appeared to be applied inconsistently by middle managers. The Union President commented how the union had been involved in making the process clearer and fairer, and ensuring that it is applied in a more consistent manner, whereas before it could be *'at the whim of a manager'*. Previously the wording was that you had to *'agree'* with your line manager but this was changed to you need to *'discuss'* holiday purchase options with your line manager.

DISCIPLINE AND GRIEVANCE

Discipline and grievance situations were another key area where the union had close involvement with the society. In the first six months of 2006, for example, the union dealt with over 100 such cases. Union members subject to disciplinary proceedings would normally have the assistance of a lay disciplinary officer, or a union-employed individual case officer. Individual case officers are employed to *'protect and promote the interests of the union members'*. Duties include representing members at hearings, providing advice to members, consulting with local managers and promoting the union within BuSoc. According to the ICO, typical disputes include holidays, time off to care for sick children, appeals against appraisal ratings, and disagreements over performance ratings. When discussing the reputation BuSoc has as a good employer, she remarked, *'It's not as good as its PR, otherwise I wouldn't be so busy.'* She explained that ICOs get involved with individual issues which often arise in relation to corporate policies, and stressed the need for the union to have a collaborative approach with management to achieve this and the importance of 'give and take'. She described her role as one of mediator following a breakdown in dialogue, but the main interaction is with union members who have an individual issue. Individual Case Officers would normally not be involved with collective union issues. For team managers, interaction with the union mostly concerned disciplinary cases concerning a member of their team, most often in relation to performance related issues. They viewed the union role primarily as one of overseeing that such cases are handled fairly and employees are treated consistently.

MANAGING CHANGE

The third main issue concerns the management of change within the organisation. The research highlighted seven main issues which were topical: outsourcing; pensions; performance management; work-life balance; relocation assistance; homeworking and healthcare provision. These are now examined in turn.

Offshoring and redundancy

Contrary to the current trend towards offshoring of customer service roles in the financial service sector, BuSoc has committed to keeping call centres in the UK and has recently opened a new contact centre in the North of England. In total, around 1000 employees work in BuSoc contact centres, and these numbers have increased in recent years. The Chief Executive argued in a company statement that offshoring is an inappropriate strategy for the organisation:

> *BuSoc is a mutual with strong links to the communities in which we operate, and we have no plans to desert these local communities in favour of overseas call centres ... call centres abroad may suit some of our competitors, but they are not the right option for BuSoc and we are aware of some commentators' concerns that some countries may not have the same level of data protection for consumers that exists in the UK.*

The union suggests that these public announcements have helped to alleviate concerns regarding job security at the administration centres. However, there was no evidence from the union that the decision was the direct result of a management–union agreement. There was the suggestion by the Call Centre Manager that historically BuSoc has never really had big redundancy programmes like other financial service organisations. As he explained, *'We don't have big redundancy programmes any more. There are some but they go out of their way to try and offer something else to someone who has been displaced.'* A Personnel Consultant echoed this view, suggesting that *'you have to do something really quite bad to find yourself not working for us anymore'*, making it difficult to distinguish between employer goodwill and union influence. Team managers also suggested that generally there was a feeling of job security among employees because consumer borrowing is high, and the company has on several occasions committed to maintaining and expanding UK operations. They suggested that where redundancies do occur, there is a need to think in advance about the impact on people, and argued that the union had been fully involved in previous redundancies. As the Personnel Consultant commented:

> *Things like that are never nice within a department, but for the business things change. There was never any feeling of God, how can they treat people like that? They made sure the people it affected had lots of support, lots of involvement with the union, knew the reason it was done, and lots of support to find new jobs as well (Personnel Consultant).*

The sense of job security was confirmed by the employee focus group statements. As employees explained:

BuSoc is a safe company to work for. I don't think there is any chance of this centre moving to India – the fact that the business wouldn't run as effectively, you can't move years of experience onto new heads (Employee Focus Group).

There is a lot of job security. They said as soon as other people started moving out there that they'd never do it (Employee Focus Group).

There is also a formal commitment in the form of the BuSoc SERA agreement, resonating with the employment security arrangements often agreed as part of formal partnership agreements. The key provisions are that:

- All statutory requirements are met.

- The business rationale for change is sound and can be justified.

- That individual consultation is conducted properly and that employees views are taken into account.

- All alternatives to redundancies are properly considered to redundancies minimum.

- The business calls for volunteers for redundancy or if this is not possible, that the selection process for:

  - Determining redundancies is fair and carried out properly
  - Decisions are communicated sensitively and effectively

- The severance terms available to employees provide reasonable compensation for loss of earnings.

- Support is made available both at the time that the possible redundancies are announced and when the decision is confirmed. This includes:

  - Sufficient time-off is given to enable an individual to look for jobs or attend interviews
  - Outplacement support is available if required
  - Counselling services made available if required

- Above all, the unions approach is to ensure that people are treated fairly.

Pensions

A second topical issue concerned pensions. BuSoc decided to end the final salary pension scheme for new employees from December 2002, and introduced a career average revalued earnings (CARE) Scheme. This was cited by all union officials as the last major conflict between the union and the management. It was claimed that the union was not consulted on this decision, and it promptly circulated a scathing communication entitled 'A Bleak Day'. The Employee Relations Manager acknowledged that *'the union were effectively informed that's what we were going to do'*, and suggested they would have preferred to have explored alternatives such as increasing employee contributions. He argued that while the union was upset because of a lack of consultation, management were also upset because *'it seemed to paint us as being villains when actually the overall package available to employees is still very good. And we've not withdrawn it for existing employees; we are still maintaining it'*. He suggested that this was a significant low point in employment relations under the previous Chief Executive.

The General Secretary, who also explained how the union was simply 'informed' of the decision, suggested that the previous Chief Executive was perceived to be very business-focused, demonstrating less concern for employee welfare. He also reinforced the view that the relationship at the time was very poor:

> It all got very nasty ... I think the current Chief Executive wouldn't do it. I genuinely think there would be an attempt to find an accommodation. Rather than, well we will just do it anyway. Which is exactly what happened in October 2001. I genuinely think that wouldn't happen today (General Secretary).

He argued that although the union view was that the changes were both unnecessary and unfair, the union had no grounds to challenge the decision on legal grounds:

> So our ability to go out and attack them publicly was severely diminished ... so while we had a real go at them, they didn't like it, our ability to get BuSoc members on [our] side was non-existent. The bank argued that it was to bring certainty to their future costs (Union General Secretary).

The union remained unhappy that the decision created 'tiers' of employment conditions which depended upon when you joined the organisation. The Union General Secretary still believes there was insufficient business justification for the change: *`BuSoc will tell you they did what they had to do for their balance sheet but we didn't think they had to do any of those things'*. However, he suggested that things have since improved, especially with the appointment of the new Chief Executive, with whom the General Secretary suggested he had established a very positive relationship. As he explained:

> *They didn't want to talk to us about pensions. Now it's a genuine dialogue about securing this scheme moving forward. I'd like to think we've secured the future of the fund. I mean you can't say categorically but hopefully. That's a good illustration of where it was from bad to good (Union General Secretary).*

The President suggested the society is still fully aware of the union goal of having all employees back on the final salary pension scheme. The Personnel Director said she *'expected them to keep mentioning it'* but that *'sometimes you do things that aren't going to be popular'*. Examination of recent documentation suggests that changes to the pension scheme are a matter of ongoing debate between senior HR and the union, several years after the change was made.

Performance management system

Conversely, the design of a new performance management system was reported to be a successful demonstration of a more open partnership approach to decision-making. The Employee Relations Manager suggested that the *'union were onboard at the beginning'*, and had extensive input in relation to the performance related pay scheme. This was confirmed by evidence obtained from the union, who wanted the new system to be 'clearer and more motivational'. Previous ratings, for example, were 'good', 'excellent' and 'exceptional', and this was changed to 'making a difference', 'outstanding' and 'inspirational'. The career discussion was also made an optional part of the process in direct response to feedback from members of the union. The forms were also simplified and a new 'Employee Proposition' was introduced, which outlined more clearly what employees can expect, and what the society expects from the employee. As the Union President commented, *'A large part of what's there now bears direct relation to what we were saying.'*

Similarly, the Employee Relations Manager commented, '*The union were onboard with that right from the very beginning, and a lot of their objectives ended up in the final product ... it's been a very good example of working well.*' Team managers also acknowledged that the union was heavily involved with the new performance management system: '*The union were very much involved in making sure that things were fair, everybody was treated fairly and the new system was the right way to go.*' However, the President did suggest that being so involved in decision-making can be a risky strategy, suggesting that '*it's a bit of a dangerous strategy because if it all goes belly up or is perceived as unfair, and we were party to it, that is a stick with which members and non-members will hit us. And if it works we'll get no thanks for it !*'

Work-life balance issues

In terms of work-life balance issues such as the provision of maternity leave, paternity leave, flexible working and sick pay, BuSoc exceeds the minimum legal requirements. Management suggested that, given the employee profile of female and part-time workers, culturally this has always been very important. Flexible working opportunities are available to all employees. For maternity and adoption leave BuSoc offers 10 weeks of full pay, for paternity leave two weeks of full pay, and carer's leave/unpaid leave for up to six months. Other benefits included:

- part-time/reduced hours

- annual hours

- term-time working

- homeworking

- flexitime

- short-term adjustments

- maternity leave paid 10 weeks, unpaid 1 year

- £200 return-to-work bonus after maternity leave

- paternity leave two weeks' full pay

- adoption leave

- IVF leave

- career breaks.

Initially many of these options were targeted at working mothers, but increasingly men are taking advantage of such flexible options as well. Such policies were presented by the union as examples of their achievements in terms of ensuring a good deal for employees, and as examples of where the union and management have worked in a co-operative manner to jointly design mutually acceptable HR policies. Employees regularly cited such policies as one of the main benefits of working for BuSoc as opposed to other local employers.

Relocation assistance

Relocation assistance was another issue negotiated by the union. The union wanted relocation assistance to apply to everybody, thus providing lower grade staff with greater career opportunities. Previously, the relocation package was very generous for senior staff, but for lower grade workers relocation was unlikely to be a viable option because of the financial implications and lack of company support. Now relocation assistance applies to all employees. The upshot of this is that senior staff no longer receive the high level of assistance they used to, as it has been spread out more evenly. On the other hand, it means workers at lower grades genuinely have the opportunity to relocate should they so wish. The President suggested this is another good example of working together to achieve mutual gains, as it helped the society save money, and it has also made relocation and therefore further career opportunities a more realistic proposition for lower grade employees. As the General Secretary remarked:

> It's another example of working together with a shared objective. BuSoc wanted to save money. It was to help them to save money. But you have got to it on the basis of what we are looking for. And we spent months just working it through (Union General Secretary).

Homeworking

Homeworking is described by BuSoc as an important component of its flexible working options, and typical homeworking roles include technology development and mortgage lending control. In the late 1990s, the policy was reviewed by a working group including corporate and operational personnel specialists, union officials, an insurance risk assessor, health and safety advisor and space consultant. The homeworking policy had to be re-designed, as the previous policy was thought to be vague and complicated, meaning that line managers were reluctant to provide homeworking contracts. For example, there had been requests from employees who wished to work hundreds of miles from their previous office, and this created many problems for the business. They have since re-designed a range of different homeworking contracts. This was cited by managers and union officials as another good example of working together with a common goal with both a good business and people rationale. For the company, there was said to be a clear business rationale for working from home in terms of office space, as well as being seen to be a modern employer in terms of corporate social responsibility. The union believed it made sense to give people the opportunity to work from home, when their job does not require them to work from the office. An agreement can be reached where workers have a formal homeworking agreement, i.e. they work from home permanently, or informally, where they have the option of working from home on an ad hoc basis. The union also agreed a Homeworking Allowance to contribute to domestic heating and lighting costs. The development of a homeworking policy was cited as a good example of where there had been extensive involvement of the Union President and Union General Secretary.

Healthcare

The business has been keen to change the healthcare policy from an insurance scheme to a trust agreement, and this has been opposed by the union 'lock, stock and barrel'. Previously, healthcare was not a negotiable item, but the General Secretary explained that, by ending union opposition to the trust agreement in the short term, he had managed to *'get it added to the list'*, giving the union more influence over this issue in the long term:

> *As a result of that they have a made a number of quite key concessions to us. Not least of all they are going to make the healthcare scheme a negotiable item. Which means when we disagree we can go to arbitration. So on the basis of doing that, they'll get what they want and we've actually come out with far more ability to influence the health scheme. Far more than we can do today. And it's all just been done by a little bit manoeuvring here and there. I'm quite pleased with that (General Secretary).*

He suggested that overall the sacrifice was worth it, because the union has a stronger influence over future healthcare policy, whereas before *'they may [have] decide[d] just to totally ignore us because they are not obliged to get our signature to it'*. Now the union can take the employer to Acas arbitration in the event of a disagreement, again underlining how powerful the ability to take the employer to arbitration appears to be.

Outcomes

To summarise, it is argued that there was sufficient prima facie evidence to suggest that the BuSoc/staff union arrangements met the criteria to qualify as a de facto partnership. However, given that this is a relationship which has evolved slowly over time, there is no direct comparison with employment relations 'pre-partnership'. The main benefits of the collaborative working relationship forged between management and the union at BuSoc can be summed up as follows.

INFLUENCE AND REGULATION OF DECISION-MAKING

Management and union respondents generally agreed that by working together on proposals and decisions, they are more able to formulate decisions which take into account the business case as well as the implications for – and likely reactions – of grassroots employees. However, the evidence suggested that in reality it was much more difficult to ascertain the regulatory effect of the union in this particular case. The clash over the end of the final salary pension scheme, which was agreed to have been the most significant incident in recent years, appeared to demonstrate few characteristics of a partnership approach in terms of decision-making or relationships, and casts doubts over the quality of the relationships between key actors at the time.

BETTER EMPLOYMENT RELATIONS

It was also argued by management and union officials that a partnership approach leads to a generally improved quality of employment relations. At the administration centre under study, employment relations have generally been more stable than in the branch network, but both parties still agreed that the regulation the union–management relationship affords, serves to minimise employee resistance, as policies are normally planned in detail before they are implemented. However, much of the negotiations regarding formal changes to HR policies and procedures appeared to be occurring at a very senior level. Many employees, line managers and union representatives demonstrated very little knowledge about how decisions about high level corporate personnel were negotiated or decided.

COLLABORATIVE RELATIONSHIPS

Another outcome of the approach was said to be good collaborative relationships at a senior level between the senior union official and senior management. Much hinged upon the dynamics of this relationship. At the time of the research, the relationship between the Union General Secretary and Chief Executive was said to be very good. However, in this case, there was less evidence of partnership behaviours and attitudes typically associated with a partnership approach.

Challenges

Despite the advantages, many challenges remained. These include the lack of an agreed common approach to employment relations, embedding a partnership culture throughout the organisation, representative efficacy and the resistance to adversity.

LACK OF AGREEMENT ON A COMMON EMPLOYMENT RELATIONS APPROACH

Management and the union agreed that the current management–union agreement is old-fashioned. It was said to assume conflict and clashes, and to focus upon on what to do when talks fail, and what can and cannot be taken to Acas for arbitration. The agenda was also narrow, with formal distinctions between negotiable and non-negotiable items. Nevertheless, at the time of the research it seemed highly unlikely that the agreement would be changed, and the Union President suggested that a new modern agreement was highly unlikely to be branded as a 'partnership agreement', for fear of the negative response of members who may perceive the union to be in management's pocket. To an extent, there appeared to be a lack of a clear approach. On the one hand, the union endorsed a challenging but collaborative approach to the management of employment relations, and were particularly critical of the formal division between negotiation and consultation. On the other hand, they were extremely wary of going down the formal partnership route for fear of appearing to be bought in. This appeared to relate to union debate in the mid-

1990s about the staff association being perceived as weak, and the need to re-badge the organisation as a staff union to reinforce perceptions of strength and independence.

EMBEDDING A PARTNERSHIP CULTURE

Embedding a partnership culture throughout the organisation was another challenge, as was employee apathy and middle management resistance, and little evidence of strong workplace activism. Employee apathy was a problem particularly within the context of the administration centre under study. The individual case officer whose role includes trying to recruit at inductions explained that younger employees now have very little knowledge of trade unions. She joked that at least before they would cite the miners' strike as an example if she asked what a union was, but suggests that now she gets a blank *'rabbit in the headlights'* look when trying to recruit younger members. The lack of interest was also attributed to the logic that, if BuSoc is such a 'good employer', why is there a need to join a union?

The Employee Relations Manager suggested that there is still a sense that being involved in the union could be career limiting, or that an employee involved in the union could be viewed as *'a bit of a liability'* by their line manager. There was employee evidence to suggest that some employees held this point of view, which is contrary to the mutual legitimacy associated with partnership. As one employee remarked, *'I would also feel that, once you have been to the union, and it's found out that you have been to the union, you are a troublemaker. It would always stay with you that you were prepared to go and speak to the union about something.'* The Call Centre Manager had a different explanation of the lack of interest: *'A lot of people are just not interested. They just want to come and do their job and go home.'* A personnel consultant expressed a similar view, explaining how *'in some of the larger departments they probably don't who their union rep is or who the health and safety person is. Most people come in, do their job and go home'*. Responses from the employee focus groups suggested that there was generally a feeling that the employer was reasonably caring and considerate, and that jobs were secure, meaning that union issues are low down their list of priorities. There was a belief among many employees that they could *'just muddle along'*. As a representative summed up, *'I think it just rumbles along and people are complacent. Until issues happen people don't really think about the union.'*

A second challenge concerned line managers. The Employee Relations Manager acknowledged that normally middle management were the least receptive to union involvement, and questioned: '*Whether our senior managers see the union as a useful business partner as opposed to an irritation and an inconvenience I'm not sure. But I think they should see it as a useful business partner.*'

An ICO speculated that often the disciplinary and grievance issues arise because the situations are mishandled at middle management level, and do not follow the formal policy agreed between senior management and the union. As she explained, '*I genuinely believe there is the will to get it right. I think the trouble is it gets stuck in middle management. A lot of work needs to be done to ensure that the policies that are devised and agreed with the union are carried out the way they are meant to.*' There was also evidence to suggest that some middle managers were worried about increased involvement raising employee expectations too much, which they believed may lead to disillusionment. This notion is illustrated by the comments below:

> *My concern is that they [employees] expect so much from us. And the more we do, the higher expectations people have. And it's trying to manage peoples' expectations, and get them to look at what the reality is. People can forget how much involvement they have actually had (Senior Collections Manager).*

> *If we could find a way to involve employees that didn't unduly raise expectations that we would be able to do everything they wanted us to do, then I'd be happy to look for those. But I can't see what it looks like. I can't visualise it ... I think if you raise someone's expectations that they will have a voice, well yes they have a voice, and will be listened to, but we still might do what we were planning to do. And then you have a load of people who think we don't listen to them (Call Centre Manager).*

REPRESENTATIVE EFFICACY

The third hurdle concerns issues of representative efficacy. Firstly, discussions with the representatives highlighted a general lack of visibility of the union, and a feeling that many members were simply interested in the monthly member staff draw. Indeed, in the contact centres the representatives admitted that recruitment was extremely difficult, as the environment makes it difficult to talk to employees, and the high staff turnover makes it difficult to keep up. The Union President suggested that there was often a difficulty selling the successes of the union because so much happens behind closed doors, and remains completely unknown to the grassroots membership. As he remarked, *'We might think it's a bloody good achievement, but how do we actually get the message across? We don't. It's hard. It's very hard.'*

Communication was also a problem, especially between representatives and their members, but also between members and the central union. For example, members cannot send emails to the union through the BuSoc network, nor can the union email members through the company email system. The union website is also poor, although money had been won from the DTI Union Modernisation Fund towards creating a more comprehensive and useful site. Some representatives admitted seldom seeking feedback from members on issues, and attributed this to the working environment of the call centre. Representatives did not seem to have reliable information regarding union membership, and the lack of email mailing lists meant email communication is difficult and time consuming.

There was also an admission of communication between management and the union failing on occasion. The Employee Relations Manager explained that this is sometimes a result of the disparity between the size of the organisation and the resources of the union. As he explained:

> *While we try to involve the union at an early stage, sometimes they find they get sent something, and it says would you read this and mind commenting to us, oh and by the way we're going to issue it two days time, and of course they have a very small team and they just don't have time almost to even read the thing, let alone make constructive comments and get involved in the change (Employee Relations Manager).*

Another issue was the quality of the union representatives. The Union President admitted that some of the representatives were lacking in confidence, in the role for wrong reasons, or simply uncommitted. The Union President questioned the capability of some of the representatives of sitting on committees with senior members of the management team, and admitted long-standing recruitment problems. Recruitment problems were reinforced by the fact that there were long lists of vacancies in union publications. Representatives complained of often feeling *'out of their depth'* when members approached them with queries. One representative explained how when approached by a member with a query she advised him to *'go and speak to the union'*, resulting in the bemused response, *'but aren't you the union?'*. There were even representatives who were clearly unaware of which constituency they represented.

Several representatives admitted that they could benefit from more time for union duties and training. Others appeared to believe that 'management knows best'.

A lack of confidence is also reflected the quote below from another representative:

> I'd like to think in the ideal world it'd have some impact but they are senior management. I'm not. They've obviously implemented something. They don't just implement it. They normally spend ages looking into it – the cost, the money and so on (Union Representative).

Some representatives did not like trying to recruit new members, arguing that they did not think people would appreciate it, or that they did not have the time to do it. Many did not really appear to be in touch with member opinion, describing difficulties 'collecting and collating all the information'. The Area Officer acknowledged that 'there is a need to get the reps active again … they are not actively recruiting or taking up issues'. The union also admitted that often they have problems recruiting suitable constituency representatives because of a 'career down the pan mentality', while two representatives speculated that some employees believed it was disloyal to get actively involved with the union as representatives because the employer was 'so paternalistic'.

RESISTANCE TO ADVERSITY

There were also concerns in relation to the ability of the current structures and processes to deal with a major event or crisis. There was an agreement that demutualization could result in a significant change in focus, and could mean that 'gradually we'd go from having a member base to having a shareholder base. And suddenly everything would be geared towards maximising profit for the shareholders'. This was also perceived to be a risk by a team manager in Lending Control:

> The only thing I would say is that if BuSoc ever decided to change track, the senior management team at the moment are committed to mutuality and the benefits it brings, but if at some stage in the future there was a case for changing that we could have a complete change of track where profit becomes the main driver. I could see that as a potential problem (Team Manager).

Another team manager expressed a similar view:

*We don't have the pressure of shareholders. Literally whatever we earn
we can plough back into the business, into employees, into members.
That makes a difference. You hear of people who have been converted
or taken over and things are never quite as nice as they were before. I
would believe it does make a difference (Team Manager).*

Also, given that the structure is reliant upon the involvement of a few
key figures, there were concerns that succession would be extremely difficult.
The Chief Executive is due to retire soon, and the Union General Secretary
may also retire in the next few years, and there were concerns of the impact
of the knowledge and relationships that would be lost. This challenge has
been acknowledged by the management and union, and efforts are currently
underway to introduce a broader structure, such as the creation of an additional
Assistant General Secretary role, to cultivate individuals capable of succeeding
the current General Secretary.

Conclusions

This chapter has presented the findings of the second case study, conducted
at BuSoc. The case is interesting for several reasons. Although there was no
formal partnership agreement between the staff union and the employer, there
was prima facie evidence to suggest that the arrangement may have qualified
as partnership, for example, because of the long history of co-operative
relationships between the employer and the staff union, and commitments
similar to many of the TUC principles of partnership. Although the term
partnership is not formally used, managers and union officials agreed that the
relationship could be described as 'partnership-style'. Employment relations
have also traditionally been stable and BuSoc, like most building societies,
has been considered to be an enlightened, paternalistic employer. Mutuality
was believed to have provided insulation from the stock market pressures
experienced in many other organisations.

The key relationships were centralised around an elite core of senior
union officials and the senior management team, and relationships between
representatives/managers and employees/union representatives. In terms of
process, the union focus was very much on pay and conditions, and discipline
and grievance issues. Union involvement in wider issues of organisational
change was less clear. The opaque nature of the decision-making processes
meant it was very difficult to judge the amount of influence the union had over

decision-making. A key question therefore, is to what extent would decisions have been the same without union input? Overall, relationships appeared much more arm's-length, and negotiations appeared to be shrouded in secrecy, contrary to the partnership ethos. There were also a range of challenges, including the effectiveness of representatives, employee apathy, the lack of a major test of the relationship, and a system heavily centred around a few key players.

Despite prima facie evidence to suggest that BuSoc and BuSoc Staff Union were working in partnership, the findings suggest that, in reality, the approach to the management of employment relations is much more traditional than it may at first appear. To conclude, in terms of process, there was mixed evidence to suggest that the BuSoc/BuSoc Staff Union arrangement could justifiably be described as a genuine 'partnership relationship'.

6

Partnership without Unions at WebBank

Introduction

This chapter presents the third case study, undertaken at the WebBank operations centre in the East Midlands. The chapter begins by providing a background to the case organisation, and to the site under study. This is followed by a review of recent employment relations at the centre, and the partnership structures. The meaning of partnership in the organisation is explored. This is followed by an examination of the process of partnership, specifically the nature of the relationships between key actors, and the way issues are handled and decisions are made. The final section outlines some of the key challenges of partnership at WebBank.

Company Profile

WebBank provides internet-based financial services and is a major UK e-commerce company. Established in the late 1990s, the company's espoused aim was to create a fresh, dynamic and distinctive organisation in the conservative finance industry. Products include savings accounts and general banking, investments and insurance. The company headquarters are in the City of London, and the company has two main administration centres, both located in the Midlands of England. As an e-bank, the company hoped that cheaper operating costs would enable them to lure new customers with attractive interest rates undercutting the high street. At the launch, the goal was to attract £5 billion of customer deposits within a five-year period, but this target was achieved in only seven months. New customers opened accounts by telephone and later the internet became the dominant medium, as the company aimed to manage the overwhelming demand by allowing new customers to sign up over the internet only. The company registered on the London Stock Exchange in 2000 and made its first profit in 2001. Currently the business accounts for over 5 per cent of UK credit card balances and employs over 2500 people.

WebBank espouses a 'purpose and values' mission statement, and central to this is the idea of being an innovative and entrepreneurial player in a conservative marketplace. It also espoused a commitment of fairness to its customers, employees and shareholders as well as the communities in which it operates. WebBank's espoused purpose and values area as follows:

- WebBank's enduring purpose is to revolutionise customers' experience of financial services driven through unleashing the power of people.

- Our core values at WebBank are honesty, integrity and respect for people.

- We aspire to be vibrant, imaginative and fair in everything we do.

- Our customers are the reason we exist and we constantly look to offer them the products and services that put them in control of their money.

- We respect our people's individuality and diversity, encouraging them to develop their careers in a stimulating environment, in keeping with our values.

- Our shareholders own the business and must be fairly rewarded for their investment.

- We work co-operatively with our suppliers and business partners, choose those who share our values and strive for mutual trust and benefit.

- We behave as good neighbours in our local communities and as a responsible citizen.

- We respect, protect and where possible enhance the quality of the environment.

The Case Site: Midlands Operations Centre

Although the company is officially headquartered in London, WebBank has two main operations sites. The main site is located in the East Midlands. Traditional industries in the area have included mining, pottery and foundry work. The city has a long tradition of aerospace, engineering, rail engineering, power generation and manufacturing. The site has grown from employing just 150 to now employing almost 2500 people. At launch the company only had a small number of employees in a city centre office, but quickly relocated to a large unit on a suburban retail park in 1999. Located on an 80 hectare out-of-town business park, the estate is built upon a former brownfield site, formerly the location of an engineering and gas works. The site consists of two main buildings and acts as the administrative head office, operations centre, technology centre, and the main customer contact centre. WebBank offices are vast open plan spaces, with breakout areas for relaxation. The environment is quite different to the other case organisations in that it is modern and purpose-built. A deliberate objective was only to have one floor in order to create a more 'egalitarian' environment.

The workforce is young (most employees are under 35 and a high proportion are 18–23), and a majority of employees are female (65 per cent). The centre employs a mix of employees including professionals, managers and customer service agents. Typical job roles in the centre include customer sales and service as the centre answers 12,000 calls per day. Most customer service roles are telephone-based, dealing with customer enquiries regarding their bank accounts. Some agents are also responsible for 'secure messaging', which involves responding to email enquiries from customers. Most employees in the call centre work on a shift basis with variable hours scheduled between 7am and midnight. In terms of career progression, it was evident that many WebBank employees perhaps begun their career as a basic service agent, and had progressed through the organisation to secure new roles in other departments, and to achieve professional qualifications in areas such as banking, marketing and personnel.

Partnership Structures at WebBank

The primary component of the partnership structure at WebBank is the Employee Forum. The Employee Forum was introduced in 2000, two years after the company was founded in 1998 and populated with three part-time employee representatives. The initiative for a representative body was said to have come from the management team, as a response to the rapid growth of the organisation. As the HR Director explained:

> We have 2000 people. You need a mechanism. It's very difficult to consult with 2000 people individually! I think we instinctively prefer as a non-union site to understand directly what people here wanted rather than hearing it through a union (HR Director).

He suggested that the introduction of the forum preceded European legislative requirements and *'fortunately the legislation is friendly to what we and the forum are doing'*. It could be speculated that the Employee Forum was a response to the 1999 Employment Relations Act, which provides for statutory union recognition if there is sufficient employee support and came into effect in June 2000. On the other hand, the creation of a representative body soon after launch may also reflect that such bodies are 'the norm' in the sector, and that it may have been taken for granted that a representative body had to be created.

At the launch of the forum in 2000, the focus was said to be on very low level issues, including canteen food, mouse-mats and the poor quality of the soap in the toilets. Indeed, one representative expressed embarrassment at some of the trivial issues he had raised with the Chief Executive. This was termed the *'sausages in the canteen'* phase. The forum's agenda was also perceived to be driven primarily by management and particularly by the HR team. Employee representatives suggested that they tended to be consulted fairly late in the process, often after decisions had already been made. In 2002 the Chief Executive was said to have expressed disappointment with the operation of the forum, and proposed a need for serious re-evaluation. Interestingly, at the same time Amicus launched a recruitment campaign, picketing outside, focusing on the policy of alleged strict toilet monitoring. Employee representatives attended a conference in summer 2002 with the HR Director in London, and had discussions with the TUC Partnership Institute and Amicus. One representative explained that: *'WebBank felt they couldn't deal with Amicus because they were too adversarial, but they took a shine to the TUC Partnership Institute ... feeling they were speaking the right language'*. Management were said to have suggested that a union would be culturally at odds with a young, innovative company such as WebBank.

The HR Director suggested that he was ambivalent, believing that the current structures were sufficient, and a trade union was not necessary. He did not suggest that the forum was necessarily there *instead of* a trade union but that *'It's almost like I don't have an attitude to unions here, because I think we've got what we need ... I don't hold that we have the forum instead of a union but practically it's true'*. He also suggested that there was no strong desire among employees for union recognition, but if that was to change *'management would have to think very hard about it'*. For management, the key concern was that trade unions are *'not as committed to the success of the company'* as internal bodies are likely to be. There was also a feeling that working with a trade union would slow down decision-making and create a prohibitive level of consultation. Another senior manager with work experience in a privatised utility described the difficulties of working in *'an entrenched union environment'* where he found for the representatives *'activism was their idea of a good time'*.

In autumn 2002, the forum representatives met again with Amicus with a view to Amicus making presentations to employees in the New Year of 2003. The three elected part-time representatives were then seconded for three months to evaluate the future of the employee forum. In 2003, the representatives recognised that there was need for some external third-party support and advice. At this point they became affiliated to the Involvement and Participation Association, who appeared to be a good source of external expertise. It was as a result of this affiliation that the seconded representatives became aware of the concept of 'partnership working' and presented their idea of a 'new' non-union employee forum to the executive team in summer 2003. The core idea was that the forum needed to be consulted early in the process rather than after decisions had been made. This involved a new system of elected full-time employee representatives supported by a network of part-time representatives, and an allocated budget and paid time off for part-time representatives to carry out their duties. The proposals were agreed by management. Any employee with more than six months service is allowed to stand for election as a representative. In autumn 2003, the three seconded representatives were elected full-time seconded employee representatives for a three-year term.

The espoused aim of the new Employee Forum was *'To represent the voice of all WebBank people, to make working life great and help drive superior business results'* In practice, it was suggested that this meant communicating with employees, bridging the relationship between management and employees, and representing employees on collective and individual issues. The new employee forum consists of three full-time representatives and 12 part-time representatives. Part-time representatives are allocated four hours per week for their duties, comparable to most union representatives, and tend to deal more with day-to-day issues within the areas in which they work. The part-time representatives generally agreed that there was sufficient opportunity to get additional time off for Employee Forum duties so long as they could balance their workload, although it was slightly more difficult for customer-facing telephone staff. The body is funded by the employer to support representatives' salaries, training, equipment and stationery and conference/travel expenses.

The representatives explained their motivation to be involved with the forum. As the current Employee Chair, a former customer relations adviser, explained:

> I was interested straight away, having been a union rep for 15 years. And in the Navy I was a Welfare Rep. I've always been interested in people. I was interested straight away and got elected (Employee Chair).

Similarly, for another full-time representative who previously worked in the contact centre:

> About a year and a half ago leaflets were dropped round, asking people if they wanted to be nominated to the forum. I looked at that and thought, I could really help with that! Because I'm seeing all sorts of things missing around the contact centre that need a voice. I thought I could really help. (Employee Representative).

For a part-time representative from Technology:

> The reason I got involved was because ... in a company like this it's very big and things go on and you think, hang on I'm not sure that's the way you should actually manage that ... or you wonder why some people get certain benefits and others don't ... A lot of people I knew shared these concerns so I thought, you know, I'll stand for election because this is what the forum is about (Employee Representative).

Again, although partnership was viewed primarily in terms of the WebBank Employee Forum structures, and specifically the relationship between the forum and management, there were also various direct employee involvement mechanisms. These included the monthly 'Life at WebBank' survey, 'fireside chats' between line managers and employees, and extensive use of electronic communication.

Definition of Partnership at WebBank

At WebBank there is no formal partnership agreement, but management did stress the need to work with representatives in a collaborative way, and were keen to avoid an adversarial style, occasionally using the language of partnership. As the HR Director explained, *'I don't experience the forum as an adversarial group whether they are agreeing or disagreeing. It's much more of a partnership.'* The term 'partnership' was used often by forum representatives. One representative admitted that before encountering the Involvement and Participation Association *'we'd never really heard of partnership before and didn't know how it worked … but it gave us a glimpse of another way of working'*. The forum Chair attempted to define the distinction between partnership and non-partnership working, suggesting that it is about establishing a common agenda and shared goals:

> *I think quite often, in the non-partnership arenas, there have been two agendas. The management have got an agenda. The union have another agenda. And the two don't always match up. So you get all sorts of conflict and time wasting. You may end up with the right result or compromise, but it takes days and days, hours and hours to get that result. With partnership, both sides know what they are aiming for. They are on the track together. Pulling in the same direction. And it doesn't take as much time to get the right result (Employee Chair).*

The representatives were unconvinced by the effectiveness of adversarial approaches, suggesting that *'an aspirational approach of working together is much more productive than the adversarial style. I don't think the adversarialism works anymore'*. This view was echoed by the Employee Chair who concluded that:

> *I like the idea of partnership. I think it makes a lot more sense. To be partners rather than enemies. I think in a partnership you are working for the same end. You are working for the good of the company, employees and customers. It just makes sense to me to do things together rather than at loggerheads all the time (Employee Chair).*

He suggested that the effectiveness of the forum hinged upon building effective high trust relationships with the management team, and that conflict and threats are ineffective. As he explained:

If we rub up managers the wrong way, they are not going to do anything with us. You end up with conflict. No good for the employees, shareholders or customers. A threatening basis is not the way to do it (Employee Chair).

For another full-time representative, working in partnership is concerned with fairness and trying to establish middle ground. As she explained, '*I think for me the forum is all about being fair. Fair to the business. Fair to the individual. There has to be middle ground in there somewhere. It's all about fairness.*'

As a non-union site, respondents were asked about the difference between having an in-house body such as the Employee Forum compared to union representation. For a senior technology manager the key difference between the Employee Forum and a trade union is that '*the Employee Forum are just as wedded to WebBank's success as everybody else, but they recognise our people feeling good is a way of building success*'. He suggested that the major benefit of the in-house Employee Forum was that the relationship was more collaborative and constructive, as they had a joint commitment to the goal of business success. As he explained, '*We are pursuing common goals, a common vision. Rather than diverging goals, that's the main thing.*' Yet he was not philosophically opposed to unions, stating how '*if they assumed trade union status, and the legal weight that carried with them, provided people had similar attitudes and approaches I'm sure that could also be successful*'. In other words, the union/non-union distinction was seen to be less important than the relationships and mode of working.

The team managers interviewed did not have much experience of trade unions, but speculated that an external union might not have a sufficient understanding of the organisational objectives:

A trade union is very much removed from WebBank. They wouldn't understand what the culture is like at WebBank, or what WebBank are trying to achieve by doing things. The forum know what the culture is like, they know what WebBank is trying to achieve and have an understanding of where the other side is coming from. So if they are in a meeting with a manager and an employee they can understand both sides (Team Manager).

There was also a lack of enthusiasm regarding trade unions from the forum representatives. For them, there was a perception that trade unions did not really add much value besides the ability to draw upon legal support in the event of an employment tribunal There were also arguments regarding the actual representativeness of trade unions, and concerns that they are governed by complex political agendas, sometimes have ulterior motives and may not understand the organisational culture. A part-time representative reiterated the view that there was probably not much additional benefit from a union beside legal support, but that the major negative was relying on precedents from other organisations and a lack of flexibility. He was also unconvinced by union claims to be more powerful in the current climate, for example, in relation to job losses:

> *All you can do is make sure that it's a fair decision. If WebBank want to move to India tomorrow who's going to stop them? No-one. We always reckon that we're there for the people and to see that they get a fair deal. That's what annoys me about the union. Saying they can do more because they have more power (Employee Representative).*

This view was echoed by another representative who was wary of the 'more-power' arguments presented by the union at the last meeting, suggesting that ultimately the business decision is likely to be the same. He stated how unions often argue how with unions, *'At the end of the day the outcome is probably the same – or less.'* He also suggested that most employees are happy with an employee representative, although a minority would prefer an external union representative. Indeed, there was a feeling amongst the representatives that unions cannot add much; one remarked, *'I'm not a member of a union and never have been, but I'm not seeing anything they can do better apart from the tribunal stuff ... I'm not seeing anything different really.* Another representative was openly hostile to the idea of unionism, following bad experiences in the 1980s:

> *My own personal opinion of unions?! Shoot the bastards ... I was in the AUEW in the 80s ... we went on strike to get the apprentices an extra £20 a week. 16 weeks with no pay. The end result? They shut the factory. I don't think WebBank needs them. I think we get to know more than a union would be told (Part-time Employee Representative).*

He also argued that an advantage of an in-house system is that it provides universal representation:

> *If I was a shop steward it'd be working for the brothers and sisters. And drumming up members. And if you aren't paying your dues you aren't part of the club. You can't play (Part-time Employee Representative).*

Employees expressed mixed views regarding the benefits of a trade union, with some believing it was unnecessary while others suggested it may be beneficial. For employees in favour, potential benefits cited included enhanced legislative standing, as opposed to a *'frivolous thing that they can get rid of if they want to'*. As supporters commented:

> *The forum ... it's a very similar thing to a union ... I've realised it isn't a union and I wish there was a union at WebBank. And the reason they get away with not having a union is that there are lots of young people ... they are not too clued up on unions. Is there a reason why they don't have a union? Is it equivalent of? It's a question mark.*

> *I don't believe, they the forum, have the legal knowledge if it did get to a really high end problem like tribunals. A union would have that legal facility.*

> *I don't know much about unions but my gut feeling tells me that an in-house forum might not be very objective. Or they might get scared. Because they work for WebBank. Because they have restrictions of their own. I'm sure they'd say it doesn't work like that ... but at the end of the day an outside body doesn't have anything to lose so to speak.*

> *I wonder how involved they will get if it goes really high up the chain ... I believe, for the basic issues around the company it's really good. But when it comes to the really serious nitty gritty it may not be as good (Employee Focus Groups).*

Conversely, others cited the advantages of an in-house forum as including greater local knowledge and a more amicable working relationship:

> *The forum have connections with the company, they've got the records, can speak to people and know how the business works ... trade unions come in and they know all the legal side and they are good, but they don't know the business side.*

> *I think with a union, you start getting power struggles, don't say this to him, say this to me, lawyers and litigation. It can create a larger problem than it actually solves.*

My preconceived notion is that it's all about strikes, a battle against management. I would see a union as that. Out for everything they want, whereas the forum are not like that. They will help you but it's not about getting everybody in the call centre to strike or causing revolt or mutiny.

You think of miners, blowing the whistle, everybody out. You had to down tools and leave the building ... but I think with the forum there isn't a need for a union, it doesn't seem like a need to put pressure on the business to bring about more worker rights because the company is more orientated to thinking of the worker (Employee Focus Groups).

However, it was clear that management retained their 'right to manage' under the partnership structure. This is made clear in the commitment document (see Appendix), which states that *'consultation = both parties views are stated and heard before a decision is made. The perspective of each party is understood by the other not necessarily agreed between them'*. The framework is based upon the IPA model of 'options-based consultation'. The process begins with business objectives being identified in terms of strategy and policy development. The management team then identify various options to move the business forward and have initial discussions with representatives. The consultation process starts before a decision is made, and affords representatives the opportunity of feeding into the process, and to suggest alternative strategies. Management then review the options and take on board the input provided to devise a revised list of options. Management then make the final decision, providing justification why a particular decision was made, and why the others were rejected. Formal decisions are then cascaded to employees by the employer, with management and representatives meeting on an ongoing basis to discuss progress and updates.

Accordingly, for the Employee Chair, the purpose is ensuring that there is a clear understanding of the rationale behind business decisions, but managers retain their right to manage. He explained, *'Whatever they decide in their area, they are the managers. The benefit for us is in knowing the rationale behind those decisions.'* However, he suggested that the forum had a right to challenge and question decisions, suggesting that *'The role of the rep is to challenge and question, the same as whether we were unionised or non-unionised. If we challenge and we question, and we understand the rationale then that's fair'*. The HR Director also made it clear that the forum is not a negotiating body, and that management and employee representatives do not necessarily have to actually agree on decisions. He clarified, *'We consult with them, we don't negotiate, so we aren't reaching an agreement about things. We are very clear that we as the company make the decision, rather than we reach an agreement with them.'* He was keen to stress that although it was not about agreeing per se, this did not mean that the representatives did not have any influence over decisions, arguing that this would mean there was no point in conducting the consultation exercise. As he explained:

> *There would be no point consulting them if what they said didn't influence. They don't have a vote on the decision, but they do have influence in the decision. We do want to be doing things that they support (HR Director).*

Indeed, another senior manager argued that early involvement of the employee representatives in decision-making can actually add value, and this appeared to be one of the key tenets of partnership working:

> *We engage them up front to help with the design, they've got a different perspective to ours so it adds value. Also being there when things are being implemented as a sounding board, a point people can go to with total anonymity and we can take action. That's where they add value (Senior Technology Manager).*

The representatives were also clear that their role was not to act in a confrontational or obstructive manner, but rather to voice the employee perspective on management proposals, and to provide feedback and constructive criticism. For them it was not necessarily about changing decisions:

> *Not that we are going to change the making of decisions. But we are in there adding some sort of knowledge and gaining understanding, and passing over our understanding of what people will feel as well. We are using our experience of the floor (Employee Chair).*

In other words, management gained insight from the coalface, while employees gained because their voice could be fed back to senior executives.

Most employees were also supportive of a non-confrontational approach to employment relations, suggesting that 1970s industrial relations are no longer desirable. As one employee commented, *'I've found you catch more flies with molasses than you do with vinegar.'* However, some employees were uncertain of how much influence the forum had, suggesting it would be difficult to identify outcomes which were the result of forum input, as opposed to what the company would have done anyway. The following quotes illustrate this ambiguity:

> *I don't know if influence is the right word. I think they have an input. Whether they have any great influence I don't know. Sway and influence. They must have otherwise it's a pointless exercise ... to judge something you need an empirical result to measure. If you don't hear the results it's difficult to know.*

> *I've got no negative thoughts about the company, I think the company is good in itself, but as to what degree the forum plays in that I don't know. Whether it's just a good company that will look after you and they don't have to do a great deal. They maybe don't need to do a great deal because the company's good anyway – you don't know (Employee Focus Groups).*

Relationships

Again, in order to understand the process of partnership it is useful to explore the realities of the relationships between the key actors. These are now discussed in turn.

SENIOR MANAGEMENT-EMPLOYEE REPRESENTATIVES RELATIONSHIPS

As mentioned earlier, the WebBank partnership is not based upon a formal agreement, but rather management and representatives described it as a more informal 'relational approach', and stressed the way people work together is more important that formal documentation. As the Vice-Chair explained, a good relationship with senior managers was believed to be more likely to lead to the objective of early involvement and consultation:

> *We put a big emphasis on building relationships because we felt, and again we researched it, that consultation at an early stage through having a really good relationship, would give us more influence than a lets-play-poker approach (Employee Vice-Chair).*

Similarly, the Chair expressed a comfortable relationship with the top management

I have a good relationship with the top people, but my relationship with middle managers is harder to crack. I was put on a People Management Committee, which involves nearly all of the Executive Committee, plus a couple of others. And I'm quite comfortable. They'll listen to me (Employee Chair).

A part-time representative also explained how *'The forum is recognised by the top management of WebBank ... they do value the input, and we are given the time and resources we want, to do what we want for the good of people'*. Overall, the evidence suggested that the relationships between the senior management interviewed and the employee representatives were generally good. The Chair is involved in many meetings, including a monthly meeting with the Chief Executive and the Director of Customer Service. Another representative has a monthly meeting with the Team Leaders in the contact centre, and the IT Director. These meetings typically involve a review of recent issues, business updates and constituency reports.

Senior management responses were also positive. As the senior IT manager commented regarding representatives:

I value them. I recognise they can do things I can't do. We've formed a good relationship over time. I have respect and find them useful in terms of the feedback and information we get from them (Senior Technology Manager).

Another manager noted that representatives who had previously been in a managerial role were particularly helpful because they could adopt more of a *'dual perspective'*. He had experience of more *'militant'* representatives in other organisations whom he thought actually created additional troubles. This was one of the main reasons he preferred the non-union body, as he believed this was more common in unionised environments. He recalled traditional 1970s unionism with intransigent shop stewards who are *'anti-establishment'* describing them as akin to *'News of the World reporters or rogue solicitors that advertise on daytime TV'*, looking for gossip and creating trouble. For him, this is because unions have to demonstrate their 'successes' and worth in order to impress fee-paying members:

If you've got a body funded by individuals who are in trouble, it's in your nature to produce stats that prove you've been really useful. [The forum is] not a business that has to produce results and show they've saved individuals from dismissal. That's not what they are about (Senior Manager).

The key limitation of these positive overall findings, however, is that relationships between managers and the representatives were patchy. The HR Director acknowledged the patchy coverage:

> *I think people who have worked with them tend to be positive about them. Others who haven't will have no relationship with them, wouldn't get involved with them, wouldn't think of involving them, and I think there will be people for whom, if the forum do get involved, there'll be a sense of what are they doing? This is my job and my decision-making!* (HR Director).

One senior manager suggested it may be useful if the forum quantified their interactions with employees more, to inform and convince management of the value they can add.

REPRESENTATIVE–MANAGER RELATIONSHIPS

The relationships between the forum representatives and the middle managers were less good, and representatives suggested a need to be integrated across all levels of management, by demonstrating that they can add value to the process:

> *We have a very good relationship with senior managers. It's middle managers where the relationships are poorer. It used to be very poor.* (Employee Representative).

> *Yesterday with middle managers, who see us a threat? I wasn't as comfortable yesterday, with those people as I was with the top people* (Employee Chair).

There was a belief that representatives were often perceived to be busybodies. Representatives acknowledged that sometimes middle management may appear to be drawn in opposing directions, and may view the forum as a hindrance to meeting their objectives. There was also the suggestion that some middle managers were wary because they knew the representatives had a good working relationship with some of the top executives, and there may be some resentment. As a part-time representative explained:

> *Wary that we have access directly to the top. Some are just wary of the fact you talk to the Chief Executive. The Chief Executive says hello to you. And they think they are the managers (Employee Representative).*

The Employee Chair also was also fairly despondent regarding a recent meeting he attended with line managers:

> *Yesterday I was quite down about it, disappointed, but then I thought it's up to them. I need to build a relationship with them so they can see the benefits we can bring, and see that we are not there to rock the boat but to actually help them. Not being confrontational at all. Some middle managers think that we are interfering really. It's certainly not perfect. But more and more people are getting educated, and seeing that we behave ourselves, and we can act responsibly for both sides (Employee Chair).*

Representatives suggested there had been some progress building relationships, but that a lot still had to be done to build the level of trust to allow the process to operate effectively. For many line managers, there was an association between the forum representatives and the representation of employees during the discipline and grievance issues. This had led to representatives being perceived as an obstruction rather than as people who add value. There was some more positive evidence to suggest, however, that some middle managers *would* use the forum for advice on handling a situation with a subordinate prior to making a decision. Occasionally, managers personally sought advice from the forum regarding an issue with an employee, or pointed people in their direction, which they viewed as a *'real accolade'*. As one representative mused:

> *There are hundreds of managers and some of them value us and some of them don't, quite frankly. And it depends on the individual manager, whether we get involved and what point we get involved. That's a journey we are on, quite frankly (Vice Chair).*

Representatives described a need to be seen to be 'professional' by the management team in order to achieve buy-in. This Vice-Chair suggested that often this was a matter of approach, for example, researching and suggesting solutions, rather than arguing and complaining. This was echoed by a part-time representative who suggested that they have had to build respect by being proactive and bringing solutions to the table rather than complaints:

We've not said 'no you can't do that' and left it at that. If they hear no,
it's 'Why not? What's your reason?' Managers don't want to hear no.
We've now got the ability to develop ideas, solutions and workarounds
(Employee Representative).

As a full-time representative commented, much depended on the individual manager:

Some Team Managers and Team Leaders, to get their buy-in to what
we actually do, and how we can make their job easier, is quite a difficult
process … some do buy in, but others are more sceptical (Employee
Representative).

She believed there was a need to demonstrate how they can actually add value to the process, making the middle manager's job easier as opposed to being perceived as a nuisance. This was said to require further relationship building, and represented a key area for future development.

EMPLOYEES AND EMPLOYEE REPRESENTATIVES

Another key relationship is the relationship between employees and employee representatives. The HR Director suggested there was a need to build awareness of what the Employee Forum do for employees. Team managers suggested that employees who had not actually approached the forum for advice would probably only have a vague notion of their purpose. A representative admitted that in the early stages the representatives had very little credibility in the eyes of employees, because they were seen to follow an agenda set by management, but that things had improved:

We had no credibility, always very much manager lapdogs, HR poodles.
Because they only ever saw us with a manager in tow. We were almost
there to legitimise it! The managers would say we are doing this, and
we have consulted with the forum (Vice Chair).

Representatives suggested their visibility had improved over time through regular 'awareness events', however, there was evidence to suggest many employees still had a limited knowledge of their role as the following employee quotes illustrate:

To be honest I don't know anything about the Employee Forum. I know that they are elected. But I'd like them to come and have a word one day and let us know what they do.

Is it them who are responsible for the cheap perfume in the atrium?

Is it because of them the toilets are getting decorated?

They might have done something revolutionary for us but we don't have a clue!

If you dig around you can probably find out, but you would have to proactively go and find out ... it's not openly volunteered.

You don't know how much of it is the company doing alright on their own or the forum saying I think we should change that and do it this way, it'd be better for the people. You don't know.

I believe they do a lot of work but it's not rolled out to us (Employee Focus Group)

Issues and Decision-Making

Again, as part of a young organisation, the East Midlands centre has experience a rapid rate of organisational change. In order to enhance understanding of the actual process of partnership, the study explored in detail how different issues have been handled, and how various decisions have been made. The section begins with a discussion of traditional 'trade union issues' such as pay and working conditions, and then proceeds to explore some context specific issues.

PAY AND WORKING CONDITIONS

The forum is not involved in the formal negotiation of pay. However, there was evidence to suggest that representatives had been involved in pay and reward discussions, although their role is quite different to traditional collective bargaining conversations. Indeed, there is evidence to suggest that their role is in the capacity of an *adviser* as opposed to a *negotiator*. At the time of the research, there were four main examples of where the employee representatives had been involved in pay and conditions discussions with management which illustrate this advisory role.

Group pension scheme

The first issue concerned changes to the WebBank pension scheme. Historically, employees had to actively 'opt in' to join the pension scheme. Following a recent check by the HR department it was discovered that over 1000 employees had never joined. The HR Director commented, *'It seemed ridiculous, people giving up money.'* The forum representatives persuaded management to change the wording on the contracts so that new employees actively have to opt out, changing the default option to opt in. This was agreed by the management team, albeit reluctantly as the HR Director still believed it was more logical to opt in than to opt out. The representatives also pushed management to backdate the payments to the time employees started as opposed to the opt-in date, at a cost of £1 million. As the HR Director explained:

> I'm not saying that we definitely wouldn't have done it if they hadn't been involved but they were very supportive of that change. Which if they hadn't been it might have been harder to get through. There is generally a perception that people should choose to do something rather than choose not to do something (HR Director).

This change was endorsed by the team managers, who suggested that the reason people were not joining the pension scheme was simply because of the long and complicated forms required to join, and the fact that new recruits received a mass of paperwork before they started it probably got overlooked.

Bonus change

The second issue concerned a change to the bonus payment system. Representatives noticed many part-time employees were refusing their bonus and discovered this was because many working mothers were in receipt of family tax credits (FTCs) which they would lose if they exceeded the earning threshold. Representatives argued the case that this was not in the interests of the business (as many employees do not have an incentive to achieve targets), and that it is clearly not in the best interests of the employee to refuse extra pay. Accordingly, they proposed alternative means of bonus reward in the form of vouchers. Following discussions between the forum and the HR Reward Team, the proposal was investigated in relation to feasibility issues such as tax and administrative implications of operating such a system. Following a pilot period, the business has now implemented a system of childcare vouchers as an alternative bonus option, without jeopardising their FTCs, and *'it became a standard part of what we do'*. There is also the option of having bonuses paid into their pension plan.

Holiday purchase scheme

A further example of forum input, concerns a representative's proposal to introduce a holiday purchase scheme, which he had heard about working in other organisations. Requests for additional holidays were a recurring issue, and there was a degree of ambiguity whether employees could take unpaid leave or not. The idea was therefore to formalise and regulate an agreed process. The scheme involves the employer offering employees the possibility to trade their holiday for a proportion of their salary up to a certain amount each year. A representative carried out a straw poll on whether a holiday purchase scheme would be desirable within WebBank. Given initial enthusiasm, he asked for a question to be included in the monthly employee survey to get a more representative employee reaction. He argued that the proposal could be framed both in terms of business rationale (less sickness and unauthorised absence which are important issues, especially in the contact centre environment) as well as the employee benefit. The Reward Team investigated the idea in detail, including the likely administrative/IT requirements of operating such a scheme and then devised some viable options and it was subsequently piloted in one business area. Following its success, the holiday purchase scheme has since been implemented across WebBank.

Pay review

Lastly, this concerns some of the representatives joining the Reward Committee to discuss the nature of the reward packages, in terms of basic salary, bonus payments and other fringe benefits.

> *Whether that was influencing or not, I don't know, we would never be involved in that before. To be invited to be part of that, and for them to take into account what we were saying (Employee Chair).*

The representatives viewed being invited to join such discussions as evidence of their success in achieving 'buy-in' from the management team, although again it must be stressed they are not attending in a traditional bargaining capacity.

DISCIPLINE AND GRIEVANCE

It was clear that a key focus of forum involvement was the conduct of discipline and grievance situations. The amount of discipline and grievance cases within WebBank was flagged by the HR Director as one of the key issues which concerned him, and the most explicit manifestations of ER problems. Typical issues included timekeeping, sickness, mis-selling and performance issues. Management and representatives suggested that in most disciplinary hearings a representative from the forum would normally be involved.

In such cases, the HR Director described the representatives as *'useful independent people'* who could re-assess a situation following a breakdown in trust between the line manager and an employee. The representatives agreed that dealing with discipline and grievance situations was one of their bread-and-butter duties. They would often attend disciplinary hearings, and offer advice to line managers and employees in advance of a hearing. To illustrate, one representative gave an example of a grievance he was currently dealing with:

> Today I have an individual, 26 weeks pregnant, requested to work out of our other site, she lives two minutes from that site. They are putting her through the wringer to agree this. The doctor is saying driving here and back is too much. And the manager involved is being an arse about it (Employee Representative).

There were further examples of the forum representatives acting as an intermediary in a case where an employee resigned, and said she would only return if they could guarantee she would not have to work with a certain line manager again. Another case involved performance management and compliance with FSA regulations. A compromise was reached where one normally high performing employee did not receive her annual pay rise because of 'red' i.e. non-compliant calls. The employee received 'two red calls' which meant she was technically not eligible for a pay rise. Previously agents were allowed four but this had been reduced to two. The representative intervened, arguing that *'when you've got a person like that, working their socks off for a whole year, and being an excellent role model that they should suffer for two red calls'.* and the outcome was that the employee was *'given a month to put together their development pack'*, and her pay would be re-reviewed by the Call Centre Manager.

However, frequent representative involvement in discipline and grievance procedures had created a problem. Team leaders/managers now mostly associated the Employee Forum with discipline and grievance procedures, and there was evidence to suggest that this had actually contributed to a certain degree of negativity by team leaders who developed a view that the forum representatives were interfering outsiders. As one young team manager commented:

> To be honest I didn't really like the Employee Forum… [at disciplinary hearings] I felt they were judging me, seeing whether I'm right or wrong, trying to catch me out. I got really uncomfortable to the point I wouldn't look forward to having a conversation with a forum rep. They made me nervous (Team Manager).

He explained how over time he had managed to build a stronger relationship with one of the representatives, and was no longer intimidated, and even going to them for advice commenting how 'they are there for me as well'.

The potential usefulness of representatives was echoed by another line manager:

> They are there where people feel they haven't been treated fairly, for example, at a disciplinary. Most people that go to a disciplinary are blind to the problem at hand. Or if they are not blind to it they don't see why it's such a problem. So for them it's not a fair process. Even if everything is as fair as it can be. The way they work is really interesting in that they've got both parties interests at hand. If they can see that, they'll tell the person it's fair, and if something is said that isn't fair, you have somebody there to support you (Team Manager).

He gave an example where a normally conscientious individual was almost dismissed because of a poor attendance record. However, after forum intervention the underlying cause was discovered to be bullying by a manager. Following a detailed investigation, the situation was resolved, with the employee reporting to a new line manager, and the development of an 'attendance plan'. The team manager believed that had there been no forum intervention, the employee would probably not have 'opened up', and would have been dismissed, and the root of the problem never identified. Yet the problem remained that for many middle managers the forum was perceived to be a nuisance, especially with managers who have limited involvement with the representatives, and typically little experience of unions either. As a team manager commented, *'If you've got managers who are quite new to the job and unsure of what you are doing then yeah, they feel a threat to you, they are almost a party scrutinising your actions.'* This tension was acknowledged by the representatives:

> *Let's face it, anytime they ever see us, it's a disciplinary so they think God, it's them again. What we've got to do it to actually educate them that we are working for all WebBank people, and not just associates. We will represent associates, line managers, team leaders, and the management have even got their own reps as well. It's working. Slowly! (Employee Representative).*

For one senior manager the key issue was achieving some sort of balance between giving employees a fair hearing, but also engaging *'common sense'* when there was clear evidence to suggest the employee had genuinely been irresponsible. He commended the Employee Forum arguing that the representatives are normally balanced in that they can send employees who have a weak case *'away with a flea in their ear'* rather than *'creating headaches with grievances that just won't go anywhere'*. He described this balanced attitude as, *'I understand what you are up against Mr Manager, but I think this guy could be treated better than he is, and that happens in the majority of cases'*. A part-time representative stressed that during disciplinary cases it is not *'us and them'*, but rather ensuring there is a fair and consistent hearing, and not necessarily backing-up a recalcitrant employee with a non-existent case. As he stated, *'We just wanted to make sure due process has been followed. You can't go from step 1 to step 5 in one move – you just can't do that'*.

MANAGING CHANGE

The third main area of involvement was around issues of managing change. Two are particularly noteworthy: the technology restructure, and the suspension of duvet days in the call centre.

Technology restructure

Firstly, a recent restructure in the Technology department was highlighted as a good example of joint-working between the management team and the representatives. There was involvement of one of the representatives in the selection process, discussing the proposals, the new job roles and the selection procedures. Representatives recalled an incident in 2003, during the early stages of the forum, when they were informed about a major restructure with redundancy implications only 24 hours before it was announced to the entire business. They suggested that this meant the only input they could offer was *'support people and nibble at the edges'*. However, there were now more examples of early involvement. It was suggested that employee representatives had been involved at a much earlier stage. The representatives suggested the initial selection procedure appeared to be slightly arbitrary – and suspected some favouritism – and consequently pushed for a more transparent procedure. It was believed that the final selection process was much fairer as a result of the dialogue. Moreover, there was a sense that sometimes managers can devise pure process models with a logical business case but *'forget the human side'*. It was proposed that the HR department occasionally focus too much on making sure that restructures and resultant redundancies are legally compliant, but overlook the human factors, and this, it was suggested, is a key area where the Employee Forum, with their additional perspective, could add value. This was echoed by another representative who commented how *'legality is the start of how we should work, not the end of how we should work'*.

Speaking of the most recent restructure, a senior technology manager hailed the benefits of the forum involvement. He described the representatives as a useful sounding board, providing valuable insight into potential employee reaction. He believed they acted as a useful feedback mechanism to the management team, as well as someone employees can talk to to allay their concerns. As he explained, *'They helped us in the design, by being available to accept feedback ... and a general sense of how things are felt by those out on the floor.'* The forum helped by providing comments the management team had not considered, and also being available to talk to those affected. Following the option-based model discussed earlier, the aim was to question and to propose alternatives. He was not part of the actual delivery mechanism, however, to ensure he was not perceived to be 'part of management'. It was suggested this provided, from a management perspective, a useful checkpoint and review mechanism throughout the entire re-organisation project. As one representative summed up:

> With that restructure we were involved from day one. It's alright saying, oh, the people will be OK. A nice process flow. Clockwork. We are doing this, this is why, and this is the business case. But they forget the human side. And sometimes HR forget that. HR need to see things are legal and watertight. But they can get wrapped up in that, forgetting the human side. And if we get involved we can suggest that.

*And if things are really bad we can suggest scrapping things that are
really bad. You can't make people redundant on Christmas Eve. You
just can't do that (Part-time Employee Representative).*

Suspension of duvet days in the contact centre

WebBank had trialled a scheme of 'duvet days' in the contact centre, in response
to suggestions by the forum representatives who had heard about such systems
working successfully in other organisations. They believed this could be a good
idea in the contact centre environment where sickness and absenteeism can
be a problem. Essentially, duvet days involve four days 'no-questions-asked'
leave which employees can take at short notice, and are specifically designed
to reduce 'sickies'. In practice, employees would have the ability to request
last-minute leave prior to the start of their shift, by requesting a duvet day from
a fixed number available on a first-come-first-served basis. In other words,
they enable employees to take leave at much shorter notice than they would
normally be expected to give. In November 2004, it was decided that there was
a lack of capacity to accommodate the four duvet days due to high sickness,
and the average service level had fallen below the 60 per cent company target.
They were also failing to meet the target of answering customer calls within 20
seconds. The representative was consulted before the change, but had a serious
concern that if the message was poorly communicated it could easily have been
misinterpreted, making the situation even worse. She highlighted that a basic
factual communication of *'duvet days have been suspended'* would have created a
lot of anger in an already overstretched and demoralised work environment in
the run up to Christmas. As she explained:

> *By consulting with us about it he was able to put out a better message
> that sat better with people working under pressure constantly. It really
> wasn't a good place to be in November! (Employee Representative).*

In other words, the representative was in touch with the general climate
in the contact centre and was able to ensure that the decision was handled
and communicated in a sensitive manner *'by putting some context around it'*.
The message was therefore delivered on the basis that the suspension was
with reluctance and only temporary, rather than a punitive response to high
absenteeism. In this way she was able to foresee and warn the management of
potentially negative consequences.

Outcomes

The main benefits were identified as collaborative relationships between senior management and employee representatives, and the regulation of decision-making.

COLLABORATIVE SENIOR MANAGEMENT–EMPLOYEE REPRESENTATIVE RELATIONSHIPS

Positive working relationships between management and employee representatives were an important outcome of the partnership working approach. This has been described as an informal 'relational' approach, based upon an agreed way of working based upon the 'options-based consultation' approach. In particular, the good relationships between the full-time employee representatives and the Chief Executive appear to be central to the success of building and operating the structure within a relatively short period of time.

REGULATION OF DECISION-MAKING

There was evidence of some strong relationships, especially between the full-time representatives and members of the senior management team, and that benefits were being derived as a result of these relationships. Management interviewees were positive about what they gained from forum representatives in terms of their input into organisational issues. They were seen as adding value, providing new perspectives, and acting as a useful checkpoint on management decision-making. Senior managers agreed that there is a need for such a system as it allows flaws to be identified and pre-emptive corrective action to be taken at an early stage. This was believed to lead to better, and more efficient, management decision-making. Senior managers agreed that often representatives had good judgment and knowledge, and were therefore useful in identifying potential employee relations 'flashpoints'. As one senior manager summed up:

> Because they are in at the front, we don't go down the road of designing something wholly inappropriate. Of course nothing is perfect, but we've already had input from people who have a different perspective. So it stops us wasting money doing things that won't work anyway (Senior Technology Manager).

Equally, representatives have experienced increased involvement over time from *'sausages in the canteen'* and *'fleas in the carpet'* to being invited to provide input on more strategic issues and being consulted earlier in the decision-making process. Their involvement now spans a wide array of both day-to-day as well as more strategic issues. It is noteworthy that while representatives had a degree of influence over the regulation of decision-making, they were not involved in actually making decisions per se. Nevertheless, it was suggested that there was a generally better climate of employment relations as a result of the mechanism, since the representatives were able to predict many problems before they occur, acting as a feedback loop for employee opinion, as well as a cathartic outlet for disgruntled employees. As the forum Vice Chair explained, *'I think compared to a union we are very slick. We are a lot more powerful than some of the old adversarial unions.'*

Both management and representatives emphasised that one of the differences between partnership and non-partnership working, is that with the former both parties express a joint commitment to business success, and try to moderate decisions with that overall goal in mind. It was proposed that while a traditional approach is normally characterised by the business trying to maximise profit while the representatives try to maximise pay and working conditions, the partnership approach operates somewhere in the middle ground. In practical terms, this meant the forum aim was 'fairness':

> *All you can do is make sure it's a fair decision ... That's what annoys me about the union. Saying they can do more than we can because they have more power. If WebBank decide tomorrow to move to India, who's going to stop them? No-one! We always reckon that we're there for people and they get a fair deal. We would have as much power as the unions (Employee Representative).*

As the Vice-Chair remarked, *'The issues haven't changed, we still get them. The way we deal with them has changed.'*

Challenges

However, several challenges to the effectiveness of the process were evident. These included difficulties embedding a partnership culture, representative efficacy and resistance to adversity.

EMBEDDING A PARTNERSHIP CULTURE

It was evident that the closest relationship was with the HR department and that forum involvement was not spread equally across business units. Indeed, there were still many examples where representatives were not consulted, and much depended on the individual departments and attitudes of managers involved. There was inconsistency across the business, and it was suggested by the representatives that managers *'are not sharing best practice'* in terms of consultation with the forum. As the HR Director acknowledged:

> *I need to put a continued emphasis on my team to include the forum, as opposed to actively exclude them. When you are trying to get something done, sometimes you don't remember to talk to everybody ... it's a frustration for me when they are not involved because I think we get better results when they are (HR Director).*

A related challenge was getting the buy-in of employees and raising the profile of the representative body. There was still a lack of awareness among employees about the forum and its role, successes and achievements. Many employees had a greater awareness of direct EI practices, and expressed a preference for raising issues directly with their line managers, unless of course it was a specific complaint about their line manager. A dilemma was present in that many ideas are communicated as though they were the idea of management. The representatives believed this allowed them to distance themselves from management decision-making, but resulted in employees not really appreciating how the forum had contributed or improved outcomes for them. Many employees remembered representatives from induction sessions, and there was a general knowledge that they existed, but a lack of clarity over their exact role.

Additionally, the HR Director expressed some concern that the forum tended to be used primarily by those lower down the organisational hierarchy, and especially those working in the call centre environment. The forum appeared to have less interaction with more senior employees. Officially there are elected representatives from the management population but they are not particularly active, and this was identified as a weakness. Several reasons may be speculated for this situation. It could be that the labour process in the call centre gives rise to more issues which are subsequently voiced. It was clear that the working environment is more regulated there than in other parts of the business where employees have more autonomy. Alternatively, managers may not consider the forum to be 'for them', or they may feel sufficiently confident to raise issues personally without representative assistance. The bias may also reflect the fact that those working in the call centre represent a large proportion of the employee population.

Middle management attitudes towards the forum may also be partly responsible. As discussed earlier, many line managers perceived the forum to be a hindrance rather than an ally. They believed that sometimes the emphasis on procedures and following processes clashed with the business objectives of dynamism and flexibility. A typical example could be a line manager's desire to change an employee's shift to accommodate changing business needs. On the one hand, the manager is pressurised to resource the team effectively, whereas on the other there is a process which they must engage in before changes can legitimately be made.

> *From a management point of view we do have quite a lot of buy-in. Especially at the top and bottom. It's the middle layer we need to infiltrate more. They are the really important people. A lot of them are the decision makers on the ground. It's the middle piece. But we are getting there I believe (Employee Representative).*

It was suggested that there was a need to demonstrate to middle managers how representatives can actually add value, and a feeling that too often they are associated as advocates of employees during disciplinaries.

REPRESENTATIVE EFFICACY

A second important challenge concerns representative efficacy. The representatives believed that there was a challenge convincing employees that they are not management poodles, but that this is difficult as grassroots employees are not aware of what goes on behind the scenes.

> *Although we are not lackeys to the management sometimes we can't change decisions. All you can do is make sure that it's a fair decision. No-one wants to be redundant but if you can show the reasons why, and explain the circumstances and what you have done to lighten the impact, they might not be happy but they'll know we did everything we could. If we can't change the decision we'll lessen the impact. Do everything we can. If you have to make two more calls per hour and you are not happy with it, we'll at least make sure you know why (Employee Representative).*

Need to dispel any myth that we work with WebBank and are therefore in service to WebBank. And are we doing what WebBank want us to do. Actually we have some pretty heated debates (Employee Representative).

Representative efficacy is also important in the eyes of senior managers. Senior managers suggested they need more grassroots feedback via the forum, especially if buy-in to the concept is going to spread across the entire business. This was a challenge, however, because managers acknowledged that many members of the management team seek value in quantifiable terms, when in reality the value added was very often more subtle and intangible. There is also the need for representatives to find the fine line between being perceived to be toothless, and being perceived to be 'militant' or 'anti-establishment'. This was a concern expressed by some managers. Much appeared to hinge upon the personalities of representatives and their ability to build a constructive rapport, as well as the previous employment relations and work experiences of individual managers.

RESISTANCE TO ADVERSITY

The third theme concerns the robustness of the forum and the ability to deal with a 'big issue'. For example, the forum has been championed since its inception by a few key players from the management community, including the Chief Executive. Similarly, the Employee Chair and Vice Chair have both been involved in the creation of the structure since 2000. A concern is the impact a major change on some of the key characters and 'champions' may have on the effectiveness of the structure. This leads to the question of the sustainability of a partnership hinged upon a few key characters and seconded representatives.

A related issue is the ability of the forum to deal with some major difficult issue. As a representative explained:

It's all nice and lovely at the minute, but we are going to hit big things. Big things will happen. Can we challenge them successfully? And have enough information to challenge? That's my concern really (Employee Representative).

There are several reasons why a major event could give cause for concern. As highlighted earlier in this chapter, the representatives are not negotiators and the structure is very much upon terms defined by management, and reliant upon employer goodwill. This leads to the question of whether the forum would have enough information – and indeed the ability to understand the information – for example, about why a department is closing down. Again, this is related to the ability of representatives, who do not have union officials or intelligence to draw upon. Representatives are increasingly involved in dealing with complicated casework around discipline and grievance and absenteeism. However, this is not to say the representatives at WebBank have been working in isolation; indeed they have forged an impressive network of contacts from whom they seek advice. For example, the representatives have arranged external training on issues including health and safety, discipline and grievance procedures, and performance management, and have worked closely with the Involvement and Participation Association.

Conclusions

The WebBank case presents a good test of partnership for several reasons. Firstly, this is one of the few explicit studies of partnership in non-union organisations. In addition, the route to partnership is interesting. The evidence suggests that as soon as the business expanded, management decided to push for a representative body, and it is possible that this reflects the norms of the sector and the fact that most of the senior management joined the organisation from other organisations in the same sector. The structure was not a response to a particular crisis, as is often the case. Though a range of formal structures exist emphasis was placed on informality and minimising burdensome procedures. This may reflect in part the cultural context: WebBank was launched with the objective of being a new, dynamic player in a traditional and conservative marketplace.

The partnership model was proposed by the representatives, following consultations with other companies and the advice of organisations such as IPA. The primary component of the partnership structure at WebBank is the Employee Forum which has evolved from a part-time forum investigating 'sausages in the canteen' to a structure with 16 representatives, three of whom are on full-time secondment to the post. The evidence suggested that most managers, employee representatives and employees were happy with the principle of non-union representation, regarding trade unions as overly political, inflexible and hostile. Partnership did not mean joint decision-making, rather, the cornerstone was early consultation with representatives before decisions had been made, affording them the ability to question, challenge and propose alternatives.

Relationships between senior management and the representatives were good, with relationships between representative and line managers/employees patchy. Areas where representatives had been involved spanned across areas of pay and conditions, discipline and grievance, and the management of change. Though they are not negotiators, they argued that through consultation they were able to persuade and influence, often securing fairer outcomes for employees by reminding management of 'the human side' of business decisions. A key question is whether, in the current climate, a union could actually deliver more.

Through the process, management benefited from input into decisions and information regarding employee opinion and morale. Representatives and employees had the opportunity to have their voice heard by the top management of the organisation. The business was able to avoid making counterproductive decisions, while workers benefited from decisions which had been discussed in detail, and were sometimes 'fairer' than they might otherwise have been. Of course several challenges remain. These include embedding a partnership culture across the entire organisation, communication, and raising employee awareness. There are also questions of how the structure and relationships could withstand a period of adversity. The representatives also have to contend with the issue of demonstrating their efficacy to both management and employees, but without appearing 'too aggressive' to alienate managers, while simultaneously not appearing 'too soft' to alienate their constituents. In short, the evidence calls into question views of non-union structures as toothless cosmetic institutions with little impact on the quality of employment relations. Indeed, not only does the case confirm the possibility of partnership without unions, it also demonstrates partnership without unions demonstrating a moderate degree of success.

7

Three Cases of Partnership Compared

Introduction

The purpose of this chapter is to compare and contrast the results from the NatBank, BuSoc and WebBank case studies outlined in the preceding three chapters. The chapter begins by outlining the different contextual factors in each organisation. It then reviews the meaning of partnership, both in terms of official policy statements as well as the understandings and interpretations of organisational actors. The aim is to then explore the process of partnership. This includes an examination of the relationships between organisational actors, and then the way decisions are made and issues are handled. The chapter goes on to explore the outcomes of partnership from the point of view of organisational actors. Finally, the chapter outlines some of the main challenges to partnership.

Context of Partnership

'Partnership' has become a portmanteau term used to refer to a wide variety of employment relations arrangements. The cases presented in the study are in many ways similar: they are all based on customer service departments in financial service organisations, and as such the type of work undertaken is comparable, as is the general employee profile. However, there are important differences between the organisations, which should be flagged. Taking account of contextual factors is important in order to test how partnership plays out in different contexts, and to avoid acontextual deterministic assumptions about the implications of partnership. These will now be discussed in turn.

ROUTES TO PARTNERSHIP

Firstly, the case studies represent three very different espoused routes to partnership: as a solution to a prolonged period of poor industrial relations; a natural evolution of employment relations; and a preferred and deliberate approach to the management of employment relations in a greenfield context.

Bad industrial relations: partnership as a solution

NatBank is in many ways typical of the current literature whereby a formal partnership deal has been struck in response to a combination of commercial and industrial relations challenges in the late 1990s. This culminated with a period where the business was losing the confidence of the City, as well as industrial action with the union over proposals to introduce performance related pay. Senior figures suggested management–union relationships were poor, and there was a realisation by senior management and union officials that the existing situation was untenable. The language of workplace partnership, as espoused by the New Labour government, TUC and IPA, was viewed as a potential solution to the industrial relations 'problem'.

Good industrial relations: partnership cements existing relationships

BuSoc has a recognition and procedural agreement with the company union it has recognised for 30 years. Unlike NatBank, there was no specific 'turning-point', but the espoused de facto partnership relationship has been built over a long time, and was said to have hinged upon forging close working relationships between union officials and members of the senior management team. BuSoc Union has a long history of stable, co-operative employment relations, and unlike NatBank, has never taken the society to Acas or engaged in industrial action. This could partly be attributed to the union's history as a staff association before it became an independent union affiliated to the TUC in the late 1990s.

Partnership as a natural evolution or response to an external threat

WebBank is an example of a non-union partnership established in 2000. It was suggested that management at WebBank did not believe union recognition was the most appropriate option for WebBank, and that it would ne inappropriate to the company's youthful entrepreneurial style, and instigated the development of an in-house representative structure in 2000. The structure is still in its infancy, and there is no long shared history as there is in the other two case organisations. Biographies of the executive team reveal they all had experience of working in unionised financial service organisations prior to joining WebBank, suggesting that perhaps despite official greenfield status, sectoral norms may have played a part in the creation of a representative body as soon as the company began to grow. Cases of non-union/greenfield partnerships are limited in the existing literature; again, presumably because they are relatively rare. As a greenfield site, WebBank could also be viewed as a positive environment for the development of a fresh and modern approach to the management of employment relations. It can be speculated that partnership here was either a response to an external threat (external union recognition/ European consultation legislation), the traditions of the parent organisation, or a natural evolution of a rapidly expanding young organisation. From the perspective of institutional theory, there is also the possibility that the company imitated the collectivist norms of the industry generally, or was influenced by perceived industry best practice. In reality, the rationale is likely to have been the result of a combination of factors.

CORPORATE GOVERNANCE

Another important point of comparison concerns corporate governance. As a mutual organisation not responsible to shareholders, BuSoc has developed a reputation as a paternalistic employer and has won various awards in relation to its employment policy. It could be speculated that this context would provide a fertile environment for partnership, given that shareholder pressure is often seen to be one of the main barriers to high trust relationships in a liberal market economy such as the UK. It is therefore interesting that they maintain a strong institutional separation between bargaining and consultation and have avoided a more opened-ended partnership agreement, although it may be speculated that the prospect of pendulum arbitration explains why the employer is reluctant to include more negotiable items, and why the union decided against a partnership agreement. On the other hand, NatBank and WebBank are PLCs, with pressure to deliver short-term results to investors. When WebBank was listed on the Stock Exchange in 2000, managers suggested that there was a palpable change in management style, as they now had to been seen to be responsible and delivering to investors. It could therefore be speculated that the PLCs represent a more challenging environment for the development of partnership relationships, and that mutual organisations operate in an environment more conducive to partnership. Equally, it could be argued that PLCs may be more proactive and actually work harder at HRM, because they do not enjoy the economic cushioning that mutuality affords, especially if they believe organisational performance requires good employment relations.

TRADE UNIONS AND IR HISTORY

Comparisons can also be made in terms of union recognition, and the particular case studies have afforded the opportunity to compare partnership in three different contexts. NatBank recognises an external trade union with which it has long relationships, and which itself is the result of a series of staff association and union mergers. BuSoc recognises an internal staff union with which it has had a relationship since 1965, and is also the result of mergers, as the representative bodies merged following business mergers. WebBank has no formal union recognition, but instead has opted for an in-house representative body known as the Employee Forum, established in 2000, two years after the company was founded. On this count it may be proposed that non-union arrangements may be less deep-rooted and that partnership is more likely to flourish in unionised contexts. Alternatively, partnership may be more likely to flourish in an environment without historical IR baggage.

PARTNERSHIPS STRUCTURES AND FORMALITY

The fourth dimension concerns the differences between the formal partnership structures. All organisations have a wide array of representative structures typically associated with organisations espousing a partnership approach. The representative structures are, unsurprisingly, the cornerstone of partnership in the three organisations, although the true test is how the structures operate in practice. Partnership structures were most formalised at NatBank. This could be attributed to their industrial relations experience, and the fact that the company is part of a large multinational organisation with experience of structures such as European Works Councils. The organisation also has a long history of working with a large national trade union as well as with an internal staff union. Formal structures were less important at BuSoc, with a much greater emphasis on relationships between key actors. There was also no formal partnership agreement, with BuSoc and the union retaining a traditional recognition and procedure agreement. Management and union officials suggested the recognition and procedure agreement is a poor reflection of the reality of the conduct of employment relations within BuSoc. For example, the formal JCNC negotiating body is ostensibly the main negotiating forum between the union and management. However, management and union officials agreed that in reality the JCNC seldom meets; with most agreements reached through more informal channels. The smaller size of the organisation and the staff union could also explain the higher level of informality. Though it was suggested that the recognition and procedure agreement does not reflect the 'new age' of industrial relations, the union was reluctant to engage with a partnership agreement. This appeared to stem from the availability of a powerful pendulum arbitration tool under the current agreement, and secondly a fear of being perceived to be too close to management. At WebBank there was also a much greater emphasis on informal relationships and again no formal partnership agreement, but a greater emphasis on developing formal partnership structures.

Definitions of Partnership

'Partnership' has become a catch-all term, leading to the problem of distinguishing between partnership and non-partnership organisations. Clearly there is a need to establish whether the organisations under scrutiny qualify as prima facie partnerships.

As Table 7.1 reveals, in each case there is an explicit commitment to organisational success. There is also a commitment to the legitimacy of interest representation. At NatBank this is referred to as the *'legitimate interests of other stakeholders'*, while at BuSoc there is an acknowledgement of the legitimacy of the union, and encouragement of union membership. A similar sentiment is expressed in WebBank documentation, suggesting the recognition of legitimate roles, interests and responsibilities although not of a union per se. The importance of trust is emphasised at NatBank and WebBank but is not an explicit component of BuSoc agreements. Information sharing and transparency is at the core of all three agreements. Similarly, issues of consultation and problem-solving are also mentioned in all organisations. Employment security and flexibility are outlined in detailed documents at NatBank and BuSoc, but at WebBank the commitment is more ambiguous, focusing more upon encouraging an understanding of the rationale behind changes, including redundancy, and why these may be deemed necessary. Issues around the quality of working life are present in all cases, and generally encompass topics such as training and development, equal opportunities and diversity. The notion of win-win outcomes is espoused by NatBank and BuSoc, suggesting that the ultimate aim is to balance issues of customer, employee and shareholder interests. This is not explicitly mentioned in WebBank documentation. However, in accordance with the IPA definition, the notion of sharing organisational success is evident.

Table 7.1   Formal definitions of partnership

Principle/Organisation	NatBank	BuSoc	WebBank
Joint commitment to organisational success (IPA) Commitment to success of the enterprise(TUC)	Securing and promoting the long-term success of NatBank	BuSoc and the union have a common objective in ensuring the efficiency and prosperity of BuSoc and its employees	Joint commitment to WebBank's success
Mutual recognition of the legitimate role and interests of all parties (IPA) Recognising legitimate interests (TUC)	Legitimate interests of other stakeholders, carry out duties in a way that demonstrates mutual trust	BuSoc acknowledges the union's duty to promote and safeguard the interests of its members; acknowledges the benefits of BuSoc employees being members of the union	Recognition for legitimate roles, interests and responsibilities
Commitment and effort to develop and sustain trust (IPA)	Carry out respective roles and duties in a way that demonstrates mutual trust	Working in a spirit of openness, trust and integrity	Trust – building trust throughout WebBank
Means for sharing information (IPA) Transparency (TUC)	Openness with information about the business, communicating openly and honestly	Regular meetings with the union; maintain effective communication and exchange information on business issues	Transparency – sharing information and organisational policy consultation
Consultation, joint problem-solving and employee involvement (IPA)	Problem-solving	Both parties agree that effective consultation and negotiation are instrumental; use appropriate channels of communication, consultation and negotiation to address issues	Meaningful consultation at all levels within WebBank
Policies to balance flexibility with employment security (IPA) Commitment to employment security (TUC)	Employability and avoiding compulsory redundancies; develop flexibility to promote commercial success	Security of employment and redundancy agreement; looks at business need to be flexible and ensure employees have maximum protection	Flexibility and understanding of why change is required; encouragement of internal movement
Focus on the quality of working life (TUC)	Promoting equality of treatment and opportunity for all, and valuing diversity	Fair treatment at work, discipline and grievance, equality, training and development	Right to be represented and to have equal opportunities within the business; exceptional training and development
Win-win (TUC)	Promoting the interests of employees, customers and shareholders	BuSoc's responsibility to manage the business in the interests of BuSoc, its employee and customers	Generating and sharing wealth with all our stakeholders
Sharing organisational success (IPA)	Recognising and rewarding exceptional performance	Prosperity for customers and employees	Sharing organisational success (bonuses and PRP)

All cases also express a commitment to recognising, rewarding and sharing organisational success.

In short, it is argued that in terms of official policy statements the commitments outlined by each organisation are remarkably similar. However, official policy statements provide limited insight into how partnership is understood, interpreted and acted upon by organisational actors on a day-to-day-basis. It is therefore essential to consider how partnership is actually interpreted and understood.

Actor Understanding of Partnership

At NatBank, partnership was defined as a modern approach to employment relations centred around a core commitment to business success. In practice this meant there should be a high level of dialogue between the union and the bank, and that decisions should be considered from both a business and employee perspective as part of an overarching problem-solving approach. This was contrasted with a traditional 'arm's length' or 'institutionalised conflict' approach. Central to the concept was discussing ideas and proposals much earlier in the process. However, partnership did *not* mean joint decision-making and the union was not expected to agree with all decisions; and occasional disagreement were believed to be a healthy and normal part of a partnership process.

At BuSoc partnership was defined more broadly as a co-operative union–management relationship. It was believed that the union and management relationship had a long history of co-operation, and that this was the approach supported by employees. It was also suggested by both managers and union representatives to be a more productive approach. The approach was described as one of '*give and take*' and '*manoeuvring*'. Again, it was suggested that one of the key differences between partnership and non-partnership was the early involvement of the union in consultation processes. The role of the union was described as one of constructively challenging management to try and ensure the fair treatment of employees. Partnership did not mean joint decision-making took place, but that the union had the opportunity to persuade, influence and challenge decision-making. As a result, the union role was often referred to as one of '*checks and balances*' on decision-making processes.

At WebBank, partnership was again described as a collaborative rather than adversarial style of employment relations. It was suggested that low trust, conflictual relationships *'do not work anymore'*, and that more can be achieved through high trust relationships. The ultimate aim was to try to ensure decisions are as fair as possible for employees, but also sensible for the business. However, management retained their 'right to manage', and stressed the forum was not a negotiating body, The emphasis of partnership was early consultation, opportunity to give feedback, and full communication in the process of implementing new business decisions.

In mapping this, the dimensions suggested by Marchington and Wilkinson (2005) in their studies of employee involvement are useful in this analysis (originally developed in Marchington et al., 1992). They propose degree, scope, form and level as means of evaluation of employee involvement initiatives and these still appear relevant today. For the purposes of partnership evaluation, however, three additional dimensions are suggested to be crucial: formality, representative level and timeliness.

Degree refers to amount of influence over decision-making. This can be mapped on a continuum with total employee/union control at one end versus managerial prerogative at the other.

In all three cases it was made clear that partnership did not mean joint decision-making, but concerned early consultation and an opportunity for union representatives and officials to comment on proposals, and feed back member views. This view was shared by management, officials and representatives in each case organisation. At NatBank partnership predominantly involved quite extensive consultation and communication. At BuSoc consultation and communication did occur, but this took place primarily between a few senior management and union figures. The WebBank case would generally be placed

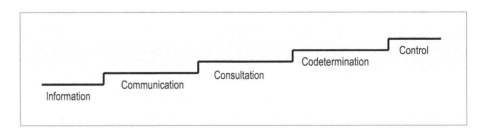

Figure 7.1   Escalator of participation (Marchington and Wilkinson, 2005)

lower down the escalator as the partnership in this organisation predominantly focused upon communication and information, with some increasing evidence of consultation, but normally when this was likely to be of explicit benefit to the business, for example, seeking ideas from the employee representatives.

Scope refers to the range of issues under discussion. In terms of scope of issues three main categories arose as integral parts of the partnership process: pay and terms and conditions, discipline and grievance, and organisational change. At NatBank the scope of discussions spans all three categories. At BuSoc the scope is more focused upon pay and conditions, and discipline and grievance. Major organisational change issues may also be discussed at high level, however there was evidence to suggest less involvement in lower level change issues of concern to grassroots employees. Conversely, at WebBank the scope of issues often concerned day-to-day issues with an immediate and direct impact on employees. Again, discipline and grievance was also a key concern. Involvement was most limited in relation to issues of pay and conditions, as employee representatives were not party to any kind of pay negotiation process.

Form of decision-making refers to the traditional distinction between direct and indirect participation. The focus of workplace partnership is typically on systems of indirect representation. Representative participation appeared to be most embedded at the NatBank centre, where employees appeared to actively engage with the union representatives, and awareness of – and confidence in – the union representatives appeared to be high. Though at BuSoc and WebBank partnership was also viewed primarily in terms of representative structures and relationships, on a day-to-day basis employees at BuSoc and WebBank were more familiar with direct mechanisms such as conversations with line managers and the company intranet than with representative channels. At BuSoc many employees suspected there could be negative repercussions of being seen to go to the union, while at WebBank most employees believed they would normally be most comfortable discussing issues with their line manager.

Formality refers to the balance between formal mechanisms of decision-making such as committees and meetings, and informal mechanisms such as ad hoc telephone calls, lunch meetings and spontaneous chats between the actors. At BuSoc a great deal of emphasis was on informal 'corridor conversations' between senior figures rather than formal structures or devolved local involvement, meaning the process was much more opaque than in the other two cases. At NatBank there was a much greater emphasis on formal structures, especially in relation to high level issues. However, representatives did stress that there was a sufficient relationship to solve many issues more informally locally, without escalating them to union officials. Informality also appeared to characterise interactions at WebBank with most actors again suggesting that often issues would be resolved through a telephone call or ad hoc meeting as opposed to arranging a formal meeting. There was, however, a system of formal meetings as well but the emphasis was on informality.

Representative level refers to the balance of involvement between local/part-time workplace representatives and full-time representatives. At BuSoc it appeared that most of the decision-making occurred at a high level between senior HR figures and heads of business areas and the Union General Secretary. Workplace representatives had a narrow role, and limited knowledge of wider business issues. Typical duties included maintaining the union notice board and attending quarterly area meetings. At both NatBank and WebBank there was a greater emphasis on local discussions between employee representatives and members/employees. As mentioned earlier, having active local representatives was an explicit aim of the union at NatBank, and at WebBank – as an in-house forum – there is no union hierarchy to contend with, so by definition the activities occurred at a local level.

Timeliness refers to the stage at which interaction would normally take place regarding decision-making. NatBank representatives suggested that under partnership they are informed at an early stage regarding most major projects and developments within the centre and the bank, normally before any decisions have been made. There was evidence to suggest that at BuSoc plans were typically shared at a later stage, and certainly local representatives would be involved at the implementation stage. It was difficult to ascertain exactly when the union would be informed, as typically this would be shared only between union officials and senior management, and therefore it was not so transparent. At WebBank the timing of involvement was said to be patchy but improving, depending on the departments and figures involved in the project, and their receptiveness to and enthusiasm for forum involvement. The findings regarding the decision-making process are summarised in Table 7.2.

Table 7.2   The decision-making process

	NatBank	BuSoc	WebBank	'Ideal' Partnership
Degree	High	Unclear	Low	High
Scope	Wide	Limited	Moderate	Wide

Table 7.2   *Concluded*

Form	Rep + direct	Rep + direct	Rep + direct	Rep + direct
Formality	High	Low	Low	Moderate
Representative level	Decentralised	Highly centralised	Decentralised	Decentralised
Time	Early	Unclear	Moderate/Late	Early

Achieving Efficiency, Equity and Voice?

The next section employs Budd's efficiency, equity and voice framework to interpret the data obtained from each case, in terms of the extent to which partnership appears to facilitate the moderation of various countervailing efficiency, equity and voice pressures.

NATBANK: UNION PARTNERSHIP AS A 'SOLUTION'

As NatBank is a large city institution, senior management made clear that efficiency was the primary objective, and that ultimately the business is owned by shareholders expecting a return on their investment. Indeed, during the 1990s industrial relations unrest was compounded by a loss of City confidence in the organisation and intense global competition. However, since the partnership was agreed in 2000, there was evidence to suggest that the business efficiency objectives are, to some extent, being regulated by the partnership mechanism. For example, like many organisations in the late 1990s, the bank began outsourcing to India to save costs and increase efficiency. However, it was suggested that with the partnership arrangement the offshoring process was more equitable than it could have been. Since partnership, an agreed union-management consultative framework has been devised. Known as a 'globalisation agreement', the document explicitly outlines both employer and union commitments regarding a fair and transparent process for the management of offshoring. The union described it as representing a number of 'hoops the organisation has to jump through'. Specific commitments include policies regarding the avoidance of compulsory redundancy where possible, generous voluntary redundancy packages, redeployment and retraining opportunities, career support and extensive notice periods. The union National Officer suggested that, although the agreement does not stop efficiency-driven offshoring policies, it does ensure that NatBank engages in early union consultation, and prevents management from making only minimal or cursory attempts to consult staff (voice), by committing them to a process which far exceeds statutory minimum requirements (equity). This contrasts with the period prior to partnership, where a previous restructuring exercise was said by representatives to have been 'presented as a fait accompli completely out of the blue', with employees reporting 'a major hoo-ha' with 'everyone extremely worried'.

NatBank management also proposed that all call centre staff should be encouraged to sell on calls, taking the efficiency view that call centres should be proactively generating new leads and additional revenue, rather than reactively servicing the customer. Prior to the relocation of several back office functions to India, many long-serving staff had little experience of customer-facing telephone work. The additional pressure associated with a blanket policy for employees to try and sell on all calls (efficiency) proved to be too stressful for many, and ultimately resulted in high employee turnover. Following protracted discussions with the union (voice), management agreed to re-introduce a customer service-only role, even though this countered their initial aim to maximise efficiency by having all call agents trying to sell on every single call. The Employee Relations Manager suggested that the corporate-level sales strategy represented a 'pure technical model' which neglected the realities and dynamics of the call centre.

Equally, union representatives cited this as an example of successful joint working, especially for experienced employees who found the pressure to sell was simply too much, but were excellent customer service advisers. This illustrates how a management policy to improve efficiency was perceived to be deeply inequitable, and this in turn had a negative impact on efficiency as attrition rapidly increased, suggesting a business case for equity also exists.

The efficiency and equity tensions are also evident from a business idea to harmonise contracts from traditional 9–5 to a staggered 8am–midnight pattern. Again, since the offshoring of most non-customer-facing roles, the administration centre was now primarily a call centre, and customers expected to be able to contact the bank at any time of the day or night. However, many long-serving staff members only worked normal office hours, resulting in shortages of evening staff, which management viewed as inefficient. Acutely concerned regarding the possibility of long-serving staff being compelled to sign new flexible contracts, the union successfully persuaded the bank through extensive dialogue (voice), to leave long-serving staff on the old working hours should they so wish, by highlighting the potential damage to morale and the associated industrial relations upheaval if this controversial change was simply imposed (equity). Management acknowledged that the negative impact of employee perceptions of inequity might negate or even outweigh the proposed administrative efficiencies of contract harmonisation. This required management and the union to return to the main issue: how they could they staff telephones in the evening to meet customer demand? It was decided that a compromise was to recruit a pool of new staff working flexible hours set to match business demand. This was not the ideal situation for the business, which would prefer all employees to work on a flexible pattern (efficiency), and neither was it the ideal situation for the union, which would have preferred to avoid what it believed was the creation of a 'two-tier' system (equity). Nevertheless, the union took the pragmatic view that their primary responsibility is to defend the interests of existing fee-paying members.

Within NatBank, voice was a prominent issue. In a workplace which had experienced significant organisational change, the local union representatives were active and enthusiastic, employees knew who their union representatives were, and support for the union was strong. There was evidence, therefore, that at NatBank the voice afforded through the partnership mechanism was moderating decision-making and mitigating the worst effects of organisational change on employees (equity). In several cases, the union was able to promote equity as a countervailing pressure against pure business decisions based on a narrow financial 'efficiency' logic. There was also evidence of a business case for equity, given that decisions which were perceived to be inequitable, were often recognised by management to be ultimately counterproductive due to the negative impact on morale, and the increase in attrition. Positive assessments of the better dialogue partnership afforded was evident among managers, union representatives and employees alike.

BUSOC: UNION PARTNERSHIP AS AN 'EVOLUTION'

The triad can also be used to evaluate partnership at BuSoc. Though there is no *formal* union–management partnership agreement in this case, a history of co-operative employment relations, and joint commitments to business success, employment security, union legitimacy, and information and consultation, appeared indicative of a prima facie case of partnership. Management and union respondents also agreed the notion of partnership best described the style of management–union relations, although the term 'partnership' was not officially used. As a mutual building society owned by members, BuSoc does not have the same commercial pressures to satisfy the Stock Exchange. BuSoc has used its historical image as an ethically guided mutual institution to its advantage both in terms of consumer marketing, as well as in its espoused approach to employment relations. Accordingly, compulsory redundancies at BuSoc are almost unknown, the business has committed not to offshore any functions abroad, and is well known in the sector for various pioneering schemes concerning work-life balance, domestic violence, homeworking and equal opportunities. Both the HR Director and Union President were keen to stress that most of their employment policies significantly exceed the UK statutory minimum arrangements (equity).

Yet some managers suggested that the general culture of organisation was 'perhaps too risk-averse', at the expense of efficiency. In employment relations terms, an example would be that the business would almost always settle tribunal claims out of court even if they believed they had a strong case, to avoid any potential damage to the 'ethical' brand image. Similarly, it was suggested that the business seldom dismissed notoriously underperforming members of staff, and this related to what was described as a very 'welfarist' and 'benevolent' culture. This led to the perception by some managers that too much focus on 'equity' may actually be inefficient for the organisation.

Though it was suggested that major conflicts between the union and management were relatively rare, the last major dispute concerned the end of the final salary pension scheme for new employees despite vehement union opposition. In this case, the efficiency aim was clearly greater than the equity concerns. Union officials opined that despite their opposition there was little they could do as the decision was 'not unlawful', and was simply presented to them as a fait accompli (minimal voice). This occurred under the leadership of the previous Chief Executive who the Union General Secretary suggested was 'strongly efficiency focused'; in contrast, he suggested that the current Chief Executive appeared to be more interested in 'his people as well profits'. In this case, the attitudes of the personalities involved appeared to be central to the process, although the suggestion that major decisions such as pension arrangements can depend on the whim of the Chief Executive and the relationship he has with union officials, appears incompatible with the notion of a strong partnership.

Some examples were cited where the union and management *had* worked together but this was mostly on a minority of relatively uncontroversial issues. For example, they jointly devised a new performance management framework which they thought was fairer for employees (equity) but clearly was driven by a desire to improve employee performance and improve business performance (efficiency). Moreover, the union was proud of its track record in negotiating pay deals which it believed were often the envy of many in the industry. Union officials stated that, on balance, BuSoc is a 'good employer', at least compared to competitors in the same sector, and this makes it difficult to assess the extent to which the union is actually making a difference, versus the extent to which it is a result of employer paternalism. On the other hand, managers suggested that the staff union was an effective medium and that since most officials are former employees, it can take a more 'balanced view' of situations.

In general terms, the equity drivers as a whole were more prominent at BuSoc than in the other case organisations, and this might have meant there was less need for the union to adopt a proactive stance than at NatBank. Moreover, within this context the grassroots interest in voice was lower. Employees were apathetic and this appeared to stem from satisfaction as opposed to disillusionment. Staff attitude surveys are normally very positive, and focus group discussions confirmed that most employees viewed BuSoc as a very good employer overall. Where dissatisfaction did occur, this was attributed to problems of implementation of local decision-making and errant line managers, rather than dissatisfaction with corporate policy itself. Union representatives were often inactive, and many had been nominated by default. Most of the negotiation and consultation occurred at a very senior level between executives and one or two senior union officials. Perhaps this is partly the case because senior union officials are the few people not employed by the society, and therefore have less fear of retribution. It is possibly more difficult for seconded officials who are due to return to work after their time on union position to voice their true concerns. Employees suggested that they would probably take more interest in employment relations matters had there been more controversial incidents, as in other organisations. Union officials also speculated that while the Executive Board are committed to mutuality for the foreseeable future, they wondered what impact demutualisation would have, and how the employment relations climate might change, as the need to deliver results to the Stock Exchange could have a negative impact on the employment relations culture.

In sum, while the equity pressure appeared to be much stronger than at NatBank, there was little evidence to confirm that this was because of a partnership relationship between the union and management, and highlights the significant possibility that BuSoc might still be a 'good' paternalistic employer irrespective of the union. For example, there was still evidence to suggest that when external forces resulted in an efficiency 'crisis', such as the problems funding the final salary pension scheme, the efficiency force would prevail over equity, with minimum voice afforded to employees or the union.

WEBBANK: NON-UNION PARTNERSHIP AS AN 'ALTERNATIVE'

WebBank was set up in the 1990s with the aim of being 'different' and 'radical' in the conservative UK banking market, offering competitive products aimed at young, educated and affluent consumers. The company does not recognise a trade union, and in this context partnership concerns an in-house representative body, affiliated to the Involvement and Participation Association, known as the WebBank Employee Forum. Management suggested that since the company was listed on the Stock Exchange two years after launch, the pressure to deliver to shareholders has had a significant impact on day-to-day operations (efficiency). Despite a high degree of UK success, WebBank was a loss-making business due to a combination of high start-up costs and the failure of an overseas expansion project, breaking into profit for the first time in 2005. In terms of voice, WebBank decided to set up an internal employee forum in preference to recognising an external trade union. It was suggested that management perceived unions to be '*too adversarial*' and '*at odds with the culture of a new organisation*'. Only five years old, the non-union forum is still evolving but appears to be run very much on terms set by management, and representatives and management were both clear about the fact that it is not a negotiating body. Most of the representatives did not seem to have a problem with this role, although one did express some doubts regarding the ability of the forum to challenge in the face of severe adversity.

However, the existence or role of the Employee Forum was not a priority for most employees, and many had limited knowledge or interest in the forum. At most, it was considered to be a 'counselling service', offering advice in the event of discipline and grievance cases. However, as was the case with NatBank, there was *some* evidence of the forum providing a useful voice channel, and acting to a degree as an efficiency-equity arbiter. For example, the forum had challenged the selection procedures being used to decide new posts following an IT restructure, which they believed were arbitrary and political. It was believed that the final selection process was much fairer as a result (equity). Moreover, there was a feeling that managers can devise pure process models in their search for efficiency, and that this is where it was believed the dialogue added value (voice and equity). The forum is also active in ensuring that disciplinary and grievance procedures are followed in a fair way and that due process is followed (equity).

A team manager recounted an incident involving a top performing employee who suddenly developed a poor attendance record. It was believed that after several warnings, an efficiency oriented decision would need to be made to dismiss the employee. The team manager admitted that he was slightly bewildered and disappointed by this, as the employee concerned was a consistently high performing member of staff, and therefore decided to ask a WebBank employee representative to help. It transpired that the employee had a poor relationship with her line manager, and believed that she had been the victim of bullying. After investigation, the team manager transferred the employee to another team, and the employee's attendance record improved significantly. The team manager believed that had there been no opportunity for forum intervention a high performing employee would probably have been dismissed, as without the voice process the root of the problem might never have been identified. In other words, management might have dismissed the employee following several warnings, on the grounds that it was the most efficient decision. However, it was believed it was better to invest some time in order to ascertain the underlying cause and to try and resolve the situation. This resulted in a decision which was both efficient for the organisation as a high performing employee was retained, but also more equitable for the worker, as she was able to air her grievance and did not lose her job as a result of a relationship breakdown. Indeed, the ostensibly efficient decision may actually have been inefficient, given that an experienced and popular employee might have been dismissed. Prior to the establishment of the forum, the culture was said to be much more 'hire and fire', but it was believed the current dialogue (voice) facilitated better efficiency and equity outcomes.

Overall though, WebBank management appeared much more interested in promoting efficiency rather than equity, and it was very much involvement on terms strictly defined and controlled by management. Even where decisions were ostensibly made in relation to equity, this was often underpinned by sound business rationale, although again this reinforces the notion that the two concepts are not mutually exclusive. As an employee representative explained, they are expected to bring solutions to the table, not to merely highlight problems. Nevertheless, managerial respondents still acknowledged the value to the business of the structure (efficiency and voice), and representatives were also generally positive about the relationship they had with managers and the effectiveness of the process.

By employing the analytical framework proposed by Budd, there was evidence to suggest that as a result of the voice and dialogue afforded through partnership, union/employee representatives were often able to moderate decisions to mitigate the worst effects for employees at NatBank and WebBank.

The research revealed that *moderation* and *mitigation* appeared to be an important characteristic of decision-making under partnership.

The framework can also be used to illustrate the dynamics of discipline and grievance at WebBank. High turnover and discipline cases were highlighted by senior managers at WebBank to be a significant problem, especially in the call centre environment. A key area of involvement for the Employee Forum was acting as an intermediary in disputes between employees and line managers, and it was believed that the forum representative provided a useful additional perspective when disputes and grievances occurred. The same regulatory effect could not be readily identified in the case of BuSoc. It was suggested that in the previous five years employment relations had generally been good, with few major controversies. The main recent incident was identified as the closing of the final salary pension scheme to new entrants. This has become a significant issue among mutual organisations, as spiralling pensions costs are seen to be eating into their ability to compete with their banking rivals. Increasing subsidies for the funds is controversial as often the main beneficiaries are executives. In 2001, the society took the decision to close the fund to new employees. A more drastic but efficient decision might have been to close the scheme to all staff. A more equitable but less efficient approach might have been for the employer to increase its contributions and lump sum payments to help maintain the fund. Yet there was little evidence of the decision being regulated by the union. Indeed the decision was said to have been imposed without consultation. So while the decision may have been to end the final salary scheme to new members only, and not perhaps the more drastic closure of the scheme which was the course of action taken by other building societies at a similar time, there was little evidence of this being a result of union involvement. At BuSoc the union has since agreed to increases in employee contributions in return for lump sum payments by the employer, but the future of the pension fund remains uncertain and is still a significant concern for the union.

To summarise, employee voice was most embedded at NatBank, and there was clear evidence demonstrating partnership acting as a countervailing pressure on efficiency-driven decisions, especially where a business case for equity could be argued by the union. At BuSoc, the equity dimension appeared to have greater prominence with the management team than in the other organisations. BuSoc was keen to demonstrate – at least in public relations terms – that it was not a ruthless City organisation, but this did not appear to be a direct result of trade union pressure. While care has to be taken when interpreting such management assertions, triangulation with responses from union representatives and employees, did seem to confirm that this was part of the paternalistic BuSoc ethos, at least in recent years. In turn, grassroots employees had less interest in voice, although a degree of voice was being provided through the interactions of union officials and senior managers. It may have been expected that the mutual organisation would have provided a fertile environment for partnership. Counter-intuitively, it appears that in this context of a fairly stagnant employment relations environment, there is actually less incentive to pursue positive partnership working, and that the relationship is in reality best described as 'traditional', with the union role limited in scope to issues around terms and conditions, and an opaque, secretive negotiation and consultation framework. Conversely, in the cases where efficiency has been under much more pressure, there appears to have been a greater impetus to engage with a more strategic approach to HRM and employment relations. At WebBank, voice was being provided to some extent through the employee forum mechanism, and there was evidence of the forum acting as a moderate countervailing pressure. Although the countervailing pressures remained fairly modest, this may be a result of the fact that the forum remains fairly new and is still evolving. The remit of the forum is also increasingly widening.

Actor Experiences and Partnership Outcomes

MANAGEMENT

Senior management respondents at all organisations were overall supportive of the principles of partnership, suggesting that partnership represents a more modern approach to the conduct of employment relations, and a departure from counterproductive adversarial relationships. This is not to say they were evangelical about partnership. On the contrary, the general view was a *pragmatic* one, in that partnership was seen to offer a more effective approach than adversarialism in terms of the regulation of the employment relationship. It appeared that management actors held an instrumental view, in that they are positive about partnership where the trade union/representative body is seen to be contributing to business success, but conversely demonstrate a very low tolerance of unions where this is not perceived to be the case.

UNIONS AND UNION/EMPLOYEE REPRESENTATIVES

Employee representatives and union officials at all organisations were also supportive of the principles of partnership. Interestingly, while officials at BuSoc were generally supportive of a co-operative approach, they were reluctant to engage with the language of partnership because of potential employee perceptions regarding the relationship. Indeed, in 1997 the union at BuSoc had actually changed its name to 'Staff Union' as opposed to 'Staff Association' in order to highlight its independence from the management. It is therefore interesting that the union with a more adversarial background chose to engage with partnership in order to free itself from a militant image and increase its legitimacy; whereas the union with a more co-operative history chose to avoid the language of partnership with the aim of reinforcing its independence from the employer. Seconded representatives at WebBank were also supportive of the partnership approach and were critical of adversarial union strategies. Many had experienced trade unions in their previous employment, and frequently recounted negative anecdotes regarding counterproductive union engagement.

EMPLOYEES

Most employees in the three cases were supportive of collaborative union–management relations. Many critically recalled incidents of union militancy such as the miners' strike, and expressed a disdain for such tactics. It was interesting that in all cases employees reflected upon the demands of the customer, and the perceptions of customers if the workers were to go on strike leaving branches closed and phone calls unanswered. Employee focus groups in all organisations revealed very little support for union militancy, acknowledging that organisations need to be competitive and that sometimes this may mean tough decisions. Across the cases for example, employees highlighted how they believed that unions can no longer always 'save jobs', but stressed that the role of unions now was to ensure that business decisions are as fair as they can be for employees.

In sum, across the cases actor attitudes to partnership were generally positive. The interesting finding across all actors in the case organisations was the level of *pragmatism and realism*. Although the actors supported the partnership principles they did not engage with uncritical utopian ideas. Employees and representatives were aware of business issues such as global competition, and the need to satisfy customers and shareholders. Most senior managers also acknowledged and accepted that unions have a job to do, and that they need to be seen to be upholding members' interests. Few expressed hostility to unions, rather ambivalence or support was the norm, especially where unions were perceived to be contributing to business success. It was at a middle management level where tensions typically arose. Middle managers may find themselves at the centre of the countervailing forces outlined, whereby they are expected to deliver business results on the one hand, but to be considerate and fair to employees on the other.

Challenges

Four main challenges to partnership were identified in the study. These include a lack of agreement as to the meaning of partnership, relationship centrality, resistance to adversity and representative efficacy. These will now be discussed in turn.

SHARED UNDERSTANDING: WHAT EXACTLY IS MEANT BY 'PARTNERSHIP'?

The first challenge is a coherence of purpose. This concerns a clear understanding of the meaning, purpose and operation of partnership between the union, representatives and management. At NatBank this was argued to be where the situation sometimes became 'blurry'. For the actors in all three cases, partnership was not necessarily about the union and management agreeing. Representatives also acknowledged that partnership did not mean joint decision-making or co-determination. The unions/forums had to persuade and convince management rather than just oppose, representing a shift to an integrative problem-solving approach. The key method was by justifying how an efficiency-based decision or proposal could actually backfire because of the potential damage if it is perceived to be inequitable, for example, resulting in high turnover, low morale and low employee satisfaction. In other words, representatives had to convince management of a business case for more equitable decisions. The representative mechanism appeared therefore to act as a useful checkpoint on management decision-making. The expectations of partnership in the critical literature are therefore set very high and perhaps at odds with reality. This study has argued that partnership can usefully be thought of as a combination of practices, processes and outcomes, and that focusing on one element is unlikely to be tenable.

RELATIONSHIP CENTRALITY: EMBEDDING A PARTNERSHIP CULTURE

Assuming a coherent shared understanding and purpose between the key actors, the next challenge is embedding this culture across the entire organisation and getting the buy-in of two other important actors: middle managers and employees. As highlighted earlier, partnership concerns a key relationship between representatives/officials and senior managers, but this creates the risk that middle managers and employees may end up disillusioned. For example, at BuSoc and WebBank it was discovered that while representatives have a good relationship with the HR department, relationships with other departments were more patchy. This was a particular risk at BuSoc, given that the main interactions occurred at an elite level.

Middle management resistance was identified as a significant barrier to the effectiveness of partnership. Managers at WebBank and BuSoc suggested that the union/employee forum was sometimes viewed as a barrier to them carrying out their job, for example, by making it difficult for them to dismiss a poorly performing member of staff. Middle management were often said to be under significant pressure resulting in them 'taking shortcuts' which sometimes did not correspond with best practice guidelines agreed at a senior level. At BuSoc the Employee Relations Manager felt some managers still viewed the union as an inconvenience or obstruction. On the other hand, some representatives still appeared to fear recrimination at BuSoc, whereas at NatBank representatives stated that they had the confidence to manoeuvre around an obstructive or unhelpful manager. Indeed, full-time officials at NatBank and BuSoc described a similar strategy. Another aspect was employee apathy towards unions and a general lack of interest, especially when things are perceived to be running smoothly. This seemed to be the case at all case organisations but especially at BuSoc, where there has been difficulty recruiting members and representatives. There was also a lack of interest in the Employee Forum at WebBank. It could be speculated that employees are less interested when they perceive stability at work, but become more interested when instability sets in, as was the case at NatBank. In other words, partnership may actually be strengthened by a period of bad weather. Clearly, establishing an embedded partnership culture across the organisation and the various actors is essential if the key management–representative relationship is to be robust, and this is likely to require the buy-in of both line managers and employees.

RESISTANCE TO ADVERSITY

This relates to the sustainability of the structure over time, following major incidents within the organisation, and the extent to which the robustness of the partnership has been tested. This could be a change of key personalities, a major incident, for example, merger, demutualisation, offshoring, or even a change in government. For example, at BuSoc there was clear concern that so much involved a few key players, and thus there was limited ownership of the partnership process, which was not widely embedded. Indeed, most union activity in this case occurred at a very senior level between top union officials and divisional directors. It was therefore unclear what would happen if the key players left the organisation. Overall, the climate has been smooth in recent years and the resistance to adversity has not been tested. It is therefore difficult to fully evaluate the union–management relationship after a period of relative stability.

The same is true at WebBank, where concerns exist regarding key representative and management figures leaving the organisation. Employee representatives also admitted that as yet the structure remains 'untested' given that there has not yet been a major incident. At NatBank, too, this could concern a change in key figures or a major offshoring exercise.

Partnership is not a static phenomenon, but rather an evolving process which changes over time. As such, partnership is likely to experience turbulence, and the key issue is how the process copes with changes, such as a change in actors or external organisational pressures, which will determine the acceptability and durability of partnership working. Just as structural engineers design tall buildings to sway in extreme weather conditions, the partnership process must also be able to flex in order to endure external pressures, and to avoid failure and ultimately total collapse.

REPRESENTATIVE EFFICACY

Representative efficacy concerns the effectiveness of representatives in the eyes of both management and employees/union members. Some managers at NatBank and WebBank raised concerns regarding representatives who they viewed to be '*anti-establishment*' or '*have a chip on their shoulder*'. It was clear that management valued arguments based on business rationale rather than '*as a matter of principle*'. This requires very different skills, which not all the representatives possessed. Management were more interested in hard business reasons for not implementing changes, such as a likely negative impact on efficiency, and were less interested in equity arguments based on a sense of '*fairness*' or '*doing the right thing*'.

It was argued by management that oppositional representatives could destabilise the process by creating conflict, but on the other hand complacent representatives could also destabilise the process because they could lack credibility in the eyes of their members. A delicate balance has to be struck in order to win and sustain the respect and credibility in the eyes of both management and employees. In the eyes of their members, representative views may not match membership views because of additional insight they have through embargoed information, and this could create tensions which undermine the legitimacy of the process. Representatives may experience isolation from grassroots members because they have extra information and see the bigger picture, thus encountering the danger of being seen to be co-opted especially when decisions are not good. Representative awareness of financial and market information could be interpreted as brainwashing. There is also the inability of representatives to demonstrate their value when much of the interactions are occurring behind closed doors, and representatives could easily be perceived to be doing nothing if things are going smoothly and blamed when things go badly. Representatives have the dilemma of proving independence and strength in a context of confidentiality, and there is the risk that this could create a chasm for the union. Sophisticated manoeuvring and 'corridor conversations' are not seen at the grassroots level whereas adversarial confrontation is much more visible. Representatives at both WebBank and NatBank were conscious of the need to ensure that employees do not perceive them to be 'in management's pocket', suggesting a need to demonstrate value to members, and management need to understand this. This is not to say that employees are keen to know the detail of decisions, but rather that they need to have trust in the union and/or their representatives.

Conclusion

This chapter has compared and contrasted the findings in terms of context, meaning, process and outcomes of partnership in the three cases. It reveals how the routes to partnership varied, and highlights the heterogeneity of partnership arrangements that exist. The organisations also differed in terms of corporate governance as well as their IR histories, recognition of trade unions, and partnership structures. This would suggest that neglecting contextual differences could lead to a very short-sighted view of partnership.

On reviewing the meaning of partnership, however, both in terms of official policy statements as well as the understandings and interpretations of organisational actors, there is a greater degree of common ground, suggesting that the three cases qualified as prima facie cases of partnership, and many of their policy commitments resonated with TUC and IPA definitions of partnership. Actor interpretations of partnership were also similar, with core concepts agreed to include a modern approach to employment relations characterised by problem-solving, early consultation and dialogue, and a dual commitment to both organisational success and the fair treatment of employees. Importantly, in no case was partnership seen to concern a process of joint decision-making between management and union/employee representatives.

The process of partnership varied between the organisations in terms of the degree of involvement, scope of issues discussed, and decision-making structures. In terms of the outcomes of decision-making processes, NatBank demonstrated clear evidence of voice being articulated and of efficiency and equity being moderated by the voice process. There was also some evidence of this in the case of WebBank. Less evidence of this process was available in the case of BuSoc, as it was more difficult to establish the extent to which business decisions had been moderated through consultation and negotiation (voice). Nevertheless, most management actors in each company were in favour of the principles of partnership, suggesting that it represented a modern approach to employment relationships, and that adversarialism was no longer appropriate. Most union officials and all union/employee representatives also supported partnership. Employee interviews are also important, as sometimes these are conflated with union views in industrial relations research. Virtually all employee interviews supported collaborative management–union relations and the ethos of partnership, and many were highly critical of militant tactics

Finally, several challenges were identified. The first was an agreement regarding what is actually meant by partnership, and the extent to which there was a shared view of what working in partnership did and did not mean in order to avoid false expectations. The second challenge was embedding a partnership culture across the organisation, and overcoming middle management resistance and employee apathy. In all cases there was the question of the sustainability of the structure over time, and the extent to which it could resist a period of severe adversity. Ensuring the representative body and representatives are perceived to be effective by employees and managers was another challenge. Clearly, representatives are expected to walk a tightrope whereby managers view them as credible and constructive, while their members view them as challenging and influential. If the balanced is tipped too much in one direction, support of management or employees may be lost and this could undermine the process. A major problem for representatives is demonstrating the effectiveness, in terms of influence, of a low key relationship, whereas with an adversarial strategy it is arguably much easier to demonstrate contribution to members because of the higher level of visibility.

The final chapter reviews these findings in light of the existing partnership literature, and draws out some of the main conclusions of the study. It then considers the implications of the study for practice.

8

Partnership Prospects

Introduction

The purpose of this chapter is to present the conclusions of the study and how they relate to the wider partnership literature. This study has sought to counter some of the limitations of the existing literature identified in Chapter 2. In an attempt to transcend the polarised debate and address the limitations of the current literature, the study is valuable in many respects. Firstly, the study focused on one sector with similar product and labour market conditions, allowing comparisons to be made between organisations operating within similar constraints. Moreover, the finance sector is an interesting as well as numerically important part of the UK and global economy. At the time of the research, in 2005/6, the sector was also highly profitable: in 2006, the British banks reported earnings of £33 billion and London-based HSBC alone reported profits of £11.9 billion. The sector also employs over 1 million people (Stuart and Martinez-Lucio, 2008), and generates a turnover equal to 14 per cent of GDP. The industry has a long history of non-union employee representation as well as trade unionism; indeed union density has remained high, at around 50 per cent in the 1990s (Gall, 2001). Moreover, despite a general image of being conservative and paternalistic (Upchurch et al., 2006), and even as 'docile' and 'strike-free' (Gall, 2001), 2005 witnessed ballots for strike action at Lloyds TSB and HSBC. In addition, the finance sector has experienced significant change and restructuring, with recent large-scale job losses at Abbey, Lloyds TSB, Clydesdale and Yorkshire Bank (EIRO Online). The 2008 financial crisis also means that considerable challenges remain across the entire financial services sector.

This study has presented comparative case studies, which are relatively scarce in the British literature, but have proved useful in the US (Kelly, 2004). This allowed a variety of circumstances to be examined which varied in terms of route to partnership, history, IR background and corporate governance. This is important given that partnership remains a nebulous and contested concept, and the acknowledgement in the recent literature that there may be different trajectories of experience (Martinez-Lucio and Stuart, 2004; Oxenbridge and Brown, 2004a, 2004b). The study has also explored a non-union example of partnership, which is again rare in the literature. It has also examined the process of partnership, and unravelled what partnership actually means in terms of the regulation of employment relations. This is useful given that most of the existing literature has tended to focus more narrowly on outcomes, and in particular, the opportunities partnership offers for trade union renewal (Terry, 2003b).

Accordingly, in order to understand more about the form and content of management–union/non-union representative relations – or what Roche and Geary (2002) refer to as the organisational micro-politics – the study explored in detail what partnership means in terms of decision-making as well as relationships between the key actors. Moreover, the study has advocated a pluralist approach, suggesting that an inherent conflict of interest does not mean that all workplace issues involve conflict (Marxism), but neither can all workplace issues be structured as a shared interest (Unitarism). Rather, in the employment relationship conflict is best regarded as 'mixed motive', with both conflictual *and* shared interests (Kochan, 2000). Employees want their employer to be successful, but employee interests of higher wages, employment security and excellent working conditions may clash with employer objectives of improving efficiency and minimising costs. The objective is achieving a stable 'negotiated order' from the expression of competing interests by 'institutionalising conflict' and by establishing an effective process of bargaining and consultation between actors (Batstone, 1984; Blyton and Turnbull, 2004). In contrast to the 1970s pluralism, however, which was dominated by trade unions, collective bargaining and joint regulation, new pluralism is characterised by a mix of union and non-union representative bodies, formal and informal structures, and a range of consultation, bargaining and negotiation. The structures and processes may have changed, but the aims of facilitating voice and institutionalising conflict remain the same.

As Stuart and Martinez-Lucio (2004b: 423) argue, employers and workers encounter simultaneously the pressures of economic efficiency and social justice. The key concerns are the 'the systems of regulation that attempt to address these issues of economic and social distribution', through, for example, statutory government regulation and collective employee representation. For pluralists, because of the inherent conflict of interest it is unwise to rely upon managerial goodwill, and equally it is not enough to rely on economic markets as proposed by neoclassical economists. This view can be contrasted with the Marxist view that a deeper class conflict exists, and that pluralist concerns for regulation are superficial. To aid analysis, the study draws on a framework proposed by Budd (2004). It is proposed that there is a need for a different way of evaluating partnership outcomes based upon the extent to which they contribute to the moderation/accommodation of the competing employment relations objectives of efficiency, equity and voice. In this way, the study avoids the use of crude employment relations outcomes – such as pay levels or job losses – as simple 'indicators' of the success or otherwise of partnership working. In order to understand issues of context, meaning and process a case study approach was deemed essential. Having summarised the rationale for the research, the following section outlines the main findings of this study in terms of the context, process and outcomes of partnership.

Context of Partnership

The first issue concerns the context of partnership. The three cases presented allowed comparisons to be made across four main dimensions: route to partnership; governance; unionisation; and formality. The key findings will now be outlined in turn.

DOES THE ROUTE TO PARTNERSHIP MATTER?

Often, partnership agreements have arisen out of industrial relations crisis (Oxenbridge and Brown, 2002, 2004a), and this may limit the scope for mutual gains (Kelly, 2004). On the other hand, where partnership has not arisen as a direct response to conflict but has evolved in more positive circumstances, there may be a greater scope for mutual gains. Specifically, in the case of WebBank – a greenfield site with a very short industrial relations history – it could be speculated that, given that there was no industrial relations baggage or embedded cultures which needed to be changed, (Hallier and Leopold, 2000), forging partnership would be easier than in an organisation with a long history. In particular, employees with limited experience of participation may welcome any attempt to increase involvement (Marchington and Wilkinson, 2005). Certainly there was evidence to suggest that to an extent this was the case, in that there were fewer expectations which needed to be changed, unlike the case at NatBank, where there was some resistance from union officials despite an official pro-partnership union stance. However, despite the long IR history at NatBank and BuSoc, most actors endorsed a partnership approach. Indeed, at BuSoc the long history of co-operative employment relations appeared to offer a fertile environment for partnership. Overall, it seems that history is not an insurmountable barrier to partnership. It is also difficult to predict how the relatively young structures at WebBank will evolve, especially as the representatives gain confidence and experience, and as the expectations of partnership actors change over time.

CAN PARTNERSHIP BE ACHIEVED IN LIBERAL MARKET ECONOMIES?

Critics suggests that it is difficult to forge a sustainable partnership in a liberal market economy due to the framework of corporate governance which puts a premium on short-term performance, quick decision-making and shareholder value, over the potential interests of other stakeholders (Sisson, 2005; Heery, 2002, Hutton, 1995). As Konzellman et al. state:

> In liberal market-based systems such as the US and the UK ... managers
> are required to pursue shareholder interests above those of labour, which
> often forces them to break implicit (psychological) contracts with labour
> in the interest of short-term shareholder value (Konzellman et al., 2006:
> 5).

In other words, organisations which have a dominant external shareholder, such as PLCs, may be constrained in their ability to commit to initiatives such as partnership (Konzellman et al., 2006). Theoretically then, BuSoc would provide a more hospitable environment for partnership than NatBank and WebBank, given that it is insulated from the fluctuations and pressures associated with stock market pressure and membership due to its mutual status. To an extent this may be true: BuSoc union officials and employees generally viewed the firm as a 'good employer', especially compared to other companies in the sector. On the other hand, this is not to say that BuSoc did not make controversial decisions without union support, such as the end of the final salary pension scheme for new employees in 2002. On the whole, however, most actors believed that the insulation mutual status affords did appear to be advantageous in enabling BuSoc to take a more stakeholder oriented approach (Kochan and Rubinstein, 2000), both in terms of providing competitive products to customers and relatively favourable conditions for employees. However, there was little evidence to suggest that this was as a result of trade union engagement. More cynically perhaps, industry commentators have suggested that although mutuality currently fits well with business strategy, further moves by 'carpetbaggers', i.e. account holders who push for mergers and conversions in order to qualify for a cash windfall or shares, remains a risk in the future. Union officials expressed concerns regarding the impact of potential demutualization in the future on employment relations, as there was a belief that mutuality was acting as an important buffer. On the other hand, managers at NatBank and WebBank admitted that pressure to satisfy the stock market *and* employees is very difficult, but equally this pressure appeared to have provided a stronger motivation to engage with partnership than was the case at BuSoc. In short, it can be concluded that the framework of corporate governance in the UK does provide some significant challenges for partnership, but that nevertheless, a degree of amelioration is still possible, and indeed that the external pressures can actually act as a catalyst to improve employment relations and to take a more strategic approach to HRM.

CAN THERE BE NON-UNION FORMS OF PARTNERSHIPS?

The partnership literature focuses almost exclusively on partnerships between trade unions and management, or what Dietz et al. (2005) refer to as a 'union-only ghetto'. This is surprising given that, inter alia, the CBI, CIPD, IPA and DTI definitions of partnership do not suggest that a union presence is an *essential* component of a partnership agreement. Admittedly, some theoretical and empirical acknowledgement of the potential of non-union partnerships has begun to emerge (Ackers et al., 2004; Badigannavar and Kelly, 2005; Butler, 2005; Dietz et al., 2005; Upchurch et al., 2006) but remains limited. Evidence on the efficacy of non-unions structures is mixed, with Knell (1999) concluding that there are negligible differences between union and non-union partnerships and IRS (2000) even concluding from its study that non-union partnerships appeared to be more 'deep-rooted' than union structures. On the other hand, research into non-union employee representation has often been pessimistic, concluding that they are toothless institutions (Blyton and Turnbull, 2004; Butler, 2005; Gollan, 2001, 2002, 2003, 2005, 2007; Terry, 1999). However, given that trade union organisation and collective bargaining has declined significantly since 1980 – indeed, in the private sector coverage of collective bargaining has fallen from 17 per cent in 1998 to 11 per cent in 2004 (Kersley et al., 2006) – and the impact of the European Information and Consultation Regulations, understanding of employment relations in non-union environments is essential. This study revealed that the non-union partnership at WebBank did appear to be significantly more constrained than agreements at NatBank, offering some support for the pessimists (Upchurch et al., 2006). Nevertheless, the difference between the bodies at BuSoc and WebBank was less clear cut, other than that the former had formally negotiable terms and conditions, and recourse to legal action and external arbitration.

In the terms of Marchington and Wilkinson (2005) the WebBank employee forum was more of an information body than a consultation/negotiating body, but did appear to be evolving into a more consultative body. However, it did also have an important role in terms of the management of discipline and grievance. As Haynes (2005) warns, there is a tendency to compare union and non-union voice, rather than non-union voice against no voice. For example, Upchurch et al. (2006: 407) describe a non-union structure where 'much information was provided by management on workplace change' but criticise the structure on the grounds that employees were not always able to 'persuade and invoke change', despite their own survey evidence which suggested that 58 per cent of employees thought the employer was good at keeping people up to date with proposed changes, and 58 per cent suggested the employer provided everyone with the chance to comment on proposed changes (Upchurch et al., 2006: 400). Two responses can be made to such conclusions. Firstly, surely management provision of information regarding workplace change is better than no information at all, and indeed their own questionnaires reveal the majority of employees were satisfied with the amount of information received. Secondly, it is unlikely that employees in both union and non-union environments will always achieve what they want, but this does not mean that the *process* has been in vain, even if the final outcome is the same. Accordingly, it is argued that the WebBank structure demonstrates a substantial degree of success, thus supporting suggestions that non-union representative voice combined with direct voice may offer an effective voice regime (Bryson, 2004). It is noteworthy that the structure is still young, and the fact that most actors appeared to be satisfied and did not express a desire for union recognition. It is also important to remember that ineffective union structures also exist. Clearly further research is required which investigates the efficacy of non-union partnerships.

SHOULD PARTNERSHIP BE FORMALISED?

The literature is inconclusive in relation to the formality of partnership, with Oxenbridge and Brown (2004a and 2004b) arguing that informal partnerships can be more successful than informal partnerships, and Heaton et al. (2002) concluding the opposite. The case studies presented here, suggest that *both* formal and informal aspects are important to a successful and enduring partnership. Actors frequently cited the importance and value of cementing strong informal relationships, and understanding how to 'play' the politics of partnership. Clearly, formal structures alone are insufficient to create a robust partnership, as this is unlikely to facilitate the attitudinal and behavioural change required. On the other hand, over-reliance on informal relationships is also a precarious strategy. This was illustrated by the situation at BuSoc where the union appeared to be in a vulnerable position due to the fact the partnership was dominated by close relationships between a few key management and union players, leading to questions of sustainability and succession. On the other hand, the relationship between BuSoc and the BuSuc Staff Union has been in existence for over 30 years, thus demonstrating some degree of stability.

Requirements for Enduring Partnership

Having discussed the contextual factors, the next section raises three important points from the study, drawing on the propositions of Haynes and Allen (2001). They suggest three requirements for an enduring partnership. Firstly, a need for clear expectations of partnership and the rules of engagement (see also Stuart and Martinez-Lucio, 2004). Secondly, the importance of process, and the extent to which the partnership process accommodates sometimes divergent interests. Thirdly, the importance of actor perspectives on partnership, and the extent to which outcomes can be considered to be mutually beneficial. These will now be discussed in turn.

DEFINITIONS, EXPECTATIONS AND THE RULES OF ENGAGEMENT

Haynes and Allen (2001) argue that there is a need for clear expectations regarding roles and behaviour to foster sufficient levels of trust which are essential to enduring partnerships (see also Cooke, 1990; Dietz, 2004; Guest and Peccei, 2001). Before considering the understandings of organisational actors it is useful to review the perspectives of academic commentators.

Among researchers, there is a lack of clear definition of what partnership actually means (Ackers and Payne, 1998; Guest and Peccei, 2001; Terry, 2003a), as well as little guidance on how to recognise a genuine example of partnership or non-partnership (Dietz, 2004). Arguably, this may reflect a polarised way of looking at a messy world, when the reality is likely to be less clear cut. This creates problems with the selection of case study organisations, and raises questions of whether researchers are actually comparing 'like with like' mentioned earlier. This is crucial, otherwise the evidence may not be of partnership failing as such, but rather 'partnership' providing a label for concession bargaining or old-style collective bargaining, and pseudo-participation masquerading as partnership (Roche and Geary, 2002).

Typically, academic definitions suggest a notion of reciprocity (Martinez-Lucio and Stuart, 2002) and 'co-operation for mutual gain' (Tailby and Winchester, 2005), coupled with the notion of proactive decision-making. Given the inherent ambiguity, the study has highlighted the need to clarify the meaning of partnership in the UK and the influential definitions of the TUC and IPA were used to confirm that NatBank, BuSoc and WebBank all represented prima facie cases of partnership (IPA, 1997; TUC, 1999). Interestingly, while NatBank had followed the TUC model, and WebBank had been inspired by the IPA model, at BuSoc the approach was more ad hoc and haphazard. The study has also proposed that partnership can be thought of more usefully as a mix of certain practices and processes. Practices typically centre round a structure of representative participation, while processes concern consultation, decision-making and actor relationships. It also proposes that associated outcomes such as sharing success, flexibility and employment security are matters for empirical investigation, rather than integral components of partnership per se.

For organisational actors, partnership also requires a clear understanding of purpose and the rules of engagement (Cooke, 1990; Stuart and Martinez-Lucio, 2004), yet, intriguingly, the understanding of partnership held by the actors in the cases did not always correspond with the interpretation adopted by the critical commentators in the academic literature. It is quite possible that the expectations of academic theorists do not match the expectations of workers and trade unionists. Critics often denounce partnership on the basis that it does not offer unions 'joint decision-making', 'joint governance' or 'co-determination'. For example, one study concludes that there was 'extant managerial hostility to any notion of joint-decision-making' (Danford et al., 2004: 185). Upchurch et al. (2006) also criticise a partnership in the finance sector on the grounds that it did not deliver 'equal dialogue' or 'economic and industrial democracy', reflecting their view that a broader issue of an inherent class conflict exists.

With regard to the present case studies, it is difficult to see how this can be presented as a justifiable criticism of partnership for two reasons. Firstly, the actors in these case studies did not believe that partnership meant co-determination of decisions. Partnership was viewed as problem-solving and as a means to promote information, consultation and dialogue at an early stage, but in all cases management and representatives unanimously agreed that within a partnership framework management retained their right to manage, and indeed to make the final decision. This was not perceived to be a particular problem; indeed, workers and employee representatives believed that on balance they *did* benefit from partnership working, and were generally positive about the outcomes, arguing that decisions were often better as a result. Secondly, it is difficult to gauge whether the situation would have been different without a partnership approach, i.e. with a traditional approach, and this is often overlooked by the critics who stress the need for negotiation and not 'just' consultation, which they dismiss as second best (see for example, Upchurch et al., 2006). There has been a shift away from negotiation to consultation in the UK for many years (Cully et al., 1999; Brown et al., 2000; Oxenbridge et al., 2003; Terry, 2003a), and there is a danger of comparing consultation under partnership with a romantic historical view of trade unionism. As Brown et al. (2000) remind us, union influence has declined over the past twenty years on both pay and non-pay issues, with the exception of health and safety where strict legislation applies. Similarly, Terry (2003a) points out that shop stewards are 'no longer joint architects of organisational policy', with or without partnership. As he asserts:

> The concept of 'joint regulation', long seen as the normative cornerstone of British industrial relations, clear evidence of unions' capacity to influence the policies and practices of employers, has to be set aside (Terry, 2003a: 460).

Despite this, Heery (2006: 452) found that union officers still view information and consultation as less central to their job than bargaining, reflecting their continued aspiration for joint regulation. However, both researchers and actors need to have a clear understanding of what is meant by partnership, and what exactly it is expected to achieve. This study has proposed that often the expectations of academic theorists or some trade union officials may not necessarily correspond with those of organisational actors, and that, in particular, employee views are seldom taken into account.

THE IMPORTANCE OF PROCESS: MUTUAL LEGITIMATION OF INTERESTS?

It is also argued that existing studies often overlook the process of partnership, and this is important if the extent to which partnership contributes to a mutual legitimation of interests is to be evaluated. In other words, does partnership change the way decisions are made? As Guest and Peccei (1992) argue in relation to downsizing, the actual process of decision-making is important as well as the final outcome. Critics, including Gall (2001) and Kelly (2004), highlight redundancies in organisations espousing partnership as evidence of the failure of partnership. However, as Dietz (2004) argues, 'one need not express surprise when large scale redundancies take place under partnership...the issue is how they are handled'. Given that 'structure does not equate with process' (Boxall and Purcell, 2003: 171) and 'good processes matter more than institutions' (Guest and Peccei, 1998: 9) there is a need to investigate the process of partnership in detail. As Freeman and Medolf (1984) argue, the efficacy of employee voice depends upon the way employers and employees interact, in other words the process of decision-making. The issue is whether voice achieves a regulatory impact (Hyman, 2005), or the 'power to persuade' (Greenfield and Pleasure, 1993). Roche and Geary (2002) have also highlighted a need to understand more about the micro-politics of partnership working. To this end, there was evidence of the partnership process exerting a moderating effect over decision-making, particularly where a 'business case for equity' could be made, resulting in decisions which accommodated the views of representatives/employees to a greater degree than they might otherwise have done.

This was an advantage of the critical incident technique, as it allowed specific issues to be identified and investigated in great detail. Accordingly, employing the analytical framework proposed by Budd (2004), there was evidence to suggest that as a result of voice and dialogue, union/employee representatives were often able to moderate decisions to mitigate the worst effects for employees at NatBank and WebBank. The same regulatory effect could not be identified in the case of BuSoc. It was suggested that in the previous five years employment relations had generally been good with few major controversies, but there was still evidence of poor process, as the decision was simply imposed unilaterally by management, with negligible union involvement. This underlines the complex relationship between process and outcomes, in that poor process need not necessarily result in poor outcomes and vice versa.

In other words, two of the cases demonstrated evidence of 'partial success' in many instances, with the voice process appearing to moderate decisions. The same could not be said in the case of BuSoc, with the most important decision in recent years being made without consultation, and limited evidence to suggest that more positive decisions were actually the result of union engagement as opposed to employer goodwill. The Budd framework is therefore useful in illustrating how – and whether – voice moderated countervailing pressures between efficiency and equity. However, an important caveat must be raised in relation to Budd's call for 'balance': what exactly is meant by *balancing the objectives of the employment relationship*? The phrase appears to suggest some kind of stable equilibrium and raises concerns, therefore, as to whether this is actually achievable (Estreicher, 2005; Adams, 2005; Hyman, 2005), thus mirroring many old 1970s debates around pluralist IR (Fox, 1974; Clegg, 1975; Hyman, 1978). It is not surprising that radical scholars such as Hyman are dismissive, as Budd acknowledges 'critical industrial relations views the labour problem as inherent in capitalism and seeks to replace it with worker ownership and socialism' (2004: 103). For liberal pluralists, on the other hand, the ideas are highly attractive and provide a useful framework for analysis (Bamber, 2005). However, it is proposed that balance may not be the most appropriate term; indeed it is difficult to imagine what a balance would look like in reality. Adams (2005: 115) proposes a slightly modified objective, 'optimality within minimally accepted bounds ... societies should attempt to optimise efficiency, equity and voice – but the result might not be an equal weighting of all three objectives'. In other words, the aim should be to achieve sufficient levels of voice and equity compatible with high levels of efficiency. This reflects the argument of Howell (2005) that, in reality, fairness is likely to be the 'junior partner', with fairness in the service of competitiveness rather than the other way round. It is therefore unlikely to be an equal measure of each. Admittedly, Budd (2005) acknowledges these criticisms, and suggests that 'balance' need not necessarily be thought of as an equal weighting between the three components, but rather as 'the search for arrangements that enhance one or more dimensions without undue sacrifices in other dimensions' (p. 196), and that they should be viewed more as a 'regulative ideal', even if it is never realised. He comments that 'respect' could be an alternative to 'balance', but suggests this creates a new question of how much respect is enough?

In many respects such arguments again reflect the controversies surrounding pluralism which existed in the 1970s, and related concerns in relation to whether the pluralist ethic even requires or implies a balance of power (Fox, 1974; Clegg, 1975: 315). Although power inequalities were a key concern for 'radical pluralists' such as Fox, the existence of a power balance was not a particular belief of liberal pluralists such as Clegg, who argued that 'the pluralist ethic does not postulate a balance of power'. As Budd (2004) acknowledges, the fact that a balance of power does not exist does not mean it is not a worthy aspiration. This study, however, prefers the use of the terms 'accommodation' or 'moderation', as it is believed that these are the most compatible with the liberal pluralist view of the employment relationship. This does not imply that there ought to be an equal weighting which new pluralism simply cannot offer, and arguably old pluralism never offered either. In short, partnership is believed to represent an attempt to make the employment relationship less imbalanced; but not an attempt to make the employment relationship balanced.

It is argued that the framework proposed by Budd is a useful heuristic device when exploring the subtle processes of partnership, though it inevitably simplifies complex relationships. Studies such as those by Kelly (2004) which rely on raw quantitative indicators, such as the number of redundancies or pay differentials, overlook the qualitative aspects such as the way the process was handled, and clearly this is also of great importance to workers. They also fail to address the impact of wider environmental factors. This reflects problems experienced in establishing a link between HRM and performance due to problems in establishing causality, inconsistency of HR practices applied, variations in the proxies used to measure high commitment HRM and performance, and the reliance on self-reported scores from HR managers (Marchington and Wilkinson, 2005). There is therefore evidence to support the arguments of Findlay and McKinlay (2003) that it is from the process of partnership itself – the benefits of both influence over management and real involvement in governance processes – that employees may stand to gain from partnership.

ACTORS' EXPERIENCES AND PARTNERSHIP OUTCOMES: MUTUALLY BENEFICIAL?

Practices must be seen to be beneficial for managers, unions and employees if the partnership is to be enduring (Haynes and Allen, 2001), but, again, this need not necessarily mean an *equal* distribution of benefits for all actors (Clegg, 1975). The study found that on balance, management, union and employee actors were all in favour of a collaborative partnership approach. Management demonstrated a degree of pragmatism, and appeared to value the additional input they received through dialogue and the facilitation of organisational change. For unions this is optimistic, given that in the two unionised organisations many senior managers acknowledged that unions 'added value' because of their knowledge of what was happening on the shop-floor (Terry, 2003a). Union officials and representatives also valued the additional resources they had been provided with under partnership, as well as the increased access to information and key management figures. This supports findings by Roche and Geary (2002) and is inconsistent with studies which predict that partnership will necessarily lead to the subordination of unions; indeed at NatBank it had actually revitalised workplace union organisation. Across the cases, employee opinion – which is often overlooked – suggested that they believed that adversarialism was no longer an appropriate union strategy. Indeed, many employees were critical of adversarial tactics, and suggested they were no longer relevant or useful. Radicals may attribute this to 'false consciousness' (Legge, 1995), but there is no reason to suggest that employees are 'cultural dopes'. Moreover, although employees all agreed that voice is important, in the case of WebBank they did not necessarily want union voice, while at BuSoc and NatBank most employees were opposed to adversarial unionism. This is consistent with surveys in the US and UK which suggest that while workers want voice, they do not necessarily want union voice (Bryson, 2004). Research has suggested that although workers still have a belief in collective action with their colleagues, they do not necessarily see a union as central to this (Diamond and Freeman, 2001). This contrasts with the critical findings of studies such as Danford et al. (2004) , which suggest a deterioration in the quality of working life, and 'the anti thesis of mutual gain' (p. 28). Overall then, the positive actor responses offer a stark contrast to the critical responses in much of the existing literature.

Critics of partnership often express disillusionment and conclude that partnership has failed to meet expectations, especially in terms of gains for unions and employees. They frequently selectively quote the remarks of Guest and Peccei (2001: 231) that 'the balance of advantage is skewed towards management' as evidence of the inherent 'failure' of partnership (see for example, Kelly, 2004; Smith and Morton, 2006). Smith and Morton (2006), for example, use this statement to support their argument that partnerships serve to 'entrench employer power'. Interestingly, this statement is often taken out of context, given that Guest and Peccei also state how 'taken overall ... the results can be seen as a positive endorsement of the concept of partnership ... evidence of a balance of advantage for management ... is not in itself an argument against partnership' (Guest and Peccei, 2001: 231). They argue that in the cases where the gains were skewed, a high trust partnership had yet to emerge. It is not then evidence of the failure of partnership per se, but rather a problem with the way partnership has been operating, and even the most ardent partnership enthusiasts acknowledge that without a coherent and integrated approach, partnership need not automatically and unambiguously lead to mutual gains (Kochan and Osterman, 1994). Indeed, it is somewhat fatalistic to argue that partnership *necessarily* leads to managerial dominance and weakens unions, given that irrespective of partnership management–union relationships are stacked in favour of the latter over the former (Wills, 2004), given the change in power relations since 1979. In short, it is argued that perhaps the benchmarks for success set by critics are often set so high it is easy to conclude that partnership is ineffective. As Stuart and Martinez-Lucio point out:

> *The expectations – both in terms of hopes and fears – generated by the term [partnership] mean that it has become all too easy to set it up as a 'straw-debate' with the aim of knocking it down (Stuart and Martinez-Lucio, 2004b: 422).*

For example, in their study of partnership in a non-union retail firm, Badigannavar and Kelly (2005) judge the effectiveness of partnership on the basis of the extent to which it 'meets' the TUC's six principles of partnership, and pass judgement accordingly, before concluding that 'the partnership is quite precarious as well as ineffective' (Badigannavar and Kelly, 2005: 1543). It is also noteworthy that despite the fact that some positive empirical findings are often reported in the data of critical writers, such findings are duly overlooked when they draw their pessimistic conclusions. Even the most critical studies such as Upchurch et al. (2006: 12) report that 'it is clear that the Partnership Council has been a useful forum for agreeing integrative concerns through consultation'. Clearly, employing an ideal type or aspirational model as an analytical framework against which to judge outcomes is setting a very high barrier for success. After all, even the IR optimists only suggested that partnership may allow unions to re-enter the mainstream of employment relations (Ackers and Payne, 1998); they did not argue that employment relations would be completely recast overnight. What is more difficult to judge, however, is what might have happened in organisations *without* the partnership dialogue. It is conceivable that the situation might actually have been much worse. As Pfeffer argues:

> *One should compare programmes not with some ideal but with the situation that would exist in their absence. In other words, just because a programme does not solve every problem or move the organisation all the way, particularly initially, to where it wants and needs to be does not mean that it is a failure. A programme fails when it produces either no sustained change or else change that it is dysfunctional and ineffective. Some remediation of problems in managing the employment relation is certainly better than nothing at all' (Pfeffer, 1994: 206).*

Indeed, several benefits were found in the three cases confirming other studies, including increased legitimacy of the representative body, improved decision-making, constructive collaborative relationships and improved employment relations generally (Guest and Peccei, 2001; Roche and Geary, 2002; Oxenbridge and Brown, 2004).

Yet in the terms used by Kelly (2004), none of the case studies could possibly be described as labour-parity (i.e. high product demand, tight labour market and high union density) which he suggests is a prerequisite for genuine co-operation, and – as he predicts of financial services partnerships – would best be described as employer-dominant. Yet it would be unfair – and inaccurate – to characterise the partnerships as little more than union compliance and employer dominance. Upchurch et al. (2006: 18) report that four fifths of employees in their study believed their representatives put forward their views at meetings, three fifths believed they were effective, and two thirds believed management sometimes/frequently asked for their views, yet the authors conclude 'partnership had proved relatively ineffective for employee voice'. For reformists, however, what really matters is the extent to which partnership delivers some benefits to employees, as well wider benefits to the economy and society as a whole. There is therefore a need to reconsider the benchmarks for success, and perhaps more attention needs to be paid to the expectations and perceptions of the actors themselves, and not those of academic theorists.

The evidence from this study suggests that the primary advantage of partnership was that actors believed often decisions were more palatable as a result of the partnership process, and this is clearly very important. As Dietz et al. (2005) contend:

> We would argue that the litmus-test for all partnerships – unionised or not – is the quality of the joint problem solving processes in the terms we suggested earlier: of giving significant influence to employees over organizational decision-making early in the process ... and in delivering regular, acceptable mutual gains for all parties (Dietz et al., 2005: 302).

Admittedly, the partnerships may not actually have *balanced* the objectives of the employment relationship in terms of efficiency, equity and voice (Budd, 2004). Moreover, the gains of partnership may not have flowed *equally* to employers, employees and unions. But this is not sufficient reason to dismiss the concept of partnership, else we risk throwing the baby out with the bath water. Concepts of mutuality and balancing may be useful in an aspirational sense, but the reality is likely to be less impressive than this ideal in a capitalist society. It may be partly due to the 'inappropriateness of "mutuality" as a device for conceptualising the employment relationship under partnership regimes', and that a reality of genuine mutuality is rare (Suff and Williams, 2004). Again, they are perhaps better thought of as a regulative ideal (Budd, 2004), and this wholly compatible with a pluralist conception of the employment relationship, where the aim is one of levelling the playing field. It also underlines the danger of conflating partnership (defined as a combination of practices and processes) with employment relations outcomes, which need to be considered separately. These reservations notwithstanding, partnership facilitated dialogue and voice, which promoted more considered decision-making, and the moderation of business decisions and often mitigated the impact on employees. When judged in this light, the partnerships at NatBank, BuSoc and WebBank demonstrate a modicum of success.

Challenges

Despite the positive overall conclusions, significant challenges to enduring partnerships remain, but these do not provide arguments against partnership per se. As Roche and Geary (2004) note, partnership needs to be institutionalised to a significant degree, taking root at multiple levels and operating consistently over time. They argue that partnership must operate at multiple levels, including day-to-day decision-making. Embedding partnership at all levels was found to be a challenge in all case organisations, with representatives frequently citing inconsistencies in approach, reflecting findings by Marks et al. (1998), Heaton et al. (2002) and Dietz (2004). This was normally attributed to the second challenge identified, a lack of middle management engagement with the concept of partnership working.

Middle management may perceive partnership policies as at odds with reality, restricting autonomy, slowing down decision-making, or promoting policies which they believe are fine in theory but difficult to effect in practice. They may also have a lack of skills, disdain for HR work and competing priorities. This can lead to inconsistencies in application, making it difficult to embed a partnership culture (Marchington and Wilkinson, 2005). WERS04 reveals that management are more supportive of unions where they believe they contribute to business performance (Kersely et al., 2006), but even instrumental support for unions may not be enough to form enduring partnership relationships, if it is not underpinned by a wider social legitimacy. As Boxall and Purcell remark:

Few voice systems and positive union-management relations will exist, or exist for long, unless they are valued in their own right as legitimate and morally necessary activities irrespective of their performance outcomes. They have to have social legitimacy (Boxall and Purcell, 2003: 182).

Representative efficacy was another significant challenge. As Terry states 'success in consultation is perceived to rely on force of argument and technical competence rather than on muscle' (Terry, 2003b: 493), and this may be difficult where representatives have traditionally criticised rather than engaged. This may create a gulf between representatives and their members. It is also more difficult for representatives to know what to support. While it is relatively easy to know what to support in terms of pay and conditions it is less easy to know what to support regarding changes to work organisation (Terry, 2003b). There is also a delicate balancing act to be struck by representatives between being perceived to be 'too strong' or 'too weak' (Ackers et al., 2004). If representatives are perceived to be too challenging, they may lose employer support, and employees may also disapprove of 'old-style tactics'. On the other hand, if representatives are not challenging, employers may not get the feedback and input they require, and employees are likely to view the representatives as co-opted and question their value. This supports the propositions of Ackers et al. (2004) that both *overly* adversarial approaches and weak partnership approaches are not sustainable in the long term. Nevertheless, the example of WebBank suggests the possibility that moderately weak non-union partnerships may actually be sustainable. It still seems reasonable to suggest, however, that strong and high trust partnership is most likely to be sustainable in the long term. (Guest and Peccei, 2001; Oxenbridge and Brown, 2004). This supports the findings of WERS04, that management are more likely to be supportive of trade unions where they believe they make a positive contribution to business performance (Kersely et al., 2006).

As mentioned earlier, regulatory context is often cited as a barrier to sustainable partnerships in liberal market economies such as the UK (Heery, 2002; Deakin et al., 2002, 2004, Turnbull et al., 2004). There was some evidence to support that occasionally, despite the rhetoric of partnership, decisions would be imposed on the grounds that they are deemed to be 'essential for financial reasons'. For example, at NatBank outsourcing to India was deemed essential in order to remain competitive, while at BuSoc the decision to close the final salary pension scheme was unilaterally imposed, and deemed essential to avoid further losses. It was also found that union/representative arguments were more likely to convince managers that a decision made business as well as ethical sense. However, there are limitations to this criticism, as there is no prospect of the UK adopting old-style EU corporatism, and indeed such styles may be fading there too.

Lastly, concerns must be expressed regarding the resistance of partnership to adversity, particularly in a voluntarist environment. Partnerships should not be seen in terms of a static agreement (Stuart and Martinez-Lucio, 2004b) but must be able to stand of test of time (Gall, 2001) and this is difficult to predict. Cooke (1990) suggests that in order to function, co-operative frameworks have to have processes to deal with challenges and threats, as well as positive developments. Challenges are likely to include a change in key actors/partnership champions, or a major conflict or organisational decision. This requires a commitment to the legitimacy of the actor contributions, and an acceptance of the inevitability of some conflict over divergent interests. As Haynes and Allen (2001: 181) comment 'partnership unionism represents not so much a bipolar movement from adversarialism to co-operation, but a movement from co-operation within an adversarial context, to constrained conflict within a co-operative framework'. In other words, parties need to accept the inevitability of some conflict arising within a healthy partnership. This pluralist perspective was generally accepted in the unionised environments of NatBank and BuSoc. At NatBank the partnership appears to have weathered the storm of the first five years, and the agreement has been renewed for another five years. At BuSoc there have been few tests in the last five years besides the issue of pensions, and on this particular issue partnership failed. In the non-union case of WebBank, however, management demonstrated a much more unitarist perspective, and should a major dispute arise, the ability of the structure to survive remains to be seen. As such, it remains untested. Streeck (1992) questions the sustainability of voluntary partnerships because of the asymmetry of power between management and labour, as well as issues of legitimacy and reliance upon management power. In other words, how effective can the representatives be if they are perceived by management to be obstructive or out of line with the business interest? In this respect the case of WebBank would present the most precarious partnership. Partnership advocates, however, would argue that voluntary arrangements can be sustainable with sufficient strategic integration (Kochan and Osterman, 1994).

Conclusion

To conclude, it would appear that the impact of partnership on employment relations in Britain is considerably more complex than the existing literature suggests. On balance, the study offers some support for the advocates, as well as some support for the concerns expressed by the critics. In particular, the study has argued that there is a need to understand more about the *context and process* in addition to the difficult-to-measure *outcomes*, if the realities of partnership working and a comprehensive understanding are to be achieved. To this end, it is argued that the views of the critics are too fatalistic and defeatist, and of little use to ordinary employees and managers looking for a way to improve the quality of their employment relations. It also suggests that different trajectories of experience are possible, and indeed likely. There is also a need to re-think exactly what partnership means, and what it is expected to achieve, and assess accordingly. The book has also demonstrated the value of exploring the *process* of partnership, as well as its outcomes, and Budd (2004) offers a useful framework for doing this. There is also a need to compare the actual outcomes in real contexts of decision-making shaped by partnership, and to compare outcomes not just with the 'ideal' outcome, but with the other possible alternatives.

As these cases demonstrate, several decisions were better than they could otherwise have been for staff, and the partnership approach had resulted in several compromises to the benefit of employees by mitigating the impact of decisions. Representatives also benefited from increased legitimacy. There was evidence to suggest that *without* the partnership dialogue decisions might have been more focused on short-term efficiency, with scant regard for the equity outcomes. Interestingly, management acknowledged that decisions based solely on 'profit-maximising' and 'efficiency', i.e. bad HRM, are often inefficient because they are met with staff resistance and union opposition, whereas compromises which may appear to be less efficient are actually more so because of greater legitimacy and acceptability. In other words, managers expressed the view that often there was a sound business case for equity. Partnership is unlikely to 'balance' the objectives of the employment relationship, but it is quite possible that the outcomes were more balanced than they would have otherwise been, and this is a central component of the pluralist ethic. Moreover, it is difficult to imagine what a balance would actually look like (Clegg, 1975). Partnership might not have led to the development of three stakeholder organisations, but rather three organisations which were more stakeholder oriented than they may otherwise have been. There was also little evidence of support for a more militant/adversarial approach in this context. In addition, there is evidence to suggest that an effective partnership encourages management to think more strategically and long-term, in relation to their HRM and employment relations policies. When judged in this light, the cases of NatBank, BuSoc and WebBank demonstrate various degrees of success, although of course significant challenges remain if partnership is to become an enduring model of employment relations regulation in the UK. As with other forms of participation, 'initiatives are probably more limited than the enthusiasts claim, but more constructive than the critics admit' (Marchington and Wilkinson, 2005: 415).

Implications for Practice

The findings of the research also raise some important implications for the key actors involved in partnership working. Trade unions are increasingly required to demonstrate the value they can add in the eyes of both employers and employees. Although critics argue that the risks of partnership are so high that it may be 'partnership and perish' (Tailby et al., 2005, 3), this study proposes, however, that the viability of a more heroic militant route is highly questionable. Rather, trade unions need a different approach if they are to prove they can actually add value. The study found that many employees no longer support adversarial strategies, and the WebBank case reveals how many workers are happy with non-union voice mechanisms, and are questioning what a union can add. Others were more overtly negative and viewed unions as outdated and the organisers of strikes. This echoes quantitative studies which suggest that employees appear to be doubting the effectiveness of union voice (Bryson, 2004), and relates to the paradox of unionised worker satisfaction, where union members are consistently found to be more dissatisfied than their non-member counterparts (Guest and Conway, 2004). It is possible, however, that unions raise member expectations and political consciousness but may be perceived to be failing to deliver against such expectations, making workers more aware of problems, and therefore more likely to report them (Freeman and Medoff, 1984). Even if this were true, it still presents a challenge for unions. In sum, suggestions that employees favour direct rather than representative voice, perceive non-union voice to be more effective than union voice, and that union members are the most dissatisfied, make very bleak reading for unions.

Accordingly, this study suggests that unions need to adapt to the new realities of work, and to re-think their approach, if they are to secure the support of employers, employees and government. Just as Labour re-invented itself in 1997 as a party which claims to be aware of the needs of both the business community and workers, the union movement needs to consider how it can re-invent itself as useful in the eyes of both employers and employees. Trade unions need to ensure that they offer sufficient training and support for representatives to take up the new challenging roles, so they are capable of engaging in consultation and not merely opposing or criticising. Representatives are increasingly required to challenge on the grounds of business case, and this requires different skills and approaches. The evidence suggests that unions do have an advantage through their knowledge and external intelligence. Unions may benefit from exploring how they can best share this knowledge with, and between, union representatives. They also need to improve communication with and recruitment of a new generation of never members, free-riders, and in particular younger workers. Raising the profile of trade unions at universities and colleges and increased use of the internet to raise awareness and service members may be two avenues for this. Websites such as www.worksmart.org. uk suggest that unions are shifting in this direction. Unions must also engage with the reality of the heterogeneity of channels now available to British workers and employers, as various combinations of union/non-union and direct/indirect representation are now increasingly possible. Overall, the findings lend support to the argument that partnership may be pursued by management with or without trade unions (Ackers et al., 2004). The NatBank case illustrates that unions can gain significant benefits from a strong partnership relationship. In short, the findings starkly disagree with the pessimistic views shared by Darlington (1994), Fairbrother (1996) and Kelly (1998). For unions, it may be the case that they need to learn to demonstrate strength through flexibility, as a traditional macho approach appears incompatible with the current multi-channel environment.

Employers have little to fear from partnership. However, if the representative body is to function effectively they need to accept the legitimacy of the representative body, and acknowledge the right of the body to question and to sometimes disagree. Employers may be concerned that partnership may lead to sub-optimal decisions, for example, engaging with a union which appears to defend the lowest performing employees, or compromising on decisions. Yet the evidence suggested that in the long term this was not the case. The representative bodies agreed that, on occasions, decisions regarding discipline and grievance are fair, so long as employees have the opportunity to have a fair hearing. From their perspective, the priority was ensuring that due process was followed, and that it was 'felt fair', even though the final outcome may have been the same. There were also several examples where employer compromises may have been deemed sub-optimal. However, in reality, often management suggested that the strategic decision-making which partnership encouraged allowed them to identify decisions which were actually more efficient in the long term. Employers need to recognise that attempts to constrain the representative body too much are likely to result in a structure which is mutually detrimental rather than mutually beneficial. If management treat partnership as a sign of union weakness and attempt to exploit the situation, or conversely if the union views a management preference for co-operation as indicative of management weakness, the structures and relationships are unlikely to be effective (Bryson and Freeman, 2006). Rather, weak 'fig leaf' partnerships will deliver little for employers, unions or workers. Moreover, the commitment to employee representation and collaborative working must extend far beyond the executive team or the HR department to have any real impact. In particular it is essential to get the 'buy-in' of the line managers who are actually managing people on a day-to-day basis, as this was identified as one of the main barriers to effective partnership working, resonating with earlier studies into employee involvement initiatives (Marchington et al., 1992).

Employees need to be more engaged with representation. The danger is that partnership becomes an arcane elite-level process of little relevance to workers, as was illustrated in the BuSoc example. The lack of interest may also mean that elected representatives are standing for the wrong reasons, again acting as a barrier to the construction of effective partnership relationships. Effective communication between the actors is key. The study suggested that most employees did not want information forced upon them, but rather that they were generally kept up to date, and knew how to access further information should they require it. The study also supports the notion that employees increasingly want co-operation not confrontation, where the union works with management to improve the workplace and working conditions, as opposed to a focus solely on defending workers (Bryson and Freeman, 2006).

Bibliography

Acas. (2003) *ACAS Annual Report and Resource Accounts.* London: Acas.

Ackers, P. (2002) 'Reframing employment relations: the case for neo-pluralism', *Industrial Relations Journal,* 33 (1), 2–19.

Ackers, P., Marchington, M., Wilkinson, A. and Dundon, T. (2004) 'Partnership and voice: with or without trade unions: changing British management approaches to participation', in M. Stuart and M. Martinez-Lucio (eds) *Partnership and Modernisation in Employment Relations.* London: Routledge, 39–75.

Ackers, P. and Payne, J. (1998) 'British trade unions and social partnership: rhetoric, reality and strategy', *International Journal of Human Resource Management,* 9 (3), 529–549.

Adams, R. J. N. (2005) 'Efficiency, equity, and voice as moral imperatives', *Employee Responsibilities and Rights Journal,* 17 (2), 111–117.

Bacon, N. (2001) 'Employee Relations' in T. Redman and A. Wilkinson (eds) *Contemporary Human Resource Management.* London: FT Prentice Hall, 193–214.

Bacon, N., Samuel, P. (2009) 'Partnership agreement adoption and survival in the British private and public sectors', *Work, Employment and Society* 23: 231–248.

Bacon, N. and Storey, J. (2000) 'New employee relations strategies in Britain: towards individualism or partnership?', *British Journal of Industrial Relations,* 38 (3), 407–427.

Badigannavar, V. and Kelly, J. (2004) 'Labour-management partnership in the UK public sector' in Kelly, J. and Willman P. (eds) *Union Organization and Activity.* London: Routledge.

Badigannavar, V. F. and Kelly, J. F. (2005) 'Labour-management partnership in the non-union retail sector', *International Journal of Human Resource Management,* 16 (8), 1529–1544.

Bain, P. and Taylor, P. (2000) 'Entrapped by the "electronic panopticon"? worker resistance in the call centre', *New Technology Work and Employment*, 15 (1), 2–18.

Bain, P. and Taylor, P. (2004) 'No passage to India? UK unions, globalisation and the migration of call centre jobs', *Work, Employment and Society Conference*.

Bamber, G. J. K. (2005) 'The geometry of comparative industrial relations: efficiency, equity and voice', *Employee Responsibilities and Rights Journal*, 17 (2), 119–122.

Batstone, E. (1984) *Working Order: Workplace Industrial Relations Over Two Decades* Oxford: Blackwell.

Batt, R. (2002) 'Managing customer services: human resource practices, quit rates, and sales growth', *Academy of Management Journal*, 45 (3), 587–597.

Beale, D. (2004) 'The promotion and prospects of partnership at Inland Revenue: employer and union hand in hand?' in M. Stuart and M. Martinez-Lucio (eds) *Partnership and Modernisation in Employment Relations*. London: Routledge, 216–246.

Belt, V. (2002) 'A female ghetto? Women's careers in call centres', *Human Resource Management Journal*, 12 (4), 51–66.

Blyton, P. and Turnbull, P. (2004) *The Dynamics of Employee Relations*. London: Macmillan.

Bowen, D. E. and Lawler, E. E. (1992) 'The empowerment of service workers: what, why, how, and when', *Sloan Management Review*, 33 (3), 31–39.

Boxall, P. F. and Purcell, J. (2003) *Strategy and Human Resource Management*. New York: Palgrave Macmillan.

Brown, W. Deakin, S. Nash, D. Oxenbridge, S. (2000) 'The employment contract: from collective procedures to individual rights', *British Journal of Industrial Relations*, 38 (4), 611–629.

Bryson, A. (2004) 'Managerial responsiveness to union and nonunion worker voice in Britain', *Industrial Relations*, 43 (1), 213–241.

Bryson, A. and Freeman, R. (2006) 'What voice do British workers want?', CEP Discussion Paper 731, July, London School of Economics and Political Science.

Bryson, A., Charlwood, A., and Forth, J. (2006) 'Worker voice, managerial response and labour productivity: an empirical investigation', *Industrial Relations Journal*, 37 (5), 438–455.

Budd, J. W. (2004) *Employment with a Human Face: Balancing Efficiency, Equity, and Voice*. New York: ILR Press.

Budd, J. W. C. (2005) 'Employment with a Human Face: the author responds', *Employee Responsibilities and Rights Journal*, 17 (3), 191–199.

Butler, P. (2005) 'Non-union employee representation: exploring the efficacy of the voice process', *Employee Relations*, 27 (3), 272–288.

Chell, E. (2004) 'Critical incident technique' in C. Cassell and G. Symon (eds) *Essential Guide to Qualitative Methodologies in Organizational Research*. London: Sage, 45–60.

Claydon, T. (1998) 'Problematising partnership: the prospects for a co-operative bargaining agenda' in *Human Resource Management: the New Agenda*. London: FT Pitman, 180–191.

Clegg, H. (1975) 'Pluralism in industrial relations' *British Journal of Industrial Relations*, 13(3), 309–316.

Cooke, W. N. (1990) *Labor-Management Cooperation. New Partnerships or Going in Circles?* Kalamazoo, MI: W. E. Upjohn Institute for Employment Research.

Cressey, P. and Scott, P. (1992) 'Employment, technology and industrial relations in the UK clearing banks: is the honeymoon over?', *New Technology, Work and Employment*, 7 (2), 83–96.

Cully, M., O'Reilly, A., Woodland, S. and Dix, G. (1999) *Britain at Work as Depicted by the 1998 Workplace Employee Relations Survey*. London: Routledge.

Danford, A., Richardson, M., Stewart, P., Tailby, S. and Upchurch, M. (2004) 'High performance work systems and workplace partnership: a case study of aerospace workers', *New Technology, Work and Employment*, 19 (1), 14–29.

Danford, A., Richardson, M., Stewart, P., Tailby, S. and Upchurch, M. (2005a) 'Workplace partnership and employee voice in the UK: comparative case studies of union strategy and worker experience', *Economic and Industrial Democracy*, 26 (4), 593–620.

Danford, A., Richardson, M., Upchurch, M., Tailby, S. and Stewart, P. (2005b) *High Performance Work and Partnership in the UK*. London: Palgrave.

Darlington, R. (1994) *The Dynamics of Workplace Unionism: Shop Stewards' Organization in Three Merseyside Plants*. London: Mansell.

Datamonitor. (2004) 'Contact centre component technologies 2004', (http://www.datamonitor.co.uk).

Deakin, S., Hobbs, R., Konzelmann, S. and Wilkinson, F. (2002) 'Partnership, ownership and control', *Employee Relations*, 24 (3), 335–352.

Deakin, S., Hobbs, R., Konzellman, S. and Wilkinson, F. (2004) 'Working corporations: corporate governance and innovation in Labour-Management Partnerships in Britain' in M. Stuart and M. Martinez-Lucio (eds) *Partnership and Modernisation in Employment Relations*. London: Routledge, 63–82.

Deery, S. and Kinnie, N. (2002) 'Call centres and beyond: a thematic evaluation', *Human Resource Management Journal*, 12 (4), 3–13.

Diamond, W. J. and Freeman, R. B. (2001) *What Workers Want from Workplace Organisations: A Report to the TUC's Promoting Trade Unionism Task Group*. London: Trades Union Congress.

Dietz, G. (2004) 'Partnership and the development of trust in British workplaces', *Human Resource Management Journal*, 14 (1), 5–24.

Dietz, G., Cullen, J., Coad, A. (2005) 'Can there be non-union forms of workplace partnership?', *Employee Relations*, 27 (3), 289–306.

DTI. (1998) *Fairness at Work, Cmnd 3968.* London: DTI.

DTI. (2002) *High Performance Workplaces: a Discussion Paper.* London: DTI.

DTI. (2004) *The UK Contact Centre Industry: a Study.* London: DTI.

Dundon, T. and Rollinson, D. (2004) *Employment Relations in Non-union Firms.* London: Routledge.

Dundon, T., Wilkinson, A., Marchington, M., and Ackers, P. (2005) 'The management of voice in non-union organisations: managers' perspectives', *Employee Relations*, 27 (3), 307–319.

Durr, W. (1998) *Navigating the Customer Contact Centre in the 21st Century: a Technology and Management Guide.* Advanstar Marketing Services.

Edwards, P. (2003) 'The employment relationship and the field of industrial relations' in P. Edwards (ed.) *Industrial Relations: Theory and Practice.* Oxford: Blackwell, 1–36.

EIRO. (2005) 'Job losses and strikes hit banking sector', (31 May), (http://www.eiro.eurofound.eu.int/2005/05/feature/uk0505106f.html).

Emmott, M. (2005) *What is Employee Relations?* London: CIPD.

Estreicher, S. E. (2005) 'Geometry does not a theory of employment make', *Employee Responsibilities and Rights Journal*, 17 (2), 123–126.

Fairbrother, P. (1996) 'Workplace trade unionism in the state sector', *The New Workplace and Trade Unionism.* London: Routledge, 110–48.

Fernie, S. and Metcalf, D. H. (1998) *(Not) Hanging on the Telephone: Payment Systems in the New Sweatshops.* Centre for Economic Performance, London School of Economics and Political Science.

Findlay, P. and McKinlay, A. (2003) 'Union organising in Big Blue's backyard', *Industrial Relations Journal*, 34 (1), 52–66.

Flanagan, J. C. (1954) 'The critical incident technique', *Psychological Bulletin*, 51 (4), 327–359.

Fox, A. (1974) *Beyond Contract: Work, Power and Trust Relations.* London: Faber and Faber.

Freeman, R. B. and Medoff, J. L. (1984) *What Do Unions Do?* New York: Basic Books.

Frenkel, S. J., Tam, M., Korczynski, M. and Shire, K. (1998) 'Beyond bureaucracy? work organization in call centres', *The International Journal of Human Resource Management*, 9 (6), 957–979.

Frenkel, S. J., Korczynski, M., Shire, K. and Tam, M. (1999) *On the Front Line: Organization of Work in the Information Economy.* Ithaca, NY, USA: Cornell University.

Gall, G. (1993) 'Industrial relations in clearing banks: a comment on Cressey and Scott', *New Technology, Work and Employment*, 8 (1), 67–73.

Gall, G. (2001) 'From adversarialism to partnership?', *Employee Relations,* 23 (4), 353–375.

Gall, G. (2003) *The Meaning of Militancy.* London: Ashgate.

Gall, G. (2004) 'Trade union recognition in Britain 1995–2002: turning a corner', *Industrial Relations Journal,* 35 (3), 249–270.

Gardener, E., Howcroft, B. and Williams, J. (1999) 'The new retail banking revolution', *The Service Industries Journal,* 19 (2), 83–100.

Garson, B. (1988) *The Electronic Sweatshop: How Computers are Transforming the Office of the Future into the Factory of the Past.* New York: Simon & Schuster.

Gollan, P. J. (2001) 'Tunnel vision: non-union employee representation at Eurotunnel', *Employee Relations,* 23 (4), 376–400.

Gollan, P. J. (2002) 'So what's the news? Management strategies towards non-union employee representatoin at News International', *Industrial Relations Journal,* 33 (4), 316–331.

Gollan, P. J. (2003) 'All talk but no voice: employee voice at the Eurotunnel call centre', *Economic and Industrial Democracy,* 24 (4), 509–541.

Gollan, P. J. (2005) 'Silent voices: representation at the Eurotunnel call centre', *Personnel Review,* 34 (4), 423–450.

Gollan, P.J. (2007) *Employee Representation in Non-union Firms.* London: Sage.

Greenfield, P. and Pleasure, R. (1993) 'Representatives of their own choosing: finding workers' voice in the legitimacy and power of their unions' in B. Kaufman and M. Kleiner (eds) *Employee Representation: alternatives and Future Directions.* Madison, WI: IRRA.

Guest, D., Brown, W. Peccei, R. and Huxley, K. (2008) 'Does partnership at work increase trust? an analysis based on the 2004 Workplace Employment Relations Survey', *Industrial Relations Journal,* 39 (2), 124–152.

Guest, D. and Conway, N. (2004) 'Exploring the paradox of unionised worker dissatisfaction', *Industrial Relations Journal,* 35 (2), 102–121.

Guest, D. and Peccei, R. (1992) 'Employee involvement: redundancy as a critical case', *Human Resource Management Journal,* 2 (3), 34–59.

Guest, D. and Peccei, R. (1998) *The Partnership Company: Benchmarks for the Future: the Report of the IPA Survey: Principles, Practice and Performance.* London: Involvement & Participation Association.

Guest, D. and Peccei, R. (2001) 'Partnership at work: mutuality and the balance of advantage', *British Journal of Industrial Relations,* 39 (2), 207–236.

Hallier, J. and Leopold, J. (2000) 'Managing employment on greenfield sites: attempts to replicate high commitment practices in the UK and New Zealand', *Industrial Relations Journal,* 31 (3), 177–191.

Haynes, P. (2005) 'Filling the vacuum: non-union employee voice in the Auckland hotel industry', *Employee Relations,* 27 (3), 259–271.

Haynes, P. and Allen, M. (2001) 'Partnership as a union strategy: a preliminary evaluation', *Employee Relations,* 23 (2), 167–187.

Heaton, N., Mason, B. and Morgan, J. (2000) 'Trade unions and partnership in the Health Service', *Employee Relations,* 22 (4), 315–333.

Heaton, N., Mason, B. and Morgan, J. (2002) 'Partnership and multi-unionism in the Health Service', *Industrial Relations Journal,* 33 (2).

Heery, E. (2002) 'Partnership versus organising: alternative futures for British trade unionism', *Industrial Relations Journal,* 33 (1), 20–35.

Heery, E. (2006) 'The role of union full-time officials: results', *Industrial Law Journal,* 35 (1), 102.

Heery, E., Conley, H., Delbridge, R. and Stewart, P. (2004) 'Seeking partnership for the contingent workforce' in M. Stuart and M. Martinez-Lucio (eds) *Partnership and Modernisation in Employment Relations.* London: Routledge, 274–302.

Hook, K. (1998) *The Human Face of Call Centre Management.* USA: Callcraft.

Howell, C. (1999) 'Unforgiven: British trade unionism in crisis' in G. Ross and A. Martin (eds) *The Brave New World of Labor: European Trade Unions at the Millennium.* New York: Berghahn, 26–74.

Howell, C. (2005) *Trade Unions and the State: The Construction of Industrial Relations Institutions in Britain, 1890–2000.* Princeton University Press.

Hutchinson, S., Purcell, J. and Kinnie, N. (2000) 'Evolving high commitment management and the experience of the RAC call centre', *Human Resource Management Journal,* 10 (1), 63–78.

Hutton, W. (1995) *The State We're In.* London: Random House.

Hyman, R. (1978) 'Pluralism, procedural consensus and collective bargaining', *British Journal of Industrial Relations,* 16, 16–40.

Hyman, R. (1996) 'Is there a case for statutory works councils in Britain?' in A. McColgan (ed) *The Future of Labour Law.* London: Cassell.

Hyman, R. (2004) 'Whose (social) partnership' in M. Stuart and M. Martinez-Lucio (eds) *Partnership and Modernisation in Employment Relations.* London: Routledge, 386–411.

Hyman, R. M. (2005) 'Striking a balance? Means, ends and ambiguities', *Employee Responsibilities and Rights Journal,* 17 (2), 127–130.

IPA (1997) *Towards Industrial Partnership.* London: IPA.

IPA (2004) 'Abbey Case Study', *IPA Case Study,* May.

IPA (2005) *Moving Partnership On: a Final Report.* London: IPA/Unions 21.

IRS (1999) 'United we stand', *IRS Employment Trends,* 15.06.1999

IRS (2000) 'Partnership at work', *IRS Management Review,* 17.

IRS (2000) 'Unions step up call centre recruitment drive', *IRS Employment Trends,* 701 (1 April).

Jenkins, J. (2007) 'Gambling partners? The risky outcomes of workplace partnership', *Work, Employment and Society*, 21 (4), 635–662.

Johnstone, S., Ackers, P. And Wilkinson, A. (2009) 'The partnership phenomenon in the UK: a ten year review', *Human Resource Management Journal.*

Johnstone, S., Ackers, P. and Wilkinson, A. (2010) Better than nothing? is nonunion partnership a contradiction in terms? *Journal of Industrial Relations*, 52 (2), 151–168.

Johnstone, S., Wilkinson, A. and Ackers, P. (2004) 'Partnership paradoxes: a case study of an energy company', *Employee Relations*, 26 (4), 353–376.

Johnstone, S., Wilkinson, A. and Ackers,P. (2010) Applying Budd's model to partnership in financial services, *Economic and Industrial Democracy*, forthcoming.

Johnstone, S., Wilkinson, A. and Ackers, P. (2010) Critical incidents of partnership, *Industrial Relations Journal*, 41 (4).

Kelly, J. (1996) 'Union militancy and social partnership' in P. Ackers, C. Smith and C. Smith (eds) *The New Workplace and Trade Unionism*. London: Routledge.

Kelly, J. (1998) *Rethinking Industrial Relations: Mobilization, Collectivism and Long Waves*. London: Routledge.

Kelly, J. (2000) 'The limits and contradictions of social partnership', *Communist Review*, (30), 3–10.

Kelly, J. (2004a) 'Social partnership agreements in Britain: labor cooperation and compliance', *Industrial Relations*, 43 (1), 267–292.

Kelly, J. (2004b) 'Social partnership agreements in Britain' in M. Stuart and M. Martinez-Lucio (eds) *Partnership and the Modernisation of Employment Relations*. London: Routledge, 303–332.

Kersley, B., Alpin, C. and Forth, J., et al. (2006) *Inside the Workplace: Findings from the 2004 Workplace Employment Relations Survey*. London: Routledge.

Kinnie, N. and Hutchinson, S. (2000) '"Fun and surveillance": the paradox of high commitment management in call centres', *International Journal of Human Resource Management*, 11 (5), 967–985

Knell, J. (1999) *Partnership at Work? Employment Relations Research Series*. London: DTI.

Kochan, T. (2000) 'On the paradigm guiding industrial relations theory and research', *Industrial and Labor Relations Review*, 53 (4), 704–11.

Kochan, T. and Osterman, P. (1994) *The Mutual Gains Enterprise: Forging a Winning Partnership among Labor, Management and Government*. Boston, MA: Harvard Business School.

Kochan, T. A. and Rubinstein, S. A. (2000) 'Toward a stakeholder theory of the firm: the Saturn Partnership', *Organization Science*, 11 (4), 367–386.

Kochan, T., Adler, P., McKersie, R., Eaton, A., Segal, P. and Gerhart, P. (2008) 'The potential and precariousness of partnership: the case of the Kaiser Permanente Labour Management Partnership', *Industrial Relations*, 47 (1), 36–66.

Konzelmann, S. J. (2005) 'Varieties of capitalism: production and market relations in the USA and Japan', *British Journal of Industrial Relations*, 43 (4), 593–603.

Konzelmann, S., Conway, N., Trenberth, L. and Wilkinson, F. (2006) 'Corporate governance and human resource management', *British Journal of Industrial Relations*, 43 (3).

Korczynski, M. (2002) *Human Resource Management in Service Work*. New York: Palgrave.

Legge, K. (1995) *Human Resource Management: Rhetorics and Realities*. London: Macmillan.

Leyshon, A., Signoretta, P. and French, S. (2006) 'The changing geography of British bank and building society branch networks 1995–2003', *University of Nottingham School of Geography Working Paper*, Nottingham.

Marchington, M. (1998) 'Partnership in context: towards a European model' in P. Sparrow and M. Marchington (eds) *Human Resource Management: the New Agenda*. London: FT Pitman.

Marchington, M., Goodman, J., Wilkinson, A. and Ackers, P. (1992) *New developments in employee involvement*. Sheffield: Employment Department Research 2.

Marchington, M. and Wilkinson, A. (2005) 'Direct participation and involvement' in S. Bach (ed) *Managing Human Resources: Personnel Management in Transition*. Oxford: Blackwell, 340–364.

Marchington, M., Wilkinson, A., Ackers, P. and Dundon, T. (2001) *Management Choice and Employee Voice*. London: CIPD.

Marchington, M., Wilkinson, A., Ackers, P. and Goodman, J. (1994) 'Understanding the meaning of participation: views from the workplace', *Human Relations*, 47 (8), 867–894.

Marks, A., Finlay, P., Hine, J., McKinlay, A. and Thompson, P. (1998) 'The politics of partnership? Innovation in employment relations in the Scottish spirits industry', *British Journal of Industrial Relations*, 36 (2), 209.

Martin, G., Pate, J., Beaumont, P. and Murdoch, A. (2003) 'The uncertain road to partnership: an action research perspective on "new industrial relations" in the UK offshore oil industry', *Employee Relations*, 25 (6), 594.

Martinez-Lucio, M. and Stuart, M. (2002a) 'Assessing partnership: the prospects for, and challenges of, modernisation', *Employee Relations*, 24 (3), 252.

Martinez-Lucio, M. and Stuart, M. (2002b) 'Assessing the principles of partnership: workplace trade union representatives' attitudes and experiences', *Employee Relations,* 24 (3), 305–320.

Martinez-Lucio, M. and Stuart, M. (2004) 'Swimming against the tide: social partnership, mutual gains and the revival of "tired" HRM', *International Journal of Human Resource Management,* 15 (2), 410.

Martínez-Lucio, M. and Stuart, M. (2005) '"Partnership" and new industrial relations in a risk society', *Work, Employment & Society,* 19 (4), 797–817.

Mason, B., Heaton, N. and Morgan, J. (2004) 'Social partnership strategies in two health service trusts', *Personnel Review,* 33 (6), 648–664.

McBride, J. and Stirling, J. (2002) 'Partnership and process in the maritime construction industry', *Employee Relations,* 24 (3), 290.

Menzies, H. (1996) *Whose Brave New World?: The Information Highway and the New Economy.* Toronto: Between the Lines.

Metcalf, D. (2004) 'British unions: resurgence or perdition?', *Centre for Economic Performance, Mimeo,* London: LSE.

Morris, T., Storey, J., Wilkinson, A. and Cressey, P. (2001) 'Industrial change and union mergers in British retail finance', *British Journal of Industrial Relations,* 39 (2), 237–256.

Oxenbridge, S., Brown, W., Deakin, S. and Pratten, C. (2003) 'Initial responses to the Statutory Recognition Provisions of the Employment Relations Act 1999', *British Journal of Industrial Relations,* 41 (2), 315–334.

Oxenbridge, S. and Brown, W. (2004a) 'Achieving a new equilibrium? The stability of cooperative employer-union relationships', *Industrial Relations Journal,* 35 (5), 388–402.

Oxenbridge, S. and Brown, W. (2004b) 'Developing partnership relationships: a case of leveraging power' in *Partnership and Modernisation in Employment Relations.* London: Routledge, 136–189.

Oxenbridge, S. and Brown, W. (2004c) 'A poisoned chalice? Trade union representatives in partnership and co-operative employer–union relationships' in G. Healy, E. Heery, P. Taylor and W. Brown (eds) *The Future of Worker Representation.* London: Routledge, 187–206.

Oxenbridge, S. and Brown, W. (2002) 'The two faces of partnership? An assessment of partnership and co-operative employer/trade union relationships', *Employee Relations,* 24 (3), 262–276.

Pfeffer, J. (1994) *Competitive Advantage Through People.* Boston, MA: Harvard Business School Press.

Purcell, J. (1993) 'The end of institutional industrial relations', *Political Quarterly,* 64 (1), 6–23.

Richardson, M., Stewart, P., Danford, A., Tailby, S. and Upchurch, M. (2004) 'Employees' experience of workplace partnership in the private and public sector' in M. Stuart and M. Martinez-Lucio (eds) *Partnership and Modernisation in Employment Relations*. London: Routledge, 333–355.

Richardson, M., Tailby, S., Danford, A., Stewart, P. and Upchurch, M. (2005) 'Best value and workplace partnership in local government', *Personnel Review*, 34 (6), 713–728.

Roche, W. K. and Geary, J. F. (2002) 'Advocates, critics and union involvement in workplace participation', *British Journal of Industrial Relations*, 40 (4), 659.

Roche, W. K. and Geary, J. F. (2004) 'Workplace partnership and the search for dual commitment' in M. Stuart and M. Martinez-Lucio (eds) *Partnership and Modernisation in Employment Relations*. London: Routledge, 356–385.

Roper, I. (2000) 'Quality management and trade unions in local government', *Employee Relations*, 22 (5), 442–466.

Rose, E. (2002) 'The labour process and union commitment within a banking services call centre', *The Journal of Industrial Relations*, 44 (1), 40–61.

Ross, G. and Martin, A. (1999) *The Brave New World of European Labor: European Trade Unions at the Millennium*. New York: Berghahn Books.

Samuel, P. J. (2001) 'Partnership efficacy: some preliminary evidence from trade union officials' in M. Stuart and M. Martínez Lucio (eds) *Assessing Partnership: the Prospects for and Challenges of 'Modernisation'*. Leeds: Leeds University Business School, 129–146.

Samuel, P. J. (2005) 'Partnership working and the cultivated activist', *Industrial Relations Journal*, 36 (1), 59–76.

Samuel, P. J. (2007) 'Partnership consultation and employer domination in two British life and pension firms', *Work Employment and Society*, 21 (3), 459.

Sisson, K. (1999) 'The "new" European social model: the end of the search for orthodoxy or another false dawn?', *Employee Relations*, 21 (5), 445–462.

Sisson, K. (2005) 'Personnel management and European integration: a case of indelible imprint?' in S. Bach (ed.) *Managing Human Resources*. Routledge, 45–67.

Smith, C., Child, J. and Rowlinson, M. (1990) *Reshaping Work, the Cadbury Experience*. New York: Cambridge University Press.

Smith, P. and Morton, G. (2006) 'Nine years of New Labour: neoliberalism and workers' rights', *British Journal of Industrial Relations*, 44 (3), 401–420.

Stiglitz, J. (2000) 'Democratic development as the fruits of labor', Keynote Address to the International Industrial Relations Research Association, Boston, January 25.

Storey, J. (1995) 'Employment policies and practices in UK clearing banks: an overview', *Human Resource Management Journal,* 5 (4), 24–43.

Storey, J., Cressey, P., Morris, T. and Wilkinson, A. (1997) 'Changing employment practices in UK banking', *Personnel Review,* 26 (1/2), 24–42.

Storey, J., Wilkinson, A., Cressey, P. and Morris, T. (1999) 'Employment relations in UK banking' in M. Regini, J. Kitay and M. Baethije (eds) *From Tellers to Sellers: Changing Employment Relations in the World-Wide Banking Industry.* Cambridge, Mass: MIT Press, 129–158.

Streeck, W. (1992) *Social Institutions and Economic Performance: Studies of Industrial Relations in Advanced Capitalist Economies.* London: Sage.

Stuart, M. and Martinez-Lucio, M. (2004a) 'Partnership and the modernisation of employment relations: an introduction' in M. Stuart and M. Martinez-Lucio (eds) *Partnership and the Modernisation of Employment Relations.* London: Routledge, 1–38.

Stuart, M. and Martinez-Lucio, M. (2004b) 'Where next for partnership?' in M. Stuart and M. Martinez-Lucio (eds) *Partnership and Modernisation in Employment Relations.* London: Routledge, 412–424.

Stuart, M. and Martinez-Lucio, M. (2008) 'Employment relations in the UK finance sector: between globalisation and regulation', CERIC Working Paper 1, Leeds University Business School.

Suff, R. and Williams, S. (2004) 'The myth of mutuality? Employee perceptions of partnership at Borg Warner', *Employee Relations,* 26 (1), 30–43.

Tailby, S. and Winchester, D. (2005) 'Management and trade unions: partnership at work' in S. Bach (ed.) *Managing Human Resources.* London: Routledge, 424–451.

Tailby, S., Richardson, M., Stewart, P., Danford, A. and Upchurch, M. (2004) 'Partnership at work and worker participation: an NHS case study', *Industrial Relations Journal,* 35 (5), 403–418.

Taylor, P. and Bain, P. (1999) '"An assembly line in the head": work and employee relations in the call centre', *Industrial Relations Journal,* 30 (2), 101–117.

Taylor, P., Mulvey, G., Hyman, J. and Bain, P. (2002) 'Work organization, control and the experience of work in call centres', *Work, Employment and Society,* 16 (1), 133–150.

Taylor, P. and Ramsey, H. (1998) 'Unions partnership and HRM: sleeping with the enemy?', *International Journal of Employment Studies,* 6 (2), 115–143.

Terry, M. (1999) 'Systems of collective employee representation in non-union firms in the UK', *Industrial Relations Journal,* 30 (1), 16–30.

Terry, M. (2003a) 'Can "partnership" reverse the decline of British trade unions', *Work, Employment and Society,* 17 (3), 45–472.

Terry, M. (2003b) 'Partnership and the future of trade unions in the UK', *Economic and Industrial Democracy,* 24 (4), 485–507.

Terry, M. and Smith, J. (2003) *Evaluation of the Partnership at Work Fund.* London: Department of Trade and Industry.

TUC (1997) *Partners for Progress: next Steps for the New Unionism.* London: TUC.

TUC (1999) *Partners for Progress.* London: TUC.

TUC (2002) *TUC High Performance Workplaces, Report.* London: TUC.

TUC Partnership Institute. (2002) *Partnership, Performance and Employment: a review of the evidence.* London: TUC.

Turnbull, P., Blyton, P. and Harvey, G. (2004) 'Cleared for take-off? Management–labour partnership in the European civil aviation industry', *European Journal of Industrial Relations,* 10 (3), 287–307.

Undy, R. (1999) 'Annual Review Article: New Labour's "Industrial Relations Settlement": the third way?', *British Journal of Industrial Relations,* 37 (2), 315–336.

Upchurch, M. Danford, A. Tailby, S. and Richardson, M. (2008) *The Realities of Partnership at Work.* Palgrave, London.

Upchurch, M., Richardson, M., Tailby, S., Danford, A. and Stewart, P. (2006) 'Employee representation and partnership in the non-union sector: a paradox of intention?', *Human Resource Management Journal,* 16 (4), 393–410.

Waddington, J. (2003) 'Trade union organisation' in P. Edwards (ed.) *Industrial Relations: Theory and Practice.* Oxford: Blackwell, 214–256.

Walton, R. E. and McKersie, R. B. (1965) *A Behavioural Theory of Labor Negotiations.* London: McGraw Hill.

Wills, J. (2004) 'Trade unionism and partnership in practice: evidence from the Barclays-Unifi agreement', *Industrial Relations Journal,* 35 (4), 329–343.

Wray, D. (2004) 'Management and union motives in the negotiation of partnership: a case study of the process and outcome at an Engineering Company' in M. Stuart and M. Martinez-Lucio (eds) *Partnership and Modernisation in Employment Relations.* London: Routledge, 190–215.

Yin, R. K. (2003) *Case Study Research: Design and Methods.* London: Sage Publications.

Note: some of the data from this research project also appear in a series of journal articals by the author (Johnstone, et al., 2009, 2010a, 2010b, 2010c).

Appendix

Empirical Partnership Studies in the UK 1998–2008

	Authors	Sector	Method	Focus	TU status
1	Ackers et al., 2004	Various	Case study	Employee voice	Union/non-union
2	Bacon and Storey, 2000	Various	Case study	Management strategy	Union
3	Badigannavar and Kelly, 2004	Civil service	Case study	Union organisation	Union
4	Badigannavar and Kelly, 2005	Retail	Case study	Employee outcomes	Non-union
5	Beale, 2004	Inland revenue	Case study	Historical development	Union
6	Danford et al., 2004	Aerospace	Case study	Employee voice	Union
7	Danford et al., 2005	Aerospace	Case study	Employee responses	Union
8	Danford et al., 2008	Various	Case study	Employee experience	Union/non-union
9	Deakin et al., 2004	Various	Case study	Corporate governance	Union
10	Dietz et al., 2005	Clothing	Case study	Non-union partnership	Non-union
11	Dietz, 2004	Spirits, engineering NHS	Case study	Partnership and trust	Union
12	Gall, 2001	Finance	Union interviews	IR development	Union
13	Guest and Peccei, 2001	Various	Survey	Mutuality	Union
14	Haynes and Allen, 2001	Retail/Finance	Case study	Union strategy	Union
15	Heaton et al., 2000	NHS	Case study	Union relationships	Union
16	Heery et al., 2004	Manpower/TGWU	Case study	Trade unionism	Union
17	Jenkins, 2007	Automotive	Case study	Unions/outcomes	Union
18	Jenkins, 2008	Manufacturing	Case study	Work organisation	Union
19	Johnstone et al., 2004	Utilities	Case study	Actor reactions	Union
20	Kelly, 2004a	Various	Secondary analysis	Labour outcomes	Union

	Authors	Sector	Method	Focus	TU status
21	Kelly, 2004b	Various	Secondary analysis	Labour outcomes	Union
22	Marchington et al., 2001	Various	Case study	Employee voice	Union/non-union
23	Marks et al., 1998	Spirits	Case study	Workplace change/ innovation	Union
24	Martin et al., 2003	Offshore oil	Case study	Management and union strategies	Union
25	Martinez-Lucio and Stuart, 2002	MSF	Survey	TU representative attitudes	Union
26	Mason et al., 2004	NHS	Case study	Management and union strategies	Union
27	McBride and Stirling, 2002	Maritime construction	Case study	TU representative experiences	Union
28	Oxenbridge and Brown, 2002	Various	Case study	Characteristics of partnership	Union
29	Oxenbridge and Brown, 2004b	Various	Case study	Formal and informal partnerships	Union
30	Oxenbridge and Brown, 2004a	Various	Case study	Stability of partnership	Union
31	Richardson et al., 2004	aerospace/local GVT	Case study	Employee responses	Union
32	Richardson et al., 2005	Local government	Case study	Employee experiences	Union
33	Samuel, 2005	Finance	Case study	Union workplace organisation	Union
34	Samuel, 2007	Finance	Case study	Consultation	Union
35	Stuart and Martinez-Lucio, 2004c	MSF union	Survey	Risks and trade unionists	Union
36	Suff and Williams, 2004	Vehicle parts	Case study	Employee perceptions	Union
37	Tailby et al., 2004	NHS	Case study	Union strategy	Union
38	Taylor and Ramsey, 1998	Retail	Case study	HRM & trade unions	Union
39	Turnbull et al., 2004	Aviation	Case study & survey	Institutional context	Union
40	Upchurch et al., 2008	Various	Case study	Mutuality	Union/non-union
41	Wills, 2004	Finance	Case study	Trade union organisation	Union
42	Wray, 2004	Engineering	Case study	Partnership agreement negotiations	Union

Source: Johnstone, S. Ackers, P and Wilkinson, A. (2009) The partnership phenomenon: a ten year review, *Human Resource Management Journal*

NatBank Partnership Agreement

	Bank commits to:	Union commits to:
Roles and responsibilities NatBank to manage the business balancing the interests of employees, customers and shareholders AND for Union to represent and promote interests of employees while recognising those of other stakeholders	Developing a business strategy and direction which recognises and respects the interests of employees along with other stakeholdersEnabling Union to influence the implementation of business strategy and plans by sharing these with Union during development Implementing business decisions in a fair and consistent wayCommunicating openly and honestly with our people and being the first to inform them about business plans/decisions	Acknowledging the legitimate interests of other stakeholders when seeking to challenge and influence business decisions Seeking out viable solutions to individual and collective employee issues Maintaining confidentiality Respecting NB's right and responsibility to communicate with its people first about issues affecting them when these are not in the public domain
Behaviours We will carry out our respective roles and responsibilities in a way that demonstrates mutual trust and respect	Openness with information about the business Acknowledging and facilitating the Unions' role to promote the interests of its members Listening to alternative views with an intention of problem solving Realism, practicality and pragmatism Constructive and effective communication with our people	Respecting the confidentiality of business information Shared agendas to promote the long-term success of the business Co-operation and problem solving Realism, practicality and pragmatism Constructive and effective communication with members
Accountability We will ensure all participants in NatBank/Union discussions understand their responsibilities and the issues, and are able to add value	Clearly setting out the type and scope of business change and other consultations Ensuring representatives have the authority to make and implement agreements Ensuring reps understand the spirit in which we undertake our discussions Supporting and promoting decisions once made and agreed	Developing representative structures with NB which continue to reflect the changing nature of the business Ensuring that, within Unions structure, reps have the authority to make and implement agreements Ensuring reps understand the spirit in which we undertake our discussions Supporting and promoting decisions once made and agreed
Excellence We will develop and promote high standards of performance and professionalism to secure the success of NatBank and the people who work here	Demonstrating professional management and leadership Valuing the diversity of all our people and helping them to fulfil their potential Recognising and rewarding exceptional performance Dealing with underperformance in a fair but firm manner Building on what we do well and supporting best practice	Recognising business goals and objectives Demonstrating support for the principle of continuous improvement in handling the concerns of employees Constructively providing feedback on performance systems and ideas for improvement Supporting best practice Recognising that NB will differentiate reward in line with performance

	Bank commits to:	Union commits to:
Flexibility We recognise that success depends on meeting customer needs. We will work together to promote commercial success, taking account of the interests of employees and the quality of their working life	Enabling our people to balance the demands of work and home when responding to customer requirements Working together across the Group while acknowledging that different markets will drive different needs Equipping our people with wider skills and where appropriate	Considering the needs of customers when representing the interests of employees Recognising that NB operates in a number of markets requiring different terms and condition of employment Recognising that flexibility and the development of skills is key to operating in FS
Employability We will work together to ensure that wherever possible compulsory redundancies will be avoided	Providing career counselling and outplacement support Investing in training and coaching Creating a climate which encourages self-development Opportunity to develop skills	Helping to develop a culture focusing on employability Proposing viable initiatives to support our people through change Providing wide-ranging training resources to members/reps

The WebBank Employee Forum Commitment Document

Objectives	To increase the level of employee involvement in change and business initiatives which affect employees using effective consultation
	To build and maintain effective relationships with all departments through consultation
	To represent independently and without prejudice the interests of WebBank [WB] people both collectively and individually
Primary principles	Joint commitment of the WBPF [WebBank Employee Forum] and WB will ensure WB's success
	Recognition by all for legitimate roles, interests and responsibilities of those on the WBPF
	Transparency between the WBPF and WB through effective consultation – sharing information policy consultation
	Building trust between WB people
	WB people have the right to be represented and have equal opportunities within the business
	WB people have exceptional training and effective development
Operating principles	Act for the good of WB people and WB
	Stay within the overall context of WB's strategy, support that strategy and contribute to WB's game
	Respect the WBPF principles of consultation

Source: Internal documentation

Index